PUZZLE SQUARE

BRAIN TEASERS

PUZZLE SQUARE

BRAIN TEASERS

INCLUDING SUDOKU, MATH PUZZLERS, NUMBER GRIDS, AND LOGIC PUZZLES

LUKE HALL

THUNDER BAY
P·R·E·S·S
San Diego, California

THUNDER BAY
P · R · E · S · S

Thunder Bay Press
An imprint of the Advantage Publishers Group
5880 Oberlin Drive, San Diego, CA 92121-4794
www.thunderbaybooks.com

ISBN 13: 978-1-59223-611-4
ISBN 10: 1-59223-611-1

Printed in Singapore.

1 2 3 4 5 10 09 08 07 06

INTRODUCTION

The great number of puzzles in this Puzzle Square make up
an interesting and varied collection, with something for
every member of the family. We have included logic problems
(both the long, classic puzzles and lots of quick ones that
are just the right size for solving over a cup of coffee),
picture puzzles, visual reasoning engines,
number problems, mazes, physical problems, sudoku and
other Japanese number puzzles, and even mathematical
crosswords. You can browse through this book for five
minutes and solve a quick puzzle, or you can spend an entire
day on one of the real biggies!

Don't be put off by a difficult puzzle, though—difficulty is
subjective, and you may find that the ones we struggled
with are just a breeze for you. You'll be in for many hours
of puzzle fun with this, the first Puzzle Square—look out
for the others.

1 · LOGI-5

Each line, across and down, is to have each of the five colors appearing once each. Each color must also appear just once in each shape, shown by thick lines. Can you color in this crazy quilt or mark each square with its correct letter B, G, R, V, or Y?

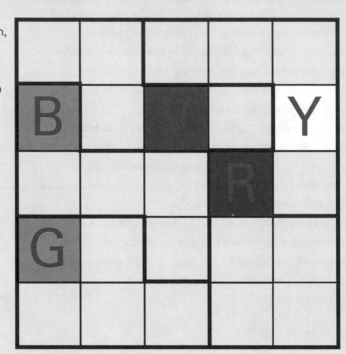

Answer on page 458

2 · CELL STRUCTURE

The object is to create white areas surrounded by black walls, so that:

- Each white area contains only one number.
- The number of cells in a white area is equal to the number in it.
- The white areas are separated from each other by a black wall.
- Cells containing numbers are not filled in.
- The black cells are linked into a continuous wall.
- Black cells do not form a square of 2 x 2 or larger.

	1		2					1	
3		4				2			3
							3		
					2				
	2		3						
						2		2	
	1								3
		2				2			

Answer on page 458

7

3 · DOTTY DILEMMA

Connect adjacent dots with vertical or horizontal lines so that a single loop is formed with no crossings or branches. Each number indicates how many lines surround it, while empty cells may be surrounded by any number of lines.

Answer on page 458

4 · TWIN SET

Two of the pictures below are identical. Can you spot the "twins" and the different detail in each of the remaining pictures?

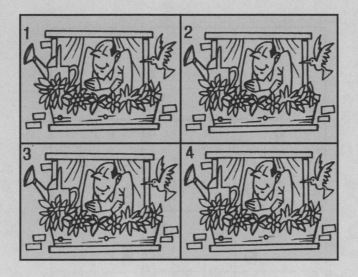

Answer on page 458

5 · SUDOKU

Place a number from 1 to 9 in each empty square so that each row, each column, and each 3 x 3 block contain all the numbers from 1 to 9.

			2		4			
9	6		7		3		8	4
	9			2			7	
	5	2	9		1	3	4	
	4	7				9	5	
3			5		9			8
		9				6		
4		5		8		7		3

Answer on page 458

6 · SQUARE NUMBERS

The numbers 1–25 are arranged randomly so that no two consecutive numbers are adjacent in any direction. One number has been entered for you. The four corner numbers are all multiples of three, and no other multiples of three are adjacent to them or to each other. The long diagonal from top left to bottom right totals 72, and the other from top right to bottom left totals 61, each diagonal containing two consecutive numbers (though not necessarily next to each other). In column 1 the lowest number is 8; 25 is somewhere in column 2; in row E the highest number is 17. The number in B2 is twice D2 and half of E2. The number in D4 is four higher than that in D1 and equals B4 plus D3, the latter being half of B5. C1 is five higher than D1; A3 plus A4 totals 23; and 24 is a chess knight's move from the 25. The 10 is farther left than 11 although they are in the same row; 13 and 19 are in the row below.

Can you locate each number?

	1	2	3	4	5
A					
B					
C				3	
D					
E					

Answer on page 458

7 · HEADS AND TAILS

The diagram shows four coins issued in different reigns by rulers of Monetaria. Can you name the monarch whose head appears on the reverse side of each of the coins lettered A–D, describe its reverse design, and say in which year it was minted?

1 No female monarch reigned in Monetaria during the 18th century.
2 The coin from the reign of Karl II bears the crossed swords on its reverse.
3 The heraldic dragon appears on coin A, which wasn't issued by William V.
4 The head on the reverse of coin D is that of Josef III.
5 The 1785 coin's reverse shows the value in a wreath of laurel leaves.
6 The coin dated 1865 is somewhere to the right of the one whose reverse design is the shield of Monetaria.

Monarchs: Josef III, Karl II, Maria, William V
Reverse designs: crossed swords, heraldic dragon, shield, wreath of laurels
Dates: 1745, 1785, 1825, 1865

| A | B | C | D |

Ruler: _____ _____ _____ _____
Reverse: _____ _____ _____ _____
Date: _____ _____ _____ _____

Answer on page 458

8 · ON THE SCENE

Each of the six objects in the lower boxes can be found in one of the lettered squares in the big picture. Find these squares and transfer the letters to the little boxes below. You should spell out the name of a world-famous university.

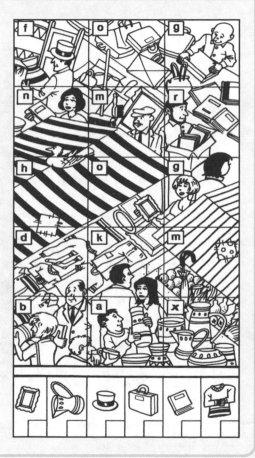

Answer on page 458

9 · TEA FOR TWO

Which two teapots are exactly identical?

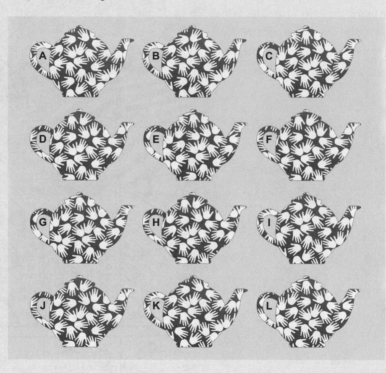

Answer on page 458

Connect adjacent dots with vertical or horizontal lines so that a single loop is formed with no crossings or branches. Each number indicates how many lines surround it, while empty cells may be surrounded by any number of lines.

Answer on page 458

11 · PATTERN MAKER

Can you place the numbered blocks into the grid to form the pattern shown?

The blocks may be placed horizontally or vertically and can be turned round.

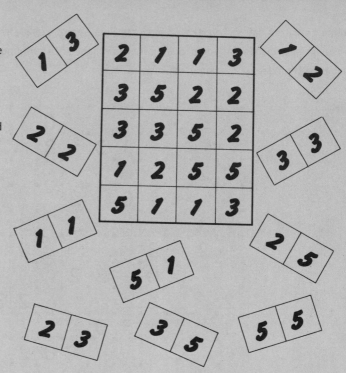

Answer on page 458

12 · WHERE THE L?

Twelve L shapes like the ones shown have been inserted in the grid. Each L has one hole in it. There are three pieces of each of the four kinds shown below, and any piece might be turned or flipped over before being put into the grid. No two pieces of the same kind touch, even at a corner. The pieces fit together so well that you cannot see the spaces between them; only the holes show. Can you tell where the Ls are?

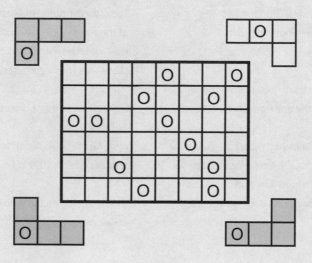

Answer on page 459

13 · LONELY VIGILS

In the later years of the Roman occupation of Britain, the garrisons in the legionary fortresses were badly depleted. In Deva, for example, they could spare only one man at a time to guard each of the four walls. From the clues given, can you indicate in the diagram the name of the soldier on each wall, his place of origin, and the number of years he had served in his legion?

1 The wall patrolled by Blunderbuss was opposite the one whose guard had twelve years' service; he was not Rictus.

2 The man on the south wall was neither Voluminus nor the one from Syria.

3 The man from Gallia had been assigned to the west wall, the one from Africa had eleven years' service behind him, and the man on the north wall had served for nine years.

4 The duty centurion making a clockwise tour of the walls would have come across Hiatus next after the man from Germania; neither of these was the longest serving legionary.

Names: Blunderbuss; Hiatus; Rictus; Voluminus
Origin: Africa; Gallia; Germania; Syria
Years' service: 9; 10; 11; 12

Starting tip: Figure out who has served for twelve years.

Answer on page 459

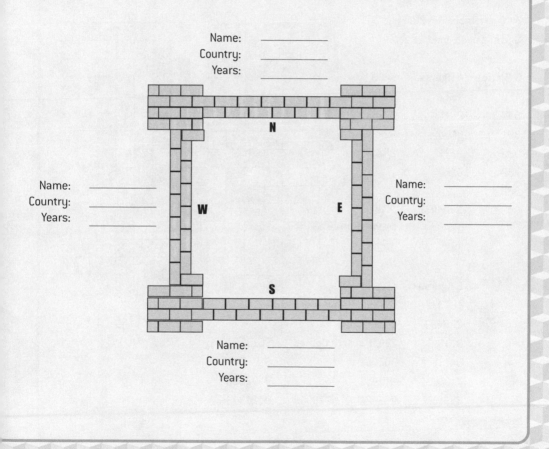

Name: _____
Country: _____
Years: _____

Name: _____
Country: _____
Years: _____

N

W

E

Name: _____
Country: _____
Years: _____

S

Name: _____
Country: _____
Years: _____

Fit the numbers into the grid.
One has been done for you.

3 figures	4 figures	5768
150	1622	5921
344	2191	7726
391	3160	8273
629	3731	9801
782	4570	
~~988~~		
943	**5 figures**	27403
	13804	28135
	14630	78836

6 figures	467169
187332	637901
228433	643115
314517	729362
341712	862561
410355	910266
435127	955925

7 figures	5613984
1230172	6157248
2482077	9102626
5273559	9921349

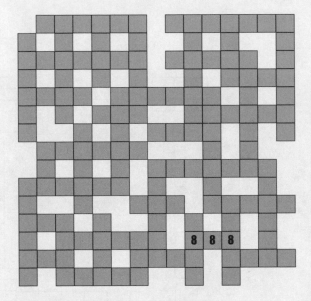

Answer on page 459

15 · ON THE SPOT

Can you place the dominoes into the grid so
that the four vertical, four horizontal, and both
diagonal rows each have a pip total of nine?

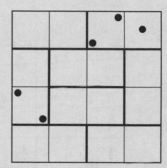

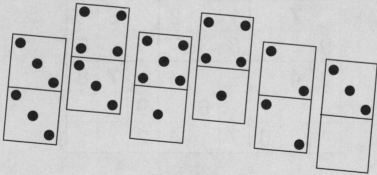

Answer on page 459

Place a number from 1 to 9 in each empty square so that each row, each column, and each 3 x 3 block contain all the numbers from 1 to 9.

		9	4		1	5		
		3		8		4		
4	1						6	2
1			5	4	6			9
	7		1		2		8	
9			8	3	7			5
3	4						7	8
		7		6		9		
		6	7		4	2		

Answer on page 459

17 · DOUBLE PUZZLE

Line up, folks, for our special offer of two puzzles for the price of one!

Puzzle One: Each color has been given a value from 1 to 7. Given the totals at the end of each line, can you work out the value of each color?

Puzzle Two: The picture is a layout of a set of color dominoes—just like ordinary dominoes but with colors instead of spots. Can you draw in the lines to show each separate domino?

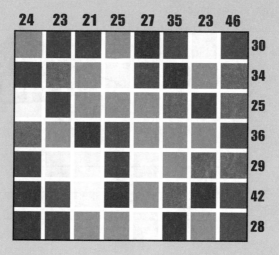

Answer on page 459

18 · KARL KRACK'S CIRCUS

Karl Krack, who owns a small traveling circus, believes that variety is the spice of life, and for each show he alters the order of his eight acts. Can you figure out what the order will be for tonight's performance?

No act is next to another with the same initials. The Clever Clowns come two acts after Fred the Fire-eater and two acts before Señor Pedro's Poodles. Jim the Juggler comes three acts before the Agilles Acrobats, but he does not open the show. The Flying Fortresses come four acts after Madame Poll's Parrots, but not immediately before the Poodles. The Crazy Carvellos are not the final act.

1	2	3	4
5	6	7	8

Answer on page 459

19 · IT FIGURES

Place a number from 1 to 9 in each empty cell so that the sum of each vertical or horizontal block equals the number at the top or on the left of that block. Numbers may only be used once in each block.

Answer on page 460

By packing numbers in the empty spaces, can you make the numbers in each of the 16 hexagons add up to 25? No two numbers in each hexagon may be the same, and you can't use zero. We've started you off.

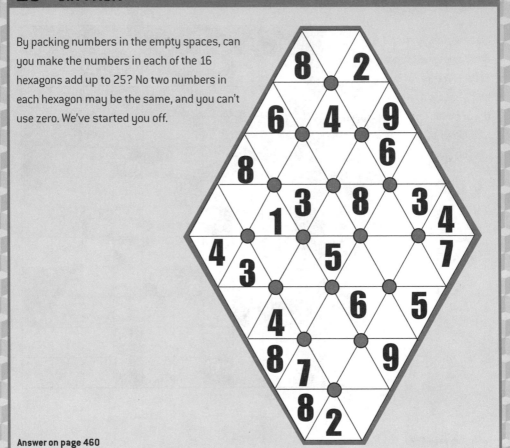

Answer on page 460

21 · FILLING IN

Each of the nine empty boxes contains a different digit from 1 to 9. Each calculation is to be treated sequentially rather than according to the "multiplication first" system. Can you fill in the empty boxes?

	×		÷		= 2
+		×		×	
	÷		+		= 10
÷		÷		−	
	+		−		= 3

$$= 2 \qquad = 2 \qquad = 6$$

Answer on page 460

Mucky Mouse has a new camera, and he's been busy taking pictures of some flowers. Can you sort his photos into five matching pairs?

Answer on page 460

23 · WHERE THE L?

Sixteen L shapes like the ones shown have been fitted into a square shape. Each L has one hole, and there are four of each type in the square. No two pieces of the same type are adjacent, even at a corner. They fit together so well that the spaces between pieces do not show. From the locations of the holes, can you tell where each L is?

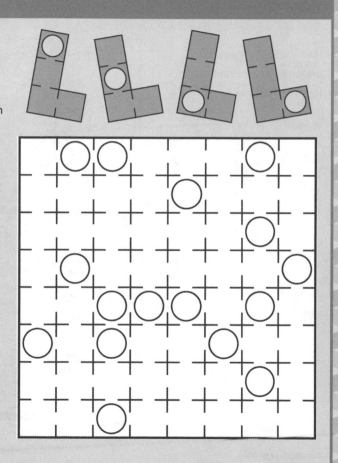

24 · SPOT THE DIFFERENCES

How quickly can you discover the ten differences between these two pictures?

Answer on page 460

25 · TRILINES

Can you draw three straight lines, each one drawn from one edge to another, so that it divides the box into five plots, each containing two different fruits?

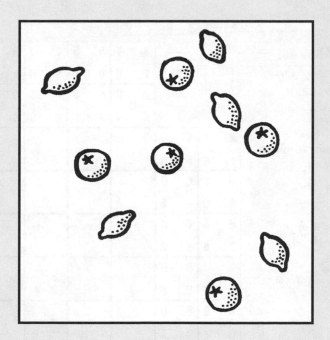

Answer on page 460

The cards eight to king of each suit, together with the ace of hearts, have been placed in a 5 x 5 square. Figures and letters showing the values 8, 9, T, J, Q, K and suits C, H, D, S have been placed on the end of each line across and down. With the ace in place and the fact that the two cards shown at the top left belong in the shaded squares, can you figure out the unique place for each card?

Top-left cards: **T S** and **K S**

		8 T / T Q — C C / H H	8 8 / 9 K — C D / S S	T J / K K — C C / H S	9 9 / J Q — C D / S S	8 J / K A — D D / H H
8 9 / T K / J K	C C / H / H S					
8 9 / T Q / Q Q	C D / D / D S					
8 8 / Q A / K A	C H / H / S S					A H
T J / J K / J K	C D / H / H S			(shaded)		
9 9 / T K / Q K	C D / D / H S				(shaded)	

Answer on page 461

Can you work out which weights will rise and which will fall when the man pulls the rope?

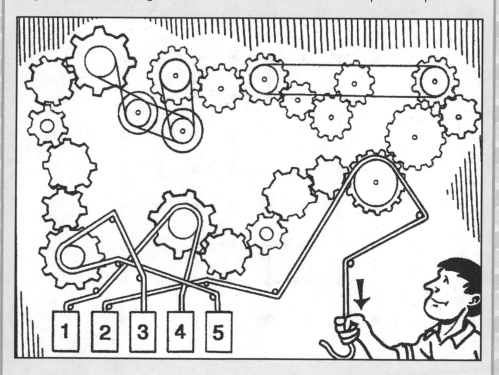

Answer on page 461

28 · ROUND TRIP

We have made a round trip through the dots in the grid below, visiting each dot once and returning to the start. Part of our path is shown; can you deduce the rest?

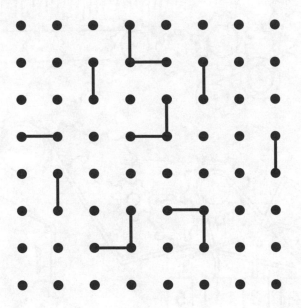

Answer on page 461

The symbols on each face have a meaning—Up, Down, Right, or Left. But each sign has a different meaning on each of the three faces. Thus, whatever is, say, on the top face cannot be on the left face or the right face. There is a meaning for each symbol that will lead to a unique path joining Start (S) to End (E) and which passes through all three faces. Can you let your brain do the logical walking and make the journey?

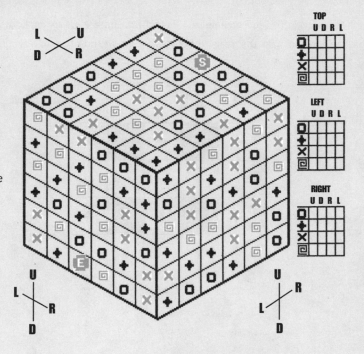

TOP

	U	D	R	L
□				
✚				
✕				
⊡				

LEFT

	U	D	R	L
□				
✚				
✕				
⊡				

RIGHT

	U	D	R	L
□				
✚				
✕				
⊡				

Answer on page 461

All the digits from 1 to 9 are used in this grid, but only once. Can you figure out their positions in the grid and make the totals work? We've given two numbers to start you off.

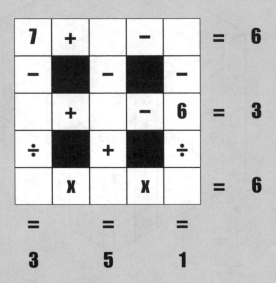

Answer on page 461

31 · MONSTER MATCH

Which two of these monsters
are exactly the same?

Answer on page 461

32 · NUMBER JIG

Fit the numbers into the grid. One has been done for you.

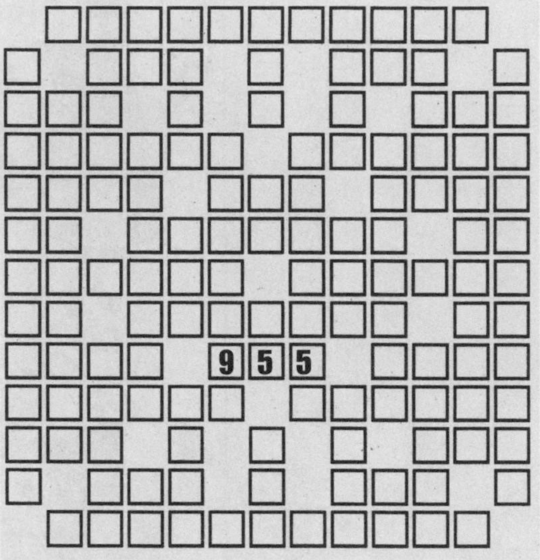

2 figures
10
21
33
42
54
56
79
87
88
95

3 figures
170
186
222
260
306
402

519
548
663
791
884
889
917
955

4 figures
1276
2245
3093
5386
6482
7910
8218
9977

5 figures
16650
20476
68308
90759

6 figures
154564
338085
416707
720503
896952
919350

7 figures
1469353
3857292
4629390
4959018

5267489
6357655

967753780

9 figures
624114298

11 figures
36870152598
41479036525

70264293061
96762458813

Answer on page 461

38

33 · BATTLESHIPS

Do you remember the old game of battleships? These puzzles are based on that idea. Your task is to find the vessels in the diagram. Some parts of boats or sea squares have already been filled in, and a number next to a row or column refers to the number of occupied squares in that row or column. The boats may be positioned horizontally or vertically, but no two boats or parts of boats are in adjacent squares—horizontally, vertically, or diagonally.

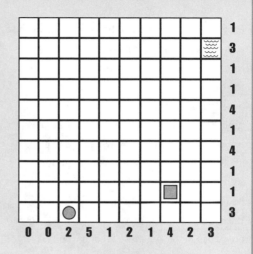

1
3
1
1
4
1
4
1
1
3

0   0   2   5   1   2   1   4   2   3

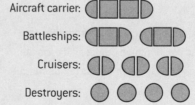

Aircraft carrier:
Battleships:
Cruisers:
Destroyers:

Answer on page 462

Peregrine Cupick, who had had some experience as a professional summer theater director, retired to Netherlipp and offered his services to the Netherlipp Players, who, duly impressed, acceded to his casting decisions for his first production of *A Midsummer Night's Dream* with unprecedented docility. However, the roles he assigned to the five leading male members were not the ones they had hoped for. Cupick had auditioned them at a reading around a table; from the clues given below, can you figure out which actor sat where, what part he was given, and which role he would have preferred?

1 Lime sat one seat clockwise from the man who had aspired to be Quince and opposite the one who was given the part of Demetrius.

2 Pitt's place was one seat clockwise from that of the man chosen to be Lysander and opposite that of the one who wanted to be Lysander.

3 The man cast as Oberon was just left of the one who got the part of Demetrius; the latter was opposite the actor who had set his heart on being Oberon.

4 Lynes sat just right of the man who wanted to play Bottom and opposite the one who was given the role of Quince.

5 Green was one seat clockwise from the selected Bottom and one seat counterclockwise from the selected Oberon and was opposite the actor who was just left of the would-be Quince.

Actors: Flood; Green; Lime; Lynes; Pitt
Roles: Bottom; Demetrius; Lysander; Oberon; Quince

Answer on page 462

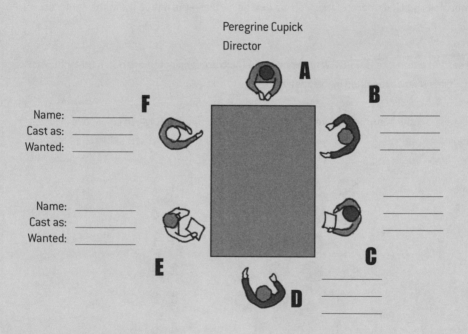

Peregrine Cupick
Director

A

B

F

Name: —————
Cast as: —————
Wanted: —————

Name: —————
Cast as: —————
Wanted: —————

—————
—————
—————

—————
—————
—————

C

E

D

—————
—————
—————

Starting tip: Work out the name of the actor in seat D.

41

35 · CODE MASTER

Just follow the rules of the classic game of Mastermind to crack the color code. The first number tells you how many of the pegs are exactly correct—the right color in the right place (✓✓).

The second number tells you how many pegs are the correct color but are not in the right place (✓). Colors may be repeated in the answer.

By comparing the information given by each line, can you figure out which color goes in which place?

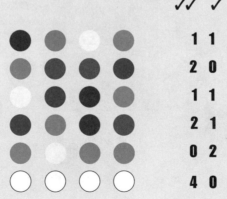

✓✓	✓
1	1
2	0
1	1
2	1
0	2
4	0

Answer on page 462

36 · SCOOP

At Justa Conesa Italian ice cream parlor, combinations of cones, scoops, and chocolate bars are charged per item:

Chocca Likka:
1 cone, 1 scoop, and
2 chocolate bars costs 80 cents

Coola Cona:
1 cone, 2 scoops, and 1 chocolate bar costs 95 cents

Plain:
1 cone and 1 scoop costs 40 cents

Can you work out the cost of one scoop of ice cream?

Answer on page 462

37 · BREAKTHROUGH

See how quickly you can break this grid down into the 28 dominoes from which it is formed.

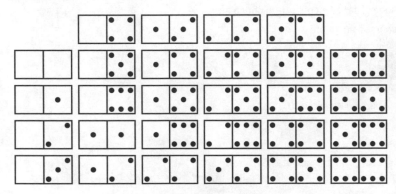

6	4	3	1	4	6	5
1	2	1	1	2	0	6
3	6	1	3	5	1	0
6	4	1	3	2	6	0
6	6	5	2	3	0	4
5	0	5	5	3	0	3
0	2	4	3	4	1	2
2	2	4	5	4	5	0

Answer on page 462

38 · INDEPENDENCE DAY

The twelve small squares each contain one of the letters or numbers making up the phrase USA JULY 4, 1776. From the clues given below, can you place the correct number or letter in each of the squares?

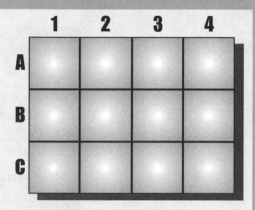

1 Horizontal row B contains three numbers but only one letter, which is not a vowel.

2 No letter or number occurs twice in any row or column.

3 The column in which a 7 appears immediately above the A is just right of the one containing the S, which is not the horizontal neighbor of either.

4 The L, which has a number in the square to its right, is in a square immediately above the 6.

5 One of the Us is immediately below the J and immediately to the left of the 1.

6 Square A2 contains a number, and C4 contains a letter.

Letters: A; J; L; S; U; U; Y
Numbers: 1; 4; 6; 7; 7

Starting tip: Begin by figuring out which is the letter in row B.

Answer on page 462

39 · IT FIGURES

Place a number from 1 to 9 in each empty cell so that the sum of each vertical or horizontal block equals the number at the top or on the left of that block. Numbers may only be used once in each block.

Answer on page 463

40 · SIX-PACK

By packing numbers in the empty spaces, can you make the numbers in each of the 16 hexagons add up to 25? No two numbers in each hexagon may be the same, and you can't use zero. We've started you off.

Answer on page 463

41 · TOTTERING TOWERS

These piles of blocks aren't the random results of a child playing but clues to a final, at present blank, pile on the right. Like the rest, that pile has one block in each of the six colors.

The numbers below the stacks tell you two things:
(a) How many adjacent pairs of blocks are actually correct in the final tower.
(b) How many adjacent pairs of blocks make a correct pair but the wrong way up.

So:

would score one in the "Correct" row if the final stack had green directly above yellow and one in the "Reversed" row if the final tower had yellow on top of green.

From all of this, can you create the tower before it finally topples?

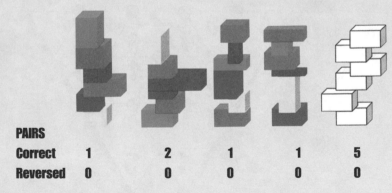

PAIRS					
Correct	1	2	1	1	5
Reversed	0	0	0	0	0

Answer on page 463

42 · SET SQUARE

All the digits from 1 to 9 are used in this grid, but only once. Can you work out their positions in the grid and make the totals work? We've given two numbers to start you off.

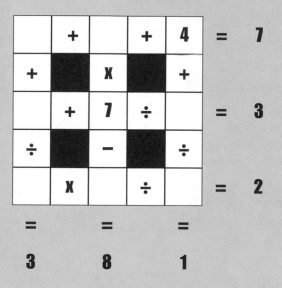

43 · LOGISTICAL

In a new science fiction movie, some of the main characters are a family of robots, identical except for the colors of their casings. From the clues below, can you figure out the color of each robot's casing and the full name of the actor who's inside it?

1 The actor who plays Roxanne, who does not have a four-letter surname, isn't Phil.

2 The yellow robot is played by the actor surnamed Jenkins, while the one whose last name is Marvin appears as Ramona.

3 Claudia, whose surname isn't Link, appears in the movie as the silver robot, which has a male name.

4 Romulus, the robot played by Selena, doesn't have a green casing.

5 George's surname is Krag.

6 Remus is the robot with the red casing.

Answer on page 463

	Blue	Green	Red	Silver	Yellow	Claudia	George	Gregory	Phil	Selena	Jenkins	Krag	Link	Marvin	Score
Ramona															
Remus															
Richard															
Romulus															
Roxanne															
Jenkins															
Krag															
Link															
Marvin															
Score															
Claudia															
George															
Gregory															
Phil															
Selena															

Record in this grid all the information obtained from the clues, by using an X to indicate a definite "no" and a check to show a definite "yes." Transfer these to all sections of the grid thus eliminating all but one possibility, which must be the correct one.

Robot	Color	First name	Surname

If it happens to be true that:

MONDAY = TODAY
TUESDAY = JUNE DAY
SUNDAY = THURSDAY
FRIDAY = BIRTHDAY

Then what day was yesterday?

Answer on page 463

In the following problems the digits 0 to 9 are represented by letters. Within each separate puzzle the same letter always represents the same digit. Can you find the correct values each time so that all sums, both horizontal and vertical, are correct? There is a clue to help start you off.

```
AB    x  CD   =  DBEB
+        +        −
FGHJ  +  FHJE  =  EGEC
FFCD  +  BGFH  =  EFHK
```

A	B	C	D	E	F	G	H	J	K

CLUE: 2 X FD = EB

Answer on page 463

46 · SIX-PACK

By packing numbers in the empty spaces, can you make the numbers in each of the 16 hexagons add up to 25? No two numbers in each hexagon may be the same, and you can't use zero. We've started you off.

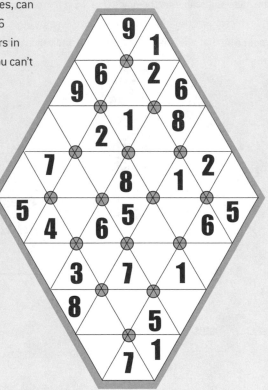

Answer on page 463

47 · SPOT THE DIFFERENCE

One of these scruffy birds is different
from the rest. Can you tell which?

Answer on page 463

Hats must be in heavy wool this year and the snowfall is light! As you can see, two sets of seesaws in the park balance beautifully. How many hats are needed to make the third seesaw level?

Answer on page 463

49 · DOT-TO-DOT

Follow the dots from 1 to 31 to reveal the hidden picture.

Answer on page 464

50 · IT FIGURES

Place a number from 1 to 9 in each empty cell so that the sum of each vertical or horizontal block equals the number at the top or on the left of that block. Numbers may only be used once in each block.

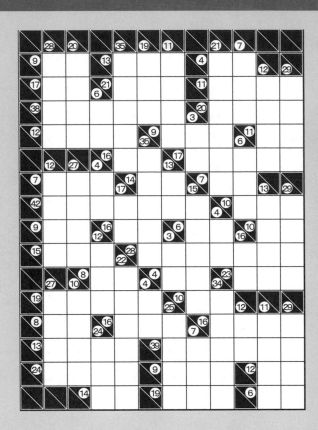

Answer on page 464

51 · SILHOUETTE

Shade in every fragment containing a dot—and what have you got?

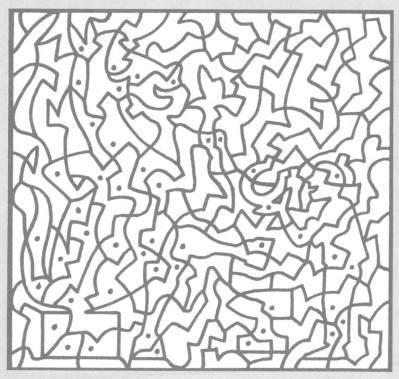

Answer on page 464

52 · CELL STRUCTURE

The object is to create white areas surrounded by black walls, so that:

- Each white area contains only one number.
- The number of cells in a white area is equal to the number in it.
- The white areas are separated from each other by a black wall.
- Cells containing numbers are not filled in.
- The black cells are linked into a continuous wall.
- Black cells do not form a square of 2 x 2 or larger.

3									
			3		3				
1									
					3				
	2								
						9			
1			5						
			9						
						6		4	
3	5		10						
9									
			5						
							4		

Answer on page 464

53 · WALKIES

Four of the six shapes on the top are hidden in the main picture. Can you spot which four and where they are?

Answer on page 464

Each circle containing a number represents an island. The object is to connect each island with vertical or horizontal bridges so that:

- The number of bridges is the same as the number inside the island.
- There are no more than two bridges between two islands.
- Bridges do not cross islands or other bridges.
- There is a continuous path connecting all the islands.

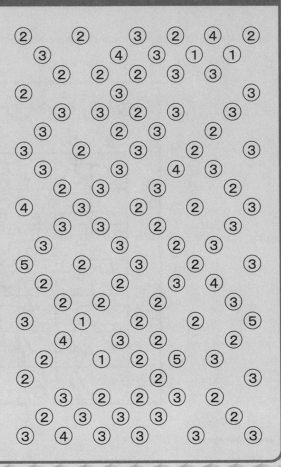

Answer on page 464

55 · SHARP'S SUPERSTORE

When Mr. Smith was appointed manager of a brand new Sharp's supermarket, he was faced with the task of stocking the shelves, following guidelines given by the area manager. Can you help Smith sort stock on Sharp's shelves?

"Don't mix commodities up on the shelves. The cookies and frozen vegetables must face the wall, but put them on opposite sides of the store. Obviously, both freezers should be back-to-back, with the fruit juices facing the frozen meat."

"All the nonconsumable items including the pet food should be stocked in the same area. I suggest the far southwest corner. The soap powder should be opposite the cleaning fluids and back-to-back with the pet food."

"All the canned produce must be on the east side of the store, with the canned meat and canned vegetables back-to-back. Put the canned fruit on a north-facing shelf and the canned meat on a south-facing shelf, opposite the baking items. The baking items should be

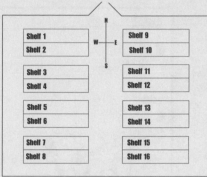

in the same row as the pet food."

"Cakes and cookies should be back-to-back, with the candy in the same row as the cakes and facing south."

"Reserve shelf 3 for the tea and coffee, and remember to find shelves for the bread and kitchenware."

Answer on page 464

Follow the dots from 1 to 34 to reveal the hidden picture.

Answer on page 465

57 · CELL STRUCTURE

The object is to create white areas surrounded by black walls, so that:

- Each white area contains only one number.
- The number of cells in a white area is equal to the number in it.
- The white areas are separated from each other by a black wall.
- Cells containing numbers are not filled in.
- The black cells are linked into a continuous wall.
- Black cells do not form a square of 2 x 2 or larger.

			1						1		
3										3	
	1					6					
							9				
				3						4	
	3										
				5			4		2		
2		4				2		2			
									2		
						2		2			
	4								2		
		3			2		2		2		
1			1			2					
											3
	1							4		1	
		5									
3				2					2		
	3						4				
					2						
		5							3	2	
					4						2
10									2		
							6				

Answer on page 465

65

58 · LATIN SQUARE

Each cell of the square below has one of the digits from 1 to 7. Each row and each column has exactly one of each digit. The clues below give the sum total of the digits in two or more cells. From these clues, can you figure out what number is in each cell?

A12=6   DEF6=18
ABCD7=10   DEFG3=11
B123=15   EFG1=6
B567=12   EFG4=16
BCD5=18   F23=8
C234=16   G23=7
CD7=5   G4567=18

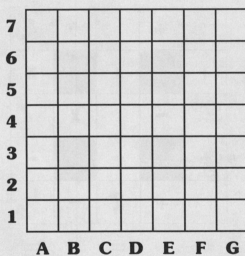

Answer on page 465

All the digits from 1 to 9 are used in this grid, but only once each. Can you work out their positions in the grid and make the totals work? We've given two numbers to start you off.

Answer on page 465

60 · LABYRINTH

Starting on the left, moving forward one hexagon at a time, try to work your way to the other side. At each step, you must follow the instruction for that column (such as x 4). There are, of course, dead ends. Go on—be amazed!

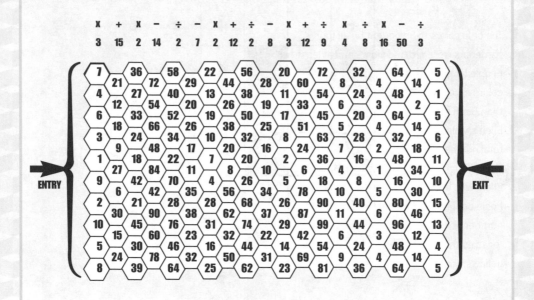

61 · BLOOMERS

Charlie Dimwit's garden center, Bloomers, has a fine display of potted plants for sale. Four gardeners each took ten pots from the stand. Each gardener took a different number of pots of the colors they selected. After they had taken their pots, there were an equal number of each color left over. From the information given, can you figure out what each gardener selected?

The only colors to be bought by all four gardeners were red and violet, and at least two people bought four colors. Rosie bought all colors except blue; she bought one less red than Geoff's greens and two more reds than Ellen's violets. The two women bought half the total number of yellow flowers between them. Percy bought all colors except green, as did Ellen, who bought twice as many blues as Rosie bought yellows. Geoff bought the same number of reds as Percy did violets, and together these totaled the same as Rosie's yellows.

Answer on page 465

62 · LATIN SQUARE

Each cell of the square has one of the digits from 1 to 7. Each row and each column has exactly one of each digit. The clues below give the total of two or more cells. From these clues, can you figure out what number is in each cell?

A567=11
ABC2=12
AB5=10
B456=7
C123=9
CDE6=15

D67=9
DEFG1=10
DEFG3=22
DEF7=6
E2345=22
F456=9

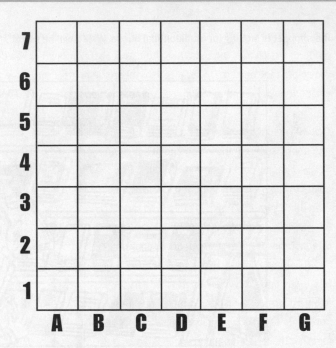

Answer on page 465

63 · FOURSOME

The shopper is looking for four identical books. Which will he select?

Answer on page 465

64 · CRIME SQUAD

The criminals involved in the four scenes on the right were soon arrested by a smart detective who spotted them in the larger picture. Can you spot them as well?

Answer on page 466

65 · ARROW NUMBERS

Each number already in the grid shows the sum of the digits in the line whose direction is shown by the arrow. Only one digit can be placed in each square. There are no zeros. For each sum, each digit can only appear once—e.g., 8 cannot be completed with 44. A sequence of digits forming a sum can only appear once in the grid. If 8 is 53 somewhere then another 8 cannot also be 53. Nor could it be 35, but must contain a different set of digits, such as 71/17, or 62/26. Can you put logic, rather than higher math, to work and find the unique solution?

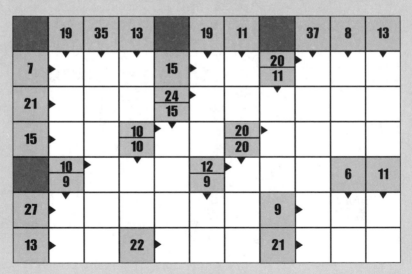

Answer on page 466

The six squares seen highlighted at the top right-hand corner of the grid are repeated in only one other place. Can you see where?

Answer on page 466

67 · WHATEVER NEXT?

Can you give the next letter in this sequence?

A D O P Q **?**

Answer on page 466

These piles of blocks aren't the random results of a child playing but clues to a final, at present blank, pile on the right. Like the rest, that one has six blocks each with a different one of the six letters.

The numbers below the stacks tell you two things:
(a) The number of adjacent pairs of blocks in that column that also appear adjacent in the final pile.
(b) The number of adjacent pairs of blocks that make a correct pair but the wrong way up.

So:

would score one in the "Correct" row if the final stack had an A directly above a C and one in the "Reversed" row if the final heap had a C on top of an A. From all of this, can you create the tower before it finally topples?

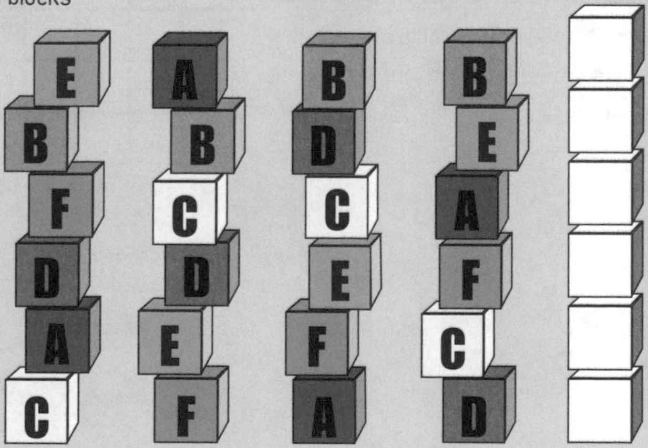

PAIRS					
Correct	0	0	0	0	5
Reversed	0	1	2	2	0

Answer on page 466

Do you remember the old game of battleships? These puzzles are based on that idea. Your task is to find the vessels in the diagram. Some parts of boats or sea squares have already been filled in, and a number next to a row or column refers to the number of occupied squares in that row or column. The boats may be positioned horizontally or vertically, but no two boats or parts of boats are in adjacent squares—horizontally, vertically, or diagonally.

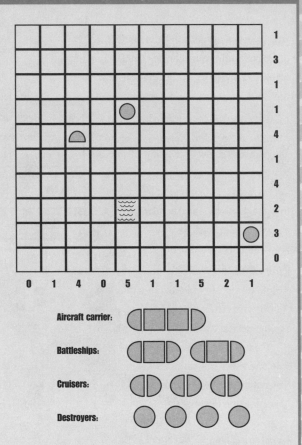

Aircraft carrier:

Battleships:

Cruisers:

Destroyers:

Answer on page 466

70 · PEN PALS

Five school friends went their separate ways to seek their fortunes. They had agreed to write to each other from time to time, but not to be bound by any "take turns" approach. In their first year after graduation it turned out that:

1 Chris wrote twice as many letters to Gainor as he did to Insley, who wrote twice as many to Al as to Ed.

2 Gainor received twice as many letters from Don as he did from Bob, who wrote four to Insley.

3 Al wrote more to Gainor than he did to Jarrett, who received three letters from Chris.

4 Harkness wrote more to Chris than Chris wrote to Harkness.

5 Don received twice as many letters form Farley as he did from Harkness.

6 No one wrote the same number to any two of the others. Each wrote and received ten letters.

From AL	■
To: BOB CHRIS DON ED	

From BOB	■
To: AL CHRIS DON ED	

From DON	■
To: AL BOB CHRIS ED	

From CHRIS	■
To: AL BOB DON ED	

From ED	■
To: AL BOB CHRIS DON	

Can you give each writer's surname and say how many letters (at least one) he sent to each of the others?

Answer on page 466

71 · HANJIE

The numbers alongside each row or column tell you how many blocks of black squares are in a line. For example: 2, 3, 5 tells you that from left to right (or top to bottom) there is a group of two black squares, then at least one white space, then a group of three black squares, then at least one white square, then a group of five black squares. Each block of black squares in the same line must have at least one white square between it and the next block of black squares.

Sometimes it is possible to tell which squares are going to be black without reference to other lines or columns. In the example below, we can deduce that any block of six black squares must incorporate the two central squares.

6

Can you complete this Hanjie puzzle, to reveal the hidden pattern or picture?

Answer on page 466

Column clues (left to right):

Column	Clue
1	6 1
2	2 2 2
3	1 4 2 3
4	2 2 2 11
5	1 2 1 3
6	2 1 2 2 1
7	2 1 1 2
8	10 5 2
9	1 1 1 1 3 1 2 2
10	1 1 1 2 5
11	1 1 1 3 8
12	9 11
13	2 5 4 3
14	2 6 1 5
15	2 7 6
16	2 5 2 3
17	2 11
18	2 8
19	2 4
20	2

Row clues (top to bottom):

Row	Clue
1	3 1
2	2 3
3	1 1 6
4	2 3 1 1
5	1 2 7
6	1 1 1 5
7	1 1 2 2 4
8	1 2 1 1 4
9	2 3 1 1 1 2
10	2 4 2 3
11	2 11
12	1 3 6
13	1 7
14	1 1 7
15	1 3 4 3
16	1 1 1 2 3
17	1 1 2 3
18	1 1 4 3
19	2 3 1 1
20	3 3 3
21	10 3
22	1 6 3
23	1 6
24	1 7
25	2 1 6

(c) Conceptis Puzzles UK10516

In a snooker break, a player alternately pots, or sinks, red balls (of which there are 15) and colored balls (of which there are six, one of each color). After a colored ball is potted, it is replaced on the table.

The point values of the balls are:

 RED 1

 YELLOW 2

 GREEN 3

 BROWN 4

 BLUE 5

 PINK 6

BLACK 7

Snooker player Bob Basher made a break of 70, which ended when he failed to pot a red. In the break, he potted the same number of blue and brown and one more pink than yellow, potting all four colors in the break.

How many of each ball were potted?

Answer on page 466

73 · SIX SQUARES

The six squares seen highlighted at the top right-hand corner of the grid are repeated in only one other place. Can you see where?

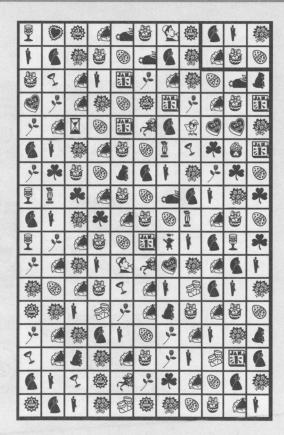

Answer on page 467

74 · THE WHEEL THING

Which two of the pictures below form a matching pair?

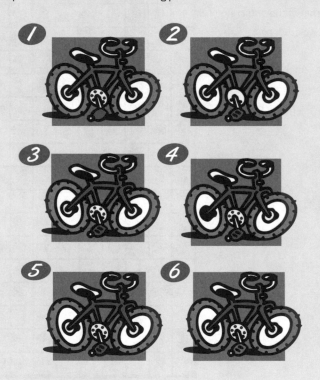

Answer on page 467

75 · DOMINO DEAL

A standard set of dominoes (0–0 to 6–6) is laid out below. Each domino is placed so that the larger number will be on the bottom:

i.e.: 3 not 6
       6   3

Those top numbers show the four numbers that form the top half of each domino in that column. The bottom numbers, below the grid, give the four bottom numbers for that column. The seven numbers on the left show the numbers that belong in that row. Can you cross-reference the facts and deduce where each domino has been placed? 3–6 is given as a start.

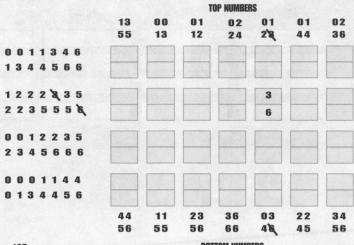

TOP NUMBERS

	13 55	00 13	01 12	02 24	01 23	01 44	02 36
0 0 1 1 3 4 6 / 1 3 4 4 5 6 6							
1 2 2 2 3 3 5 / 2 2 3 5 5 5 6					3 6		
0 0 1 2 2 3 5 / 2 3 4 5 6 6 6							
0 0 0 1 1 4 4 / 0 1 3 4 4 5 6							
	44 56	11 55	23 56	36 66	03 46	22 45	34 56

BOTTOM NUMBERS

Answer on page 467

At the Little Appenin local fair, a plant booth had a display of 25 potted plants. Four customers each bought five plants—taking one from each row and each column. So with just five plants left, each was given a free gift of a plant type she had not already bought. Madge was given the plant next to one of the ferns she purchased. The picture shows one plant bought by each customer. The chart indicates how many of some plants each purchased. (For nongardeners, the begonia is yellow, the azalea is pink, and the other two are, hopefully, obvious.) At the end of it all, which plant was left on the table and which pots did each buy or was given?

	Azalea	Begonia	Cactus	Fern
Jackie			3	
Kim				3
Laura		3		
Madge			2	2

Answer on page 467

77 · NUMBER JIG

Fit the numbers into the grid. One has been done for you.

3 figures	4 figures	40134
130	2190	48181
191	3253	50242
219	8491	50551
233	9725	52104
354		53606
419	5 figures	60885
463	12663	62271
507	13002	65018
588	19309	77123
671	20393	83118
690	26205	89031
~~807~~	29994	90460
876	31069	91203
935	31155	92186
	32194	93661
	33062	93906

6 figures

110375	546371
452706	680935
	790020

Answer on page 467

78 · SUDOKU

Place a number from 1 to 9 in each empty square so that each row, each column, and each 3 x 3 block contain all the numbers from 1 to 9.

	6	3			2	4	1	
4			5		8			7
8			1		3			6
9	8	7				1	4	
				3				
	2	4				6	9	5
7			2		1			4
6			3		9			1
	1	8	4			7	3	

Answer on page 467

79 · DOMINO SEARCH

A set of dominoes has been laid out, using numbers instead of dots for clarity, but the lines that separate the dominoes have been left out. Can you show where each domino in the set has been placed? You may find the check grid useful, since each domino is identified by its number pair and the appropriate box can be checked off when the domino has been located. To give you a start, 5–2 has been marked in.

6	1	0	3	4	3	4	1
1	6	6	3	6	5	2	2
2	0	3	1	2	3	5	1
1	3	4	2	6	1	1	0
5	4	2	6	0	5	2	5
3	0	4	0	4	6	4	4
0	3	6	0	2	5	5	5

0							
1							
2							
3							
4							
5			X				
6							
	0	1	2	3	4	5	6

Answer on page 468

80 · IT FIGURES

Place a number from 1 to 9 in each empty cell so that the sum of each vertical or horizontal block equals the number at the top or on the left of that block. Numbers may only be used once in each block.

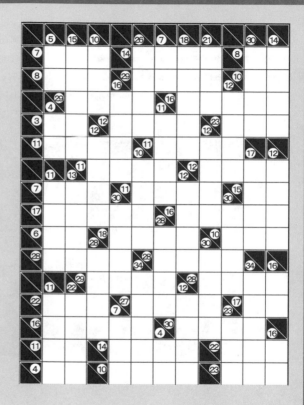

Answer on page 468

81 · BOOK BORROWING

The top shelf shows books at the start of the day, when Puzzleton Library opened. The bottom shelf shows books at the end of the day, when Puzzleton Library closed. During the day the books were all studied by various people who replaced them in different positions, and one was borrowed and taken home. Can you discover which is missing?

Answer on page 468

82 · BOXES

Pattern A, when cut out and folded along the straight lines, will make a cube-shaped box. This folded box is shown in figures 1 and 2, but in each case one face is left blank. Can you fill in the missing symbols that should appear on the blank faces? When you have done this, repeat the same procedure with pattern B and figures 3 and 4.

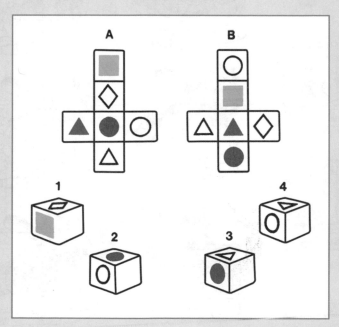

Answer on page 468

Which of the falling girls are identical?

Answer on page 468

84 · EASY AS ABC

Each row and column originally contained one A, one B, one C, one D, and two blank squares. Each letter and number refers to the first or second of the four letters encountered when traveling in the direction of the arrow. Can you complete the original grid?

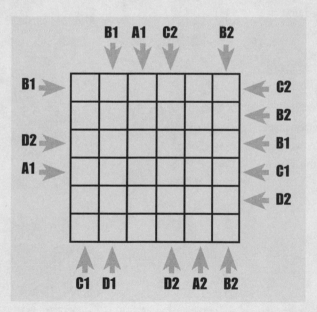

Answer on page 468

Each circle containing a number represents an island. The object is to connect each island with vertical or horizontal bridges so that:

- The number of bridges is the same as the number inside the island.
- There are no more than two bridges between two islands.
- Bridges do not cross islands or other bridges.
- There is a continuous path connecting all the islands.

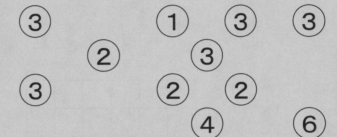

Answer on page 468

86 · BIG BREAK

In a snooker break, a player alternately pots, or sinks, red balls (of which there are 15) and colored balls (of which there are six, one of each color). After a colored ball is potted, it is replaced on the table. The point values of the balls are:

- 🔴 **RED 1**
- ⚪ **YELLOW 2**
- 🟢 **GREEN 3**

- 🟤 **BROWN 4**
- 🔵 **BLUE 5**
- 🩷 **PINK 6**
- ⚫ **BLACK 7**

Snooker player Bob Basher, otherwise known as the Bristol Breeze, made a break of 71, which ended when he failed to pot a red. In the break he potted two more pinks than greens and two more yellows than blues, potting only these four colors in the break.

How many of each ball were potted?

Answer on page 468

87 · SIX-PACK

By packing numbers in the empty spaces, can you make the numbers in each of the 16 hexagons add up to 25? No two numbers in each hexagon may be the same, and you can't use zero. We've started you off.

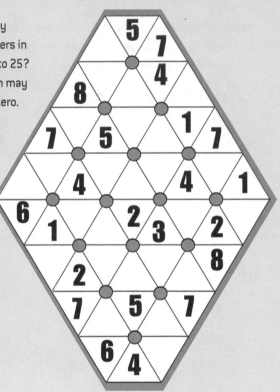

Answer on page 468

88 · BATTLESHIPS

Do you remember the old game of battleships? This puzzle is based on that idea. Your task is to find the six vessels in the diagram. Some parts of boats or sea squares have already been filled in, and a number next to a row or column refers to the number of occupied squares in that row or column. A row or column with nothing next to it does not necessarily mean that there are no ship parts there. The boats may be positioned horizontally or vertically, but no two boats or parts of boats are in adjacent squares—horizontally, vertically, or diagonally.

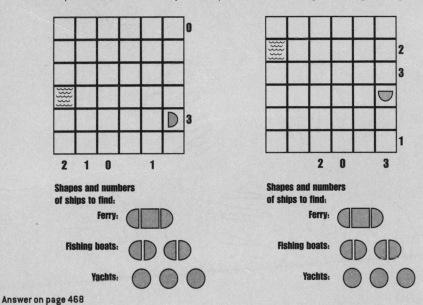

Shapes and numbers
of ships to find:

Ferry:

Fishing boats:

Yachts:

Answer on page 468

Which are the only two pieces that will fit together perfectly to form a complete circle?

Answer on page 469

90 · NUMBER JIG

Fit the numbers into the grid.
One has been done for you.

3 figures	4 figures	39792
172	2933	40013
296	3461	42618
317	6514	48887
366	9943	49980
413		50468
541	**5 figures**	52789
552	11903	67158
622	14712	72422
673	15704	72431
707	21014	73538
745	26817	75368
818	29306	77213
820	29317	86261
914	30115	92065
	37304	93371
	39610	93770

6 figures	876421
493918	933016
763081	946152

Answer on page 469

91 · LOGI-5

Each line, across and down, is to have each of the five colors appearing once each. Each color must also appear just once in each shape, shown by thick lines. Can you color in this crazy quilt, or mark each square with a letter by which the color can be identified?

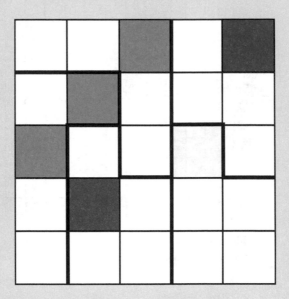

Answer on page 469

92 · SPOT THE DIFFERENCE

Can you tell which one of these
pictures is different from the
others?

Answer on page 469

93 · TEE TIME

Three old-timers play a weekly game of golf on the Golden Lawns 18-hole, par 72, course. Each score at every hole falls into one of five categories. Each golfer gets a different result, greater than zero, in each category. Also, no category has the same result for another player, i.e., if a player has two eagles, he has a different number in the other four and no other player has two eagles. With the score details below and the information given, can you fill in their card? Nick's bogeys were the same as Barry's pars and Parnell's double bogeys, and together they totaled the same as Parnell's pars, which were one more than Nick's birdies, which were one more than Barry's double bogeys, which were the same as Parnell's eagles, and these last two together totalled Barry's birdies. The total number of eagles was more than the double bogeys but less than the bogeys.

	Eagle −2	Birdie −1	Par 0	Bogey +1	Double Bogey +2	FINAL SCORE
Parnell Darma						
Nick Jackliss						
Barry Clayer						

Answer on page 469

94 · ON THE SPOT

Can you place the dominoes into the grid so that the four vertical, four horizontal, and both diagonal rows each have a pip value of nine?

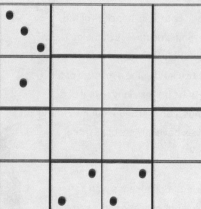

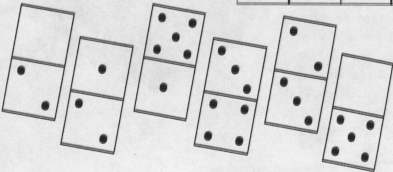

Answer on page 469

95 · FLOWER POWER

Patriotic Pete sells bunches of red, white, and blue flowers in the market. Some bunches have just a single color, some two, and some a mixture of all three. If he brings along a total of 80 bunches, can you figure out how many bunches have flowers of all three colors?

The number of bunches with both red and blue but no white is the same as that with blue only, and together they total the number with both red and white but no blue. The number with white only is double that with all three, which is one less than red only, which is the same as that with both blue and white but no red. Fifty-five bunches had white flowers in them.

Answer on page 469

These joggers are so pleased with themselves for doing some exercise over Christmas that they've decided to treat themselves to extra helpings of cake when they get back. Follow the trails to discover which runner is after each cake.

Answer on page 469

97 · BLOOMERS

Charlie Dimwit's garden center, Bloomers, has a fine display of potted plants for sale. Four gardeners each took ten pots from the stand. Each gardener took a different number of pots of the colors they selected. After they had taken their pots, there were an equal number of each color left over. From the information given can you work out what each gardener selected?

The two gardeners whose names begin with A bought seven blues between them. George bought twice as many yellows as reds. The two women each bought the same number of yellows. Barbara bought no blues or violets. The two men bought half the sold number of blues, but neither bought any greens. Anne bought one more green than violets, and the total of the two was one more than Barbara's reds. Albert also bought some fertilizer, but that has nothing to do with the puzzle.

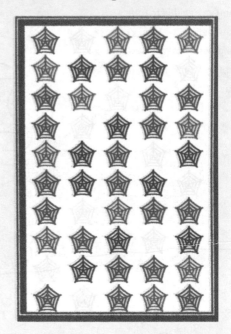

Answer on page 469

A set of dominoes has been laid out, using numbers instead of dots for clarity, but the lines that separate the dominoes have been left out. Can you, armed with a sharp pencil and keen brain, show where each domino in the set has been placed? You may find the check grid useful, since each domino is identified by its number pair and the appropriate box can be checked off when the domino has been located.

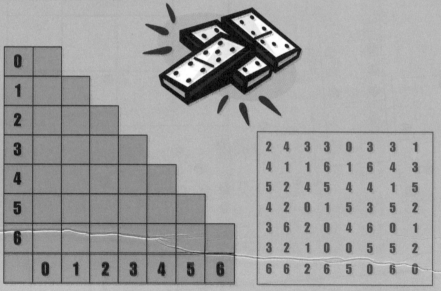

	0	1	2	3	4	5	6

2	4	3	3	0	3	3	1
4	1	1	6	1	6	4	3
5	2	4	5	4	4	1	5
4	2	0	1	5	3	5	2
3	6	2	0	4	6	0	1
3	2	1	0	0	5	5	2
6	6	2	6	5	0	6	0

Answer on page 469

99 · ON THE SPOT

Can you place the dominoes into the grid so that the four vertical, four horizontal, and both diagonal rows each have a pip total of eight?

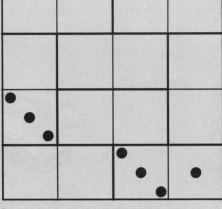

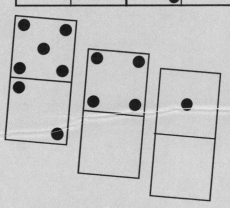

Answer on page 469

Place a number from 1 to 9 in each empty square so that each row, each column, and each 3 x 3 block contain all the numbers from 1 to 9.

			5		4		1	
6	8				9		7	
		9				3		
3	5			7				8
			2		1			
1				4			5	9
		2				5		
	9		3				4	2
	4		6		8			

Answer on page 470

101 · PAINT BOXES

In each of the pictures on the right, there is a different amount of paint dripping from the brush. Starting with picture F, can you put these pictures in order, so that in each new picture the paint drip is larger than before?

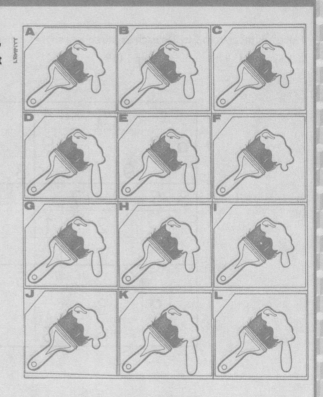

Answer on page 470

102 · GIVING IT THE BOOT

Four boys were fishing in a shallow stream, each wearing a different colored pair of boots. From the clues given below, can you identify the boys in positions 1 to 4 and figure out the color of the boots each was wearing?

First names: Darren; Garry; Johnny; Shaun
Surnames: Brook; Burne; Poole; Waters
Boots: black; brown; green; red

Starting tip: Start by working out the first name of the boy in position 1.

1 The boy in the red boots is somewhere to the left of Shaun, whose surname is not Brook.
2 Darren Poole is somewhere to the right of the youth in the brown boots.
3 Wader number 3 is Johnny; the surname of the boy in position 2 is not Burne.
4 The green boots are worn by a boy wading alongside Garry, while Waters is standing next to his friend whose boots are black.

First name: _____ _____ _____ _____

Surname: _____ _____ _____ _____

Boots: _____ _____ _____ _____

Answer on page 470

103 · IT FIGURES

Place a number from 1 to 9 in each empty cell so that the sum of each vertical or horizontal block equals the number at the top or on the left of that block. Numbers may only be used once in each block.

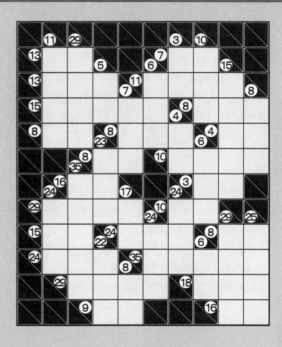

Answer on page 470

Which one of the two contacts will be touched when the mechanic turns the handle as shown?

Answer on page 470

Rearrange these matches to make 14 squares.

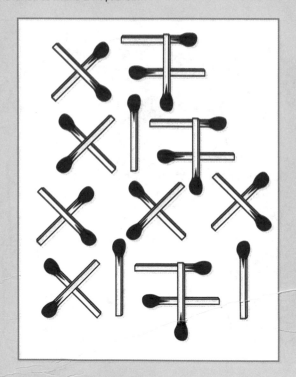

Answer on page 470

Charlie Dimwit's garden center, Bloomers, has a fine display of potted plants for sale. Four gardeners each took ten pots from the stand. Each gardener took a different number of pots of the plants they selected. After they had taken their pots, there was an equal number of each plant left over. From the information below can you figure out what each gardener selected? In case you are tempted to rush out to Bloomers, the gardenias are now sold out!

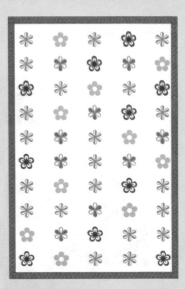

Connie bought twice as many African violets as begonias and the same number of begonias as Debbie, who bought two less African violets than begonias. Arthur bought half the number of begonias as Barry bought cyclamens, and Barry bought no begonias. Debbie was the only one not to buy cyclamens, and Arthur bought no African violets but twice as many jasmines as Barry.

Answer on page 470

107 · SQUARE FILL

How many squares, of all sizes, are more black than white in this picture?

Answer on page 470

108 · DOTTY DILEMMA

Connect adjacent dots with vertical or horizontal lines so that a single loop is formed with no crossings or branches. Each number indicates how many lines surround it, while empty cells may be surrounded by any number of lines.

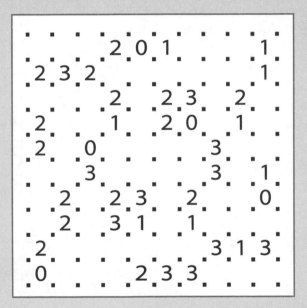

Answer on page 471

109 · CELL STRUCTURE

The object is to create white areas surrounded by black walls, so that:

- Each white area contains only one number.
- The number of cells in a white area is equal to the number in it.
- The white areas are separated from each other by a black wall.
- Cells containing numbers are not filled in.
- The black cells are linked into a continuous wall.
- Black cells do not form a square of 2x2 or larger.

	2	3								3
								3		
			3			3	4	1		
5		2								
	4				5					
					5					
							4			3
						2				
3	4		3							
						2		1		
2			3				3			
		1				2				4
	3		5							
						3		2		3
		3								
3		4								
			4							
			5						4	
							1			3
	3	3	3			5				
		1								
3							5	4		

Answer on page 471

120

Can you spot the ten differences between these two pictures?

Answer on page 471

111 · STRAWBERRY SHARES

Can you carve up this ornate cake, cutting along the intersecting lines only, to produce eight equally sized portions? Each portion is to be decorated with one square of chocolate, one iced cake, a blob of cream, and one strawberry.

Answer on page 471

112 · ALPHABET ECHO

In the grid, each letter of the alphabet appears twice and there are four blanks. Neither the same or any two consecutive letters of the alphabet appear in the same row, column, or diagonal. A and Z are not treated as consecutive in this puzzle. Beside each row and column appear two numbers; the black number shows how many vowels appear in that row or column, and the blue number shows how many of the letters are in the first half of the alphabet, i.e., A–M. Using the additional clues below, can you fill in the grid?

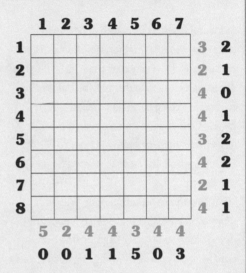

Letters that are repeated:

In the first four rows	D, F, M, P, S, U, Y
In the last four rows	A, C, L, O, Q, T
In the first four columns	B, D, G, K, N, Q, R, V
In the last four columns	C, E, H, I, M, O, P, S, U, X, Z

In adjacent rows   D, F, M, O, P, Q, S, U, Y
In adjacent columns   B, H, I, K, X, Z

JRY and FIR read diagonally downward. One column contains three blanks, but there are none in the left-hand column. One G is in the top row, but there are no Bs in row 6.

Answer on page 471

Inspector Drayne of the Yard pulled up in his car at the door of Whartson Hall, home of Lord and Lady Mole. He entered the hall. Swiftly his eyes traveled around the interior. Not waiting for them to come back, he stepped blindly forward and tripped over a scullery maid. A large butler helped him to his feet.

"This way, sir. The body is waiting for you in the library."

Passing through another door, Drayne stopped in horror. He had seen death before many times—but never like this. The body of Lord Mole lay on a Persian rug, his head caked in a thick, glutinous yellow liquid. It was obvious he had been battered to death.

Drayne turned to the local detective who was leaning against a constable.

"Where was each person at the time of the murder?"

The detective cleared his throat, cleaned his glass eye, and varnished his nails.

Answer on page 471

"Lady Mole says she was in the card room; the Honorable Reginald Ackney in the billiard room; Reverend Rash, the lounge; Lance O'Boyle, the morning room. Miss Felicity Bytes was in the study. Spott, the butler, and Wicklow, the maid, were in the cloakroom."

"Thank you. Now it's obvious that . . ."

A sobbing interrupted his train of thought, which went off the rails. The maid he had tripped over was having her arm set in plaster, but Drayne was sure her tears were not for that. He looked at her, stern but kindly.

"Please, sir. I was told to say we were together by Mr. Spott. But we wasn't."

"Were you alone?"

"If you please, sir, yes, sir."

An inner light in Drayne's mind signalled green, and his train of thought shunted back on track. "Not only was Wicklow here, lying," he said, "but I know for a fact that not one of you was in the room you claimed to be in. And each of you was alone—except one—the murderer!

"I shall now take a statement from each of you, and it had better be the truth this time."

It was.

Lady Mole recalled that Reverend Rash was in a room next to hers but Wicklow was not. The Honorable Reginald, who thought himself quite good with numbers, was in a room with fewer doors than the one her ladyship was in but more than the one occupied by Lance O'Boyle.

Reverend Rash seemed flustered. "Well, yes. I'm sure there was a lady in one room next to mine and a man in another. But I don't know who was in the third—you see, the door to that room was shut at the time."

Felicity Bytes stated candidly that Reverend Rash had not been in the lounge, because she had been in a room next to it.

Spott declared that he had not been in a room adjacent to either Wicklow or the Honorable Reginald. He also confirmed that there was no door between the billiard room and the study. Wicklow sobbed out between her tears that Mr.

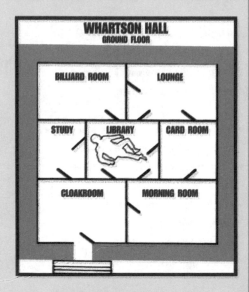

O'Boyle had been in a room next to hers.

Drayne was stumped. He wrung his hands and then his wife. She agreed to warm his dinner in the oven.

To the assembled suspects he had but one thing to say. "I haven't a clue who was in the library—will somebody please confess?" No one did, so—whodunnit?

Each circle containing a number represents an island. The object is to connect each island with vertical or horizontal bridges so that:

• The number of bridges is the same as the number inside the island.
• There are no more than two bridges between two islands.
• Bridges do not cross islands or other bridges.
• There is a continuous path connecting all the islands.

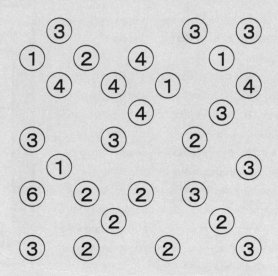

Answer on page 472

115 · TENTACKLE

Eight children are camping, two to each tent, and some have given us a couple of clues as to how to find them. The trouble is their senses of direction are as bad as their cooking, and in each case only one direction is true while the other is an exact opposite, so that east should read west, etc. Directions are not necessarily exact, so north could be north, northeast, or northwest. To help you, one child is already tucked into a sleeping bag.

Kate says: "I'm west of Jenny and south of Sally."
Megan says: "I'm east of Lisa and south of Naomi."
Rita says: "I'm west of Megan and south of Kate."
Sally says: "I'm west of Paula and north of Lisa."

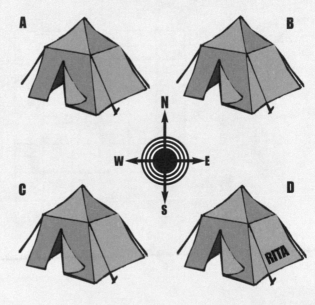

Answer on page 472

116 · EASY AS ABC

Each row and column originally contained one A, one B, one C, one D, and two blank squares. Each letter and number refers to the first or second of the four letters encountered when traveling in the direction of the arrow. Can you complete the original grid?

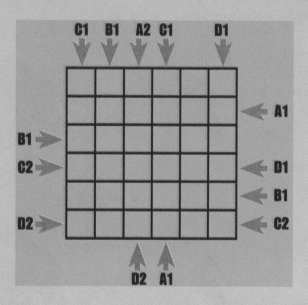

Answer on page 472

117 · STAR LINES

With one continuous line, connect all the circles (starting from Pisces, the fish) and, with another continuous line, connect all the triangles (starting from Gemini, the twins). The lines must not cross!

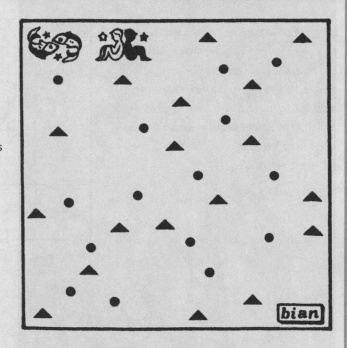

Answer on page 472

118 · WHERE THE L?

Sixteen L shapes like the ones below have been inserted into a square shape. Each L has one hole, and there are four of each type in the square. No two pieces of the same type are adjacent, even at a corner. They fit together so well that the spaces between pieces do not show. From the locations of the holes, can you tell where each L is?

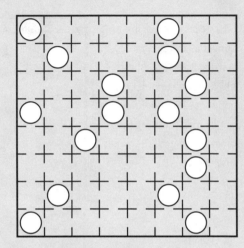

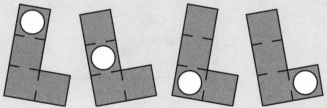

Answer on page 472

Which two cubes can be constructed from the template?

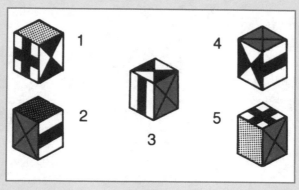

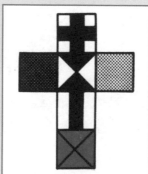

Answer on page 472.

Connect adjacent dots with vertical or horizontal lines so that a single loop is formed with no crossings or branches. Each number indicates how many lines surround it, while empty cells may be surrounded by any number of lines.

```
 0       2 0       3   1
    2          2      1
 2    3          3 0
    1    3              1
    3       0    1 0    2
 2    2 3    1       1
 1             1    2
    3 3             0    1
    2       3          1
 2    1       2 1       3
```

Answer on page 472

121 · DOUBLE PUZZLE

Line up, folks, for our special offer of two puzzles for the price of one!

Puzzle One: Each color has been given a value from 1 to 7. Given the totals at the end of each line, can you work out the value of each color?

Puzzle Two: The picture is a layout of a set of color dominoes—just like ordinary dominoes but with colors instead of spots. Can you draw in the lines to show each separate domino?

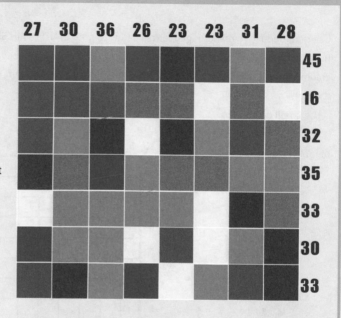

Answer on page 472

122 · LOGI-PATH

Use your deductive reasoning to form a pathway from START to FINISH moving in either direction horizontally or vertically (but not diagonally). The number at the beginning of every row or column indicates exactly how many boxes in that row or column your pathway must pass through.

The small diagram is given as an example of how it works.

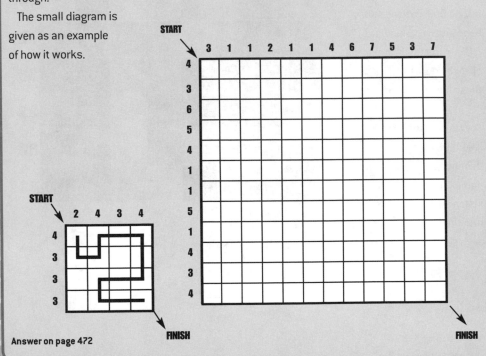

Answer on page 472

123 · ARTIST'S MAZE

Can you work your way through this maze, starting from the flower at the top and finishing at the bottom of the chair?

Answer on page 473

124 · SUDOKU

Place a number from 1 to 9 in each empty square so that each row, each column, and each 3 x 3 block contain all the numbers from 1 to 9.

7			3	4				5
		2			5			
	1					6		
2			1				7	
3								8
	4				2			9
		5					1	
			6			9		
4				7	8			2

Answer on page 473

125 · PILE UP

These piles of blocks aren't the random results of a child playing but clues to a final, at present blank, pile on the right. Like the rest, that one has six blocks each with a different one of the six letters.

The numbers below the stacks tell you two things:
(a) The number of adjacent pairs of blocks in that column that also appear adjacent in the final pile.
(b) The number of adjacent pairs of blocks that make a correct pair but the wrong way up.

So: 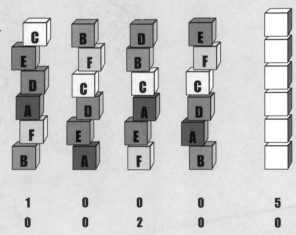 would score one in the "Correct" row if the final stack had an A directly above a C and one in the "Reversed" row if the final heap had a C on top of an A. From all of this, can you create the tower before it finally topples?

PAIRS					
Correct	1	0	0	0	5
Reversed	0	0	2	0	0

Answer on page 473

Which one of the numbered pieces can be used to repair the cat's mug?

Answer on page 473

127 · NUMBER KROSS

See how quickly you can fit all these numbers into the grid. We've filled one figure in to start you off.

3 figures
180
215
~~309~~
405
581
618
747
941

4 figures
1152
2145
3576
4336
5174

6713
7564
8105

5 figures
13131
15209
20415
21775
31001
33403
40756
43519
50221
57391
67890

69104
70395
71878
82701
90417

6 figures
151617
170154
278145
279156
313108
351057
417934
428496
543716

601537
629313
656667
770198

854352
931867
990173

3 0 9

Answer on page 473

128 · ALL OF A FLUTTER

Bean's party costume has attracted lots of butterflies! Can you see which type of butterfly is the only one to appear three times in this picture?

Answer on page 473

Each circle containing a number represents an island. The object is to connect each island with vertical or horizontal bridges so that:

- The number of bridges is the same as the number inside the island.
- There are no more than two bridges between two islands.
- Bridges do not cross islands or other bridges.
- There is a continuous path connecting all the islands.

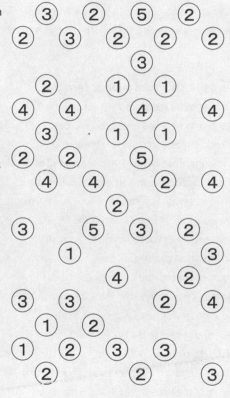

Answer on page 473

130 · SQUARE NUMBERS

The digits, ranging from 1 to 9, in each of the five lines and columns in this square add up to 23; three have been inserted. From the clues given below, can you fill in the rest?

	1	2	3	4	5
1					5
2					
3					
4					
5	3				5

1 In every line there are three odd and two even digits, as there are also in columns 1, 3, and 4; column 2 has four even and column 5 five odd digits. There are no repeated digits in any line, but column 1 has a repeated odd digit, as does column 5; the other columns have no repeated digits.

2 The two 9s are in lines 1 and 4, the two 8s are in two other successive lines, and the two lines that contain a 7 have a line separating them; the three 1s are in successive lines, and the three 2s are in odd-numbered lines. Only in line 3 is there no 3, and only in line 4 is there no 5; there are no 5s in columns 1 and 2.

3 In lines 2 and 3 the highest digit immediately precedes the lowest, but in line 4 the lowest

immediately precedes the highest. In line 1 the second digit is one higher than the fourth, but in line 5 the second is lower than the fourth.

4 The square at the intersection of line 3 and column 4 does not contain 5; the square at the end of line 3 contains an odd digit.

Starting tip: Figure out in which lines the 8s appear.

Answer on page 473

131 · DOT-TO-DOT

Follow the dots from 1 to 45 to reveal the hidden picture.

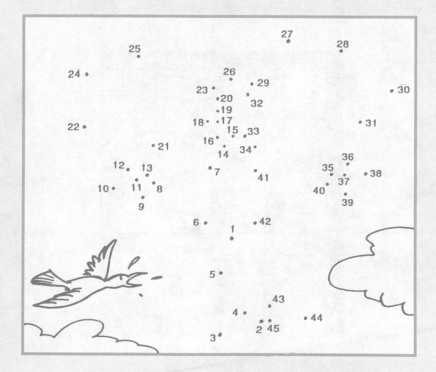

Answer on page 474

Place a number from 1 to 9 in each empty cell so that the sum of each vertical or horizontal block equals the number at the top or on the left of that block. Numbers may only be used once in each block.

Answer on page 474

133 · SILHOUETTE

Shade in every fragment containing a dot—and what have you got?

Answer on page 474

134 · WHO'S WHO?

From the information given here, can you match each girl to her sister?

Answer on page 474

135 · SPOT THE DIFFERENCES

See how quickly you can spot the
ten differences between these
two clowns.

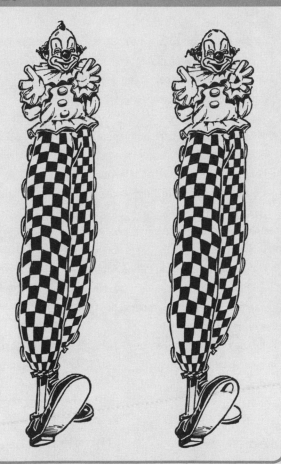

Answer on page 474

136 · ORIENT EXPRESS ALIASES

One day in the late 1920s, the *chef de train* of the Orient Express received a discreet warning that the passengers in the first four sleeping compartments were — well, not all they appeared to be. From the clues given below, can you work out the name in which each compartment had been reserved, and uncover the real name of its occupant?

1 Maxwell Van Skyler, the notorious American confidence trickster, occupied the compartment next to that of the man masquerading as Danish physics professor Nils Knudsen.

2 The man in compartment 4, who was not Russian spy Boris Zugov, was not posing as Middle Eastern playboy Prince Karim Al-Aziz.

3 Compartment 2 had been booked in the name of Sir Percival Gascoyne, described as a British diplomat.

4 Enrico Leone, the Italian jewel thief, traveled in compartment 1.

5 Franz Schmidt, the German anarchist, was two compartments away from the man posing as French aristocrat the Duc de Chomette.

Assumed names: Duc de Chomette; Prince Karim Al-Aziz; Professor Nils Knudsen; Sir Percival Gascoyne.

Real names: Boris Zugov; Enrico Leone; Franz Schmidt; Maxwell Van Skyler.

Starting tip: First figure out the real name of the passenger in compartment 4.

	1	2	3	4
Alias:	___	___	___	___
Real name:	___	___	___	___

Answer on page 474

137 · SQUARED OFF

The empty 4 x 4 grid was originally filled with the numbers from 1 to 16 inclusive. No two consecutive numbers were adjacent (including diagonally) or in the same row or column. Each of the sixteen numbers given in the full grid is the sum of the horizontal and vertical neighbors of the corresponding square in the original grid. Can you work out where the sixteen numbers originally were?

20	23	15	25
17	37	37	20
42	23	41	21
11	41	13	24

Answer on page 475

138 · BRIDGES

Each circle containing a number represents an island. The object is to connect each island with vertical or horizontal bridges so that:

- The number of bridges is the same as the number inside the island.
- There are no more than two bridges between two islands.
- Bridges do not cross islands or other bridges.
- There is a continuous path connecting all the islands.

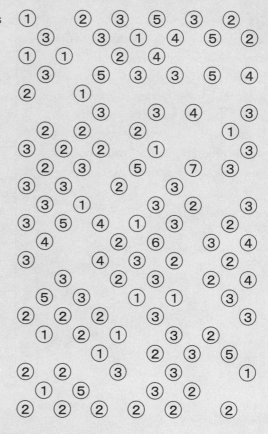

Answer on page 475

139 · SILHOUETTE

Shade in every fragment containing a dot—and what have you got?

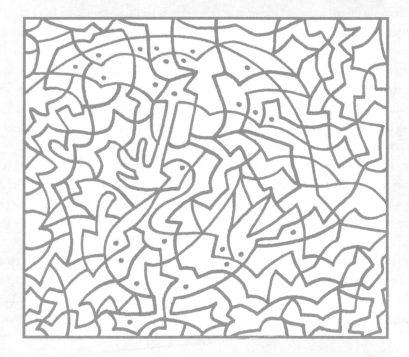

Answer on page 475

140 · WHICH CAR?

The game "Which Car?" is a card game using 36 different cards. Each card depicts a car of a particular make: either a Ford, a Lincoln, or a Chevrolet; a particular model: a sports car, a sedan, or an SUV; and the cars are red, green, blue, or silver. In this particular game, five children took part. They were each dealt seven cards, with the seventh being dealt face up. The 36th card was placed face down on the table. Each player in turn then stated (more or less!) which cards he or she did not have and then gave an indication of the most or least numbers of cards held of any combination of make, model, or color. In this game, no one held more than three cards in any category. George's exposed card was a green Ford sedan. He said he had no red and no blue Fords, no Chevrolet sports cars, and no Ford SUVs.

Anna's exposed card was a green Chevrolet SUV. She said she had no Ford sports cars, no silver Fords, no Ford SUVs, no red Lincolns, and no Chevrolet sedans. Katy's exposed card was a blue Chevrolet sedan. She said she had no red cars, no silver Lincolns, and no blue Fords. Richard's exposed card was a silver Lincoln sedan. He said he had no Chevrolet SUVs, no Lincoln sports cars, and no Ford sedans.

Jane's exposed card was a red Ford sports car. She said she had no red Chevrolet, no Ford sedans, no green Fords, no Chevrolet sports cars, and no silver Lincolns. George then said that he had more blue cars than any other color and more Lincolns than any other make. He said he had one sedan, one green car, and one silver. Anna said she had more Lincolns than any other make and more sedans than any other model, the latter of which were all

Answer on page 475

different colors. She said she had one blue car. Katy said she had more green cars than any other color and one sports car. She said she had more Chevrolets than any other make, all different models and colors. Richard said he had more Fords than any other make, all different colors. He said he had more SUVs than any other model, only one green car, and more reds than any other color, plus one silver sports car. Jane said she had more Ford cars than any other make, all different colors, and only one blue car.

At this stage, Richard was able to identify the 36th card because he had failed to declare a further single card of a particular color. Can you now evaluate each hand and name the 36th card?

	Ford			Lincoln			Chevrolet		
	Sp	Se	SUV	Sp	Se	SUV	Sp	Se	SUV
Red									
Green									
Blue									
Silver									

141 · SQUARED OFF

This empty 4 x 4 grid was originally filled with the numbers from 1 to 16 inclusive. No two consecutive numbers were adjacent (including diagonally) or in the same row or column. Each of the sixteen numbers given in the full grid is the sum of the horizontal and vertical neighbors of the corresponding square in the original grid. Can you work out where the sixteen numbers originally were?

20	21	24	17
23	41	40	25
39	28	40	28
5	37	14	19

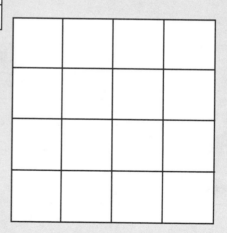

Answer on page 475

142 · CELL STRUCTURE

The object is to create white areas surrounded by black walls, so that:

- Each white area contains only one number.
- The number of cells in a white area is equal to the number in it.
- The white areas are separated from each other by a black wall.
- Cells containing numbers are not filled in.
- The black cells are linked into a continuous wall.
- Black cells do not form a square of 2 x 2 or larger.

				5					
									4
5					3		2		
	6			2					
					5			2	
				3					2
3									
					4				

Answer on page 475

143 · IT'S MAGIC

This magic square can be completed using every other number from 23 to 71. To give you a start, we have entered every 3 and all the numbers that are multiples of 3. Can you complete the square so that the five numbers in each row, column, and diagonal add up to the magic total? That total—and close your eyes now if you don't want to be told—is 235.

Answer on page 475

Each of the empty boxes contains a different digit from 1 to 9. Each calculation is to be treated sequentially rather than according to the "multiplication first" system. Can you fill in the empty boxes?

	X		÷		=	4
−		+		X		
	+		÷		=	4
+		−		−		
	+		−		=	4

=	=	=
4	4	3

Answer on page 475

145 · ISLANDS IN THE SUN

Four couples booked vacations on different islands for themselves and their two children. From the clues given below, can you match the couples, work out their surnames and the names of their children, and say which island paradise each foursome visited?

1 Rebecca is Charles's sister.

2 Keith and Angela's son is not the boy named Darren Morris.

3 Judy Langton's holiday location was not Cyprus, and her son's name is not Ian.

4 Chris is Garry's father, and Gail is the daughter of Lance, who did not visit the Canaries.

5 Violet is Fiona's mother; she is not married to Perry, and she is not Mrs. Chadwick, who spent her holiday in Crete.

6 Bridget and her husband took their children to Majorca.

Husband	Wife	Surname	Son	Daughter	Location

Answer on page 476

146 · CELL STRUCTURE

The object is to create white areas surrounded by black walls, so that:

* Each white area contains only one number.
* The number of cells in a white area is equal to the number in it.
* The white areas are separated from each other by a black wall.
* Cells containing numbers are not filled in.
* The black cells are linked into a continuous wall.
* Black cells do not form a square of 2 x 2 or larger.

4		4			4			3	
	3								
		3							
	3						4		
	3				3				
	5				5				

147 · PILE UP

These piles of blocks aren't the random results of a child playing but clues to a final, at present blank, pile on the right. Like the rest, that one has six blocks each with a different one of the six letters. The numbers below the stacks tell you two things:

(a) The number of adjacent pairs of blocks in that column that also appear adjacent in the final pile.
(b) The number of adjacent pairs of blocks that make a correct pair but the wrong way up.

So: 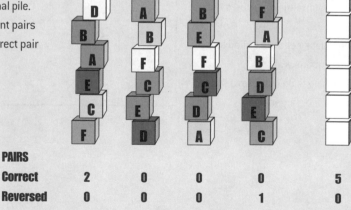 would score one in the "Correct" row if the final stack had an A directly above a C and one in the "Reversed" row if the final stack had a C on top of an A. From all of this, can you create the tower before it finally topples?

PAIRS					
Correct	2	0	0	0	5
Reversed	0	0	0	1	0

Answer on page 476

148 · BACKHANDER

Which one of these five archers is seen from the back in the top left-hand corner?

Answer on page 476

Which two numbers continue this sequence?

Answer on page 476

150 · A BOX IN THE SHED

When Joe needed something for a job around the house, he would say, "They're in a box in the shed." The four boxes shown in the diagram standing next to each other on a shelf, all of different colors, each contain a different number of useful items. From the clues given below, can you work out the full details?

1 The 43 nails of assorted sizes are not in the brown box.

2 There are 58 items in the blue box.

3 The screws are in the green box, one of whose immediate neighbors on the shelf contains the washers, and the other the largest number of items.

4 The carpet tacks are in box C.

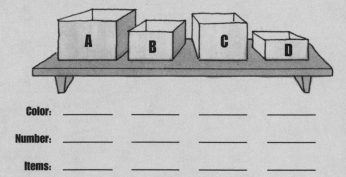

Color: _____ _____ _____ _____

Number: _____ _____ _____ _____

Items: _____ _____ _____ _____

Box colors: blue; brown; green; red

Number: 39; 43; 58; 65

Items: carpet tacks; nails; screws; washers

Starting tip: First figure out the color of the box containing the nails.

Answer on page 476

151 · SIX-PACK

By packing numbers in the empty spaces, can you make the numbers in each of the 16 hexagons add up to 25? No two numbers in each hexagon may be the same, and you can't use zero. We've started you off.

Answer on page 477

Although it's a quiet time for building jobs, these five merchants are busy supplying the needs of five builders who each need a different item for a different project.

Can you put the facts into place?

1 Alf Pryce is shopping at Hodsup, who do not sell stone, but he does not want wood, which is for the conservatory, which is not being built by A. Cowerboy.
2 T. Brakes wants sand.
3 The ballast is for the path. Cy Berman is building a bungalow.
4 The customer at BricksRus is building a garage, but this is not Val Heegham or A. Cowerboy, and none of these three wants cement or stone.

5 Neither Just Slates nor Mortar Mart sells stone, and the latter does not supply wood.

MERCHANT	CUSTOMER	ITEM	JOB
BRICKSRUS	A. COWERBOY	BALLAST	BUNGALOW
	ALF PRYCE	CEMENT	CONSERVATORY
	CY BERMAN	SAND	GARAGE
	T. BRAKES	STONE	PATH
	VAL HEEGHAM	WOOD	WALL
HIRAN HIRE	A. COWERBOY	BALLAST	BUNGALOW
	ALF PRYCE	CEMENT	CONSERVATORY
	CY BERMAN	SAND	GARAGE
	T. BRAKES	STONE	PATH
	VAL HEEGHAM	WOOD	WALL
HODSUP	A. COWERBOY	BALLAST	BUNGALOW
	ALF PRYCE	CEMENT	CONSERVATORY
	CY BERMAN	SAND	GARAGE
	T. BRAKES	STONE	PATH
	VAL HEEGHAM	WOOD	WALL
JUST SLATES	A. COWERBOY	BALLAST	BUNGALOW
	ALF PRYCE	CEMENT	CONSERVATORY
	CY BERMAN	SAND	GARAGE
	T. BRAKES	STONE	PATH
	VAL HEEGHAM	WOOD	WALL
MORTAR MART	A. COWERBOY	BALLAST	BUNGALOW
	ALF PRYCE	CEMENT	CONSERVATORY
	CY BERMAN	SAND	GARAGE
	T. BRAKES	STONE	PATH
	VAL HEEGHAM	WOOD	WALL

Answer on page 477

In order to answer that all-important social question, how many flies are there around the grease spot, six dice are thrown. The answers to the first three throws are given.

So what is the answer for the fourth throw?

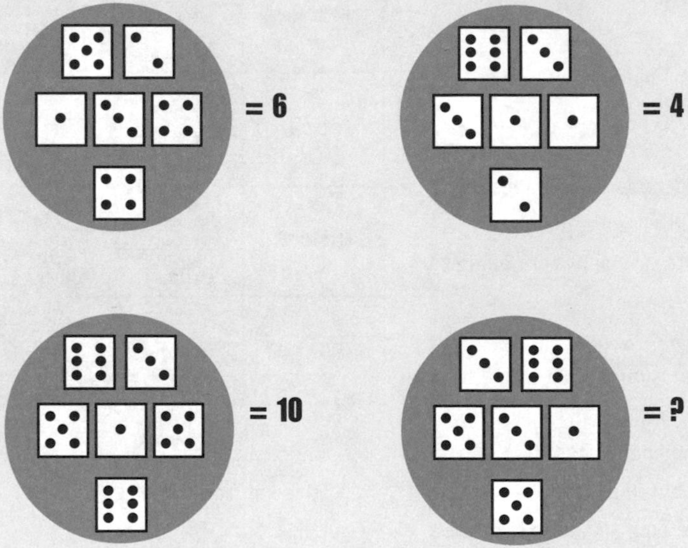

= 6

= 4

= 10

= ?

Answer on page 477

154 · MIRROR IMAGE

There are four pairs of mirror images below. Can you identify the pairs, and find the odd one out?

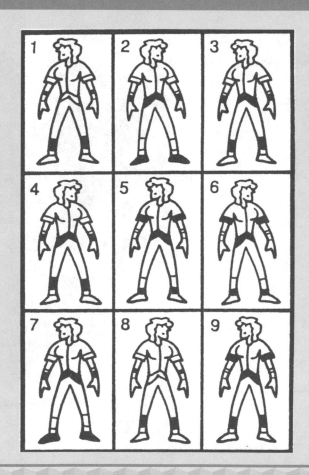

Answer on page 477

155 · SEARCH FOR A RAINBOW

The seven colors of the rainbow (red, orange, yellow, green, blue, indigo, violet) appear just once in the correct order in this grid, running in either a forward or backward direction, either vertically, horizontally, or diagonally. Can you locate the rainbow?

Answer on page 477

How many forks are needed to balance scale C?

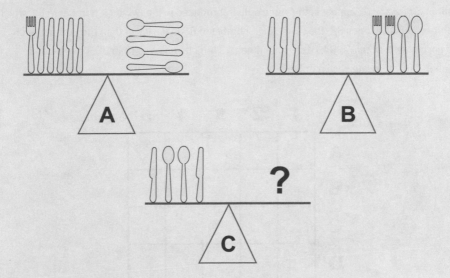

Answer on page 477

157 · SQUARE NUMBERS

The numbers 1 to 25 are arranged randomly in a 5 x 5 square so that no two consecutive numbers are adjacent in any direction or in the same row, column, or long diagonal. The corner numbers are all prime; A4 is twice A3; E2 is four times E3, and E4 is twice C4. The single-digit numbers in C2 and D2 appear in the same order reproduced in the two-digit number in B1, which is prime; B3 is five times B2. The single-digit number in B5 is ten lower than the number in C5 and six higher than that in B4. D1 is three times D3 but eleven lower than D5. D4 is an odd number. Can you locate each number?

	1	2	3	4	5
A					
B					
C					
D					
E					

Answer on page 477

Shade in every fragment containing a dot—and what have you got?

Answer on page 477

Each number already in the grid shows the sum of the digits in the line whose direction is shown by the arrow. Only one digit can be placed in each square. There are no zeros. For each sum, each digit can only appear once—e.g., 8 cannot be completed with 44. A sequence of digits forming a sum can only appear once in the grid. If 8 is 53 somewhere then another 8 cannot also be 53. Nor could it be 35 but must contain a different set of digits, such as 71/17, or 62/26. Can you put logic, rather than higher math, to work and find the unique solution?

Answer on page 477

	11	19	17		6	18	21	16	11	8
14				39						
24				23 / 13						
15					7 / 18				20	6
	10	22 / 20					8 / 22			
18					8 / 10			11 / 12		
4			14 / 9			18 / 11				
18					21 / 14				10	17
	12	11 / 23					15 / 16			
9				10 / 16			12 / 29			
10			12 / 21			13 / 9				
30					9 / 17				19	11
	10	12 / 7					13 / 5			
33						18				
15						28				

160 · NUMBER SEARCH

The number 123456 appears just once in this grid, running in either a forward or backward direction, either vertically, horizontally, or diagonally. Can you locate it?

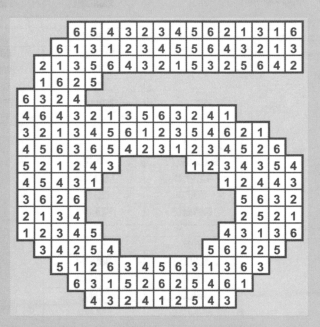

Answer on page 478

161 · BOWLING TEAM

The members of the Basham bowling team make a splendid sight. Can you identify these four colorful characters?

1 Tom, the doctor, is not the man sporting the long beard.

2 The mailman is not Alf, who wears a monocle.

3 George is not the lawyer, who even bowls in his panama hat.

ALF	
BLACKSMITH	DOCTOR
LAWYER	MAILMAN
BEARD	CRAVAT
MONOCLE	PANAMA

GEORGE	
BLACKSMITH	DOCTOR
LAWYER	MAILMAN
BEARD	CRAVAT
MONOCLE	PANAMA

FRED	
BLACKSMITH	DOCTOR
LAWYER	MAILMAN
BEARD	CRAVAT
MONOCLE	PANAMA

TOM	
BLACKSMITH	DOCTOR
LAWYER	MAILMAN
BEARD	CRAVAT
MONOCLE	PANAMA

Answer on page 478

162 · COLOR BLIND

Police Officer Friendly's informer, Slippery Sid, is none too helpful when it comes to pointing out which of various colorful characters keeps his car behind which colored garage door. The only thing that we do know is that no garage has either a door, car, or an owner's name with the same color in it. From Sid's statement see if you can fill in the form correctly.

The red car is two places to the left of the Jaguar, and the gray car is one place to the right of Mr. Gray's car, which isn't a VW. Mr. Green's car, the Lancia, and the blue car are in adjoining garages, but none has a red door, and the green car, the Skoda, and Mr. Pink's car are also in adjoining garages with the named make being the middle car in each case. There is also an Opel; Mr. Blue and Mr. White are the other two owners, and the other car color is white.

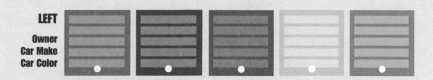

LEFT
Owner
Car Make
Car Color

Answer on page 478

163 · FRAME UP

Henry is a faithful supporter of Coppleton Basketball Club, and he attends matches whenever possible. He has decided that the supporters should have some recognition, and he has persuaded Madge, one of the women providing refreshments, to take a photo. Henry is in position F, and your job is to provide the other names. Left and right are as you look at the photo, and in front and behind are not necessarily directly so unless stated, i.e., it is true to say that A is behind K.

1 Agnes is behind Emily and to the right of Isaac.

2 David is behind Joyce and to the right of Keith.

3 Isaac is behind David and to the right of Lydia.

4 Clive is to the right of Beryl and behind Lydia.

5 Grace is to the left of Isaac and in front of Agnes.

6 Beryl is in front of Felix and to the right of Joyce.

7 Keith is to the right of Henry and behind Agnes.

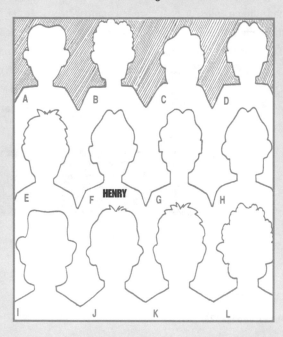

Answer on page 478

164 · BLACK AND WHITE

In a negative, everything that is really black appears white and everything that is really white appears black.

Can you see which one of A, B, and C is shown as a negative?

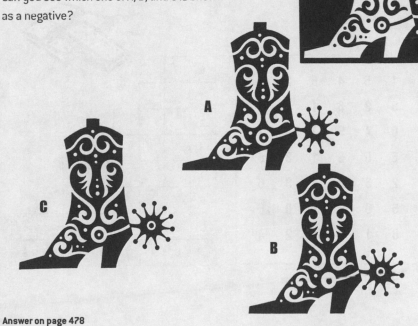

Answer on page 478

165 · DOMINO SEARCH

A set of dominoes has been laid out, using numbers instead of dots for clarity, but the lines that separate the dominoes have been left out. Can you show where each domino in the set has been placed? You may find the check grid useful, since each domino is identified by its number pair and the appropriate box can be checked off when the domino has been located. To give you a start 6–4 has been marked in.

0	0	1	5	4	5	2	6
1	0	5	3	6	1	4	2
3	5	0	4	5	3	4	1
2	5	6	5	6	1	3	6
2	3	2	3	2	4	3	6
0	0	5	0	2	1	0	**6**
4	3	6	1	1	4	2	**4**

0							
1							
2							
3							
4							
5							
6					X		
	0	1	2	3	4	5	6

Answer on page 478

Fit the numbers into the grid. One has been done for you.

3 figures
128
285
396
586
793
861
950

4 figures
1218
1809
2237
3354
4026
5302
6195

6233
8139
9303

5 figures
25510
32165
51995
78163
92851

6 figures
108392
122589
210101
329406
403625

411074
525008
606340
726493
783914
803103
895105
938118

7 figures
1438116
2117055
3248813
5246319
5360241
8302269
9372688

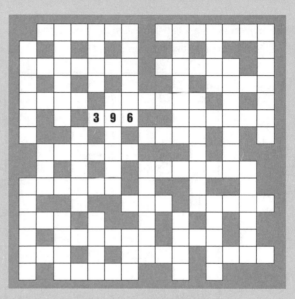

Answer on page 478

167 · SUDOKU

Place a number from 1 to 9 in each empty square so that each row, each column, and each 3 x 3 block contain all the numbers from 1 to 9.

2	6				3			1
				8		4		7
	8	3	7			9		
1						5		
	9			4			8	
		2						3
		8			2	6	9	
6		4		1				
5			6				2	8

Answer on page 478

168 · TAKE FIVE

Can you complete the 5 x 5 block so that each of the following symbols appears in all vertical and horizontal lines?

Symbols:

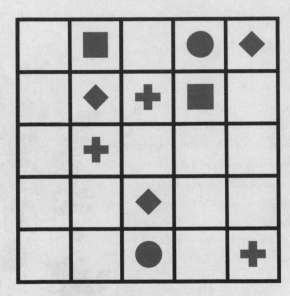

Answer on page 478

169 · FLOWER POWER

Patriotic Pete sells bunches of red, white, and blue flowers in the market. Some bunches have just a single color, some have two, and some a mixture of all three. If he brings along a total of 80 bunches, can you work out how many bunches have flowers of all three colors?

Half the bunches contain red flowers, and a quarter of the bunches have both blue and white. There is one more bunch with red flowers only than there are with both blue and white but no red. The total number of those with both red and white but no blue and red and blue but no white is five greater than the number containing red only.

How many bunches have all three colors?

Answer on page 478

170 · BRIDGES

Each circle containing a number represents an island. The object is to connect each island with vertical or horizontal bridges so that:

- The number of bridges is the same as the number inside the island.
- There are no more than two bridges between two islands.
- Bridges do not cross islands or other bridges.
- There is a continuous path connecting all the islands.

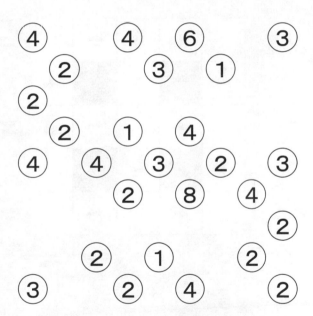

Answer on page 479

All the digits from 1 to 9 are used in this grid, but only once. Can you work out their positions in the grid and make the totals work? We've given two numbers to start you off.

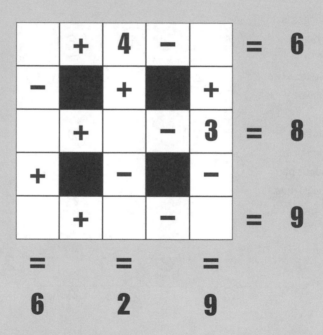

Place a number from 1 to 9 in each empty square so that each row, each column, and each 3 x 3 block contain all the numbers from 1 to 9.

	7		2		4		1	
	4	2	1		6	7	9	
2			6	9	5			4
	9	4		2		1	3	
8			4	1	3			5
	3	1	9		8	2	5	
	5		3		2		4	

Answer on page 479

Eight men and eight women are playing bridge at four tables, as shown. At the game in hand, dummy is in a different position at each table, and the contract at each is in a different suit and for a different number of tricks—this number also differs in each case from the table number. With the following clues, can you position each person and also say who is dummy and name the contract being played at each table?

Roger (South) is dummy at his table, which is numbered one lower than Connie's and one higher than Harry's, both of whom are in a different position from Roger and from each other, neither being dummy. Fred and Gordon are partners at the remaining table, neither being dummy. Alan (West) is at a table where the contract is four spades. Tessa (dummy) is one table counterclockwise from Eddie, at whose table the contract is for one trick more than on table 1.

Dummy at table 4 is the person whose name comes first alphabetically at that table. Jane and Dot are in the same position at different tables whose numbers are two apart; this is also true of Kate and Lola, the first-named in each case being at the lower-numbered table. From his seat, Peter, who is not at table 2, can see table 2 but not table 4; his contract is in diamonds, while Michael's table is going for hearts, but one fewer.

Susie (dummy) has Jane on her left and Harry on her right; her partner is Peter, and the contract is for one more trick than the table number. Connie has Dot on her left, who is not in the same position as Fred. Tessa, whose table is playing a red-suit contract, is in the same relative position as Babs.

Answer on page 479

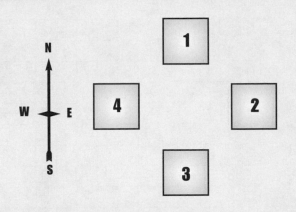

	Table 1	Table 2	Table 3	Table 4
N				
E				
S				
W				
Contract				

The numbers in the squares tell you how many of it and its neighbors are to be filled in. A square can have up to eight neighbors. Using logic alone, can you fill in the pixels and create an admirable portrait?

1	2	3
8	X	4
7	6	5

0		0		2		5		5		2		0		0
	1		4		6		6		6		3		0	
0		4		7		5		7		8		2		0
	4		8		4		5		8		7		2	
2		7		4		6		7		7		7		3
	7		6		6		6		3		6		8	
3		6		7		6		3		3		6		4
	3		5		6		2		2		2		3	
0		1		5		3		2		3		1		0
	0		0		3		2		1		2		0	
0		0		1		3		3		4		1		0
	0		0		1		3		5		3		0	
0		2		3		3		5		6		3		2
	4		6		6		4		4		5		5	
4		8		9		8		5		6		7		6
	8		8		9		6		5		4		6	
4		7		7		8		8		8		6		6
	4		4		8		7		7		4		6	
1		2		4		8		8		8		6		6
	0		0		4		5		5		3		4	

Answer on page 479

175 · KARL KRACK'S CIRCUS

Karl Krack, who owns a small traveling circus, believes that variety is the spice of life, and for each show he alters the order of his eight acts. Can you figure out what the order will be for tonight's performance? The Flying Fortresses will perform immediately after Jim the Juggler, and Fred the Fire-eater is immediately before the Crazy Carvellos. The Clever Clowns are in action three acts after Señor Pedro's Poodles and three acts before the Agilles Acrobats. Madame Poll's Parrots are two acts after the Flying Fortresses.

1	2	3	4
5	6	7	8

Answer on page 479

See how quickly you can break this grid down into the 28 dominoes from which it was formed.

0	0	3	6	4	2	3
3	4	4	4	4	5	2
0	5	5	0	5	5	6
4	3	3	6	6	6	2
4	5	3	0	5	1	3
6	2	2	0	1	1	1
1	5	2	0	2	4	1
1	3	6	6	2	1	0

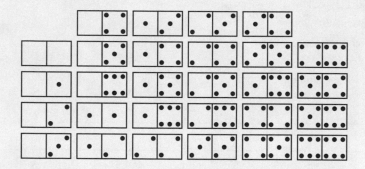

Answer on page 479

177 · DOTTY DILEMMA

Connect adjacent dots with vertical or horizontal lines so that a single loop is formed with no crossings or branches. Each number indicates how many lines surround it, while empty cells may be surrounded by any number of lines.

Answer on page 479

Can you work out how
many bricks are missing
from this wall?

Answer on page 480

179 · IT FIGURES

Place a number from 1 to 9 in each empty cell so that the sum of each vertical or horizontal block equals the number at the top or on the left of that block. Numbers may only be used once in each block.

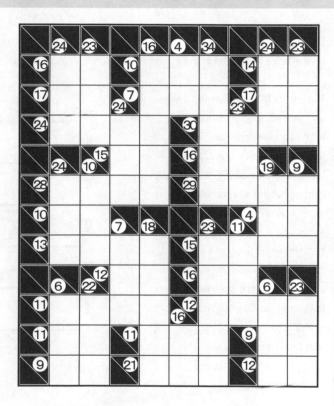

Answer on page 480

180 · SQUARE LETTERS

The letters of the alphabet, excluding Z, are entered randomly into a 5 x 5 square so that no two consecutive letters are in the same row or column, or in a diagonal in any direction.

The letters NQG can be read downward as can TMO. Square E5 is a vowel. D is immediately left of V and immediately above I, which is not in column 2. Row D begins and ends with a vowel, the first alphabetically preceding the latter. Q and T are at opposite ends of a row, and K and S are at the top and bottom respectively of a column. U is diagonally immediately below W. E and R can both be seen on the same long diagonal. C is diagonally adjacent to H; Y is to the immediate right of F, and X is in a corner square.
Can you locate each letter?

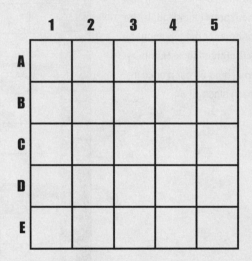

	1	2	3	4	5
A					
B					
C					
D					
E					

Answer on page 480

Connect adjacent dots with vertical or horizontal lines so that a single loop is formed with no crossings or branches. Each number indicates how many lines surround it, while empty cells may be surrounded by any number of lines.

```
  2 2 1 1 3 1 1 3
                  3
  3 2 0 2 0 2 1 2
1
  3 3 2 1 2 2 2 3
                  1
  3 1 1 0 2 3 2 2
2
  3 1 2 3
            2 1 3 3
                      0
  3 2 0 2 2 3 1 1
2
  2 3 1 0 3 1 1 3
                  1
  2 2 2 2 2 2 2 2
1
  3 1 3 1 2 2 1 2
```

Answer on page 480

182 · LOGI-PATH

Use your deductive reasoning to form a pathway from START to FINISH moving in either
direction horizontally or vertically (but not diagonally). The number at the beginning of every
row or column indicates exactly how many boxes in that row or column your pathway must
pass through. The small diagram is given as an example of how it works.

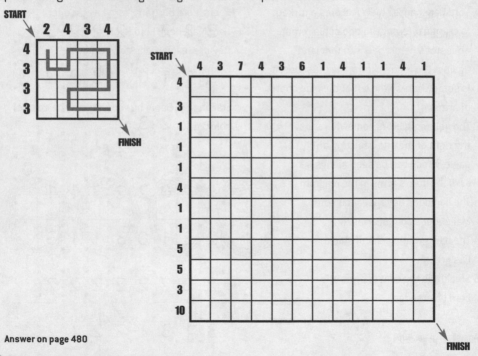

Answer on page 480

183 · ARMS AND THE MAN

Four hereditary peers own the coats of arms featured in the diagram. From the clues given below, can you name the owner of each of the shields lettered A to D, say which heraldic device appears on each, and figure out the background color of each coat of arms?

1 Lord Rackham's shield features a turkey, in cryptic reference to one of his remote ancestor's heroic deeds in that land against the infidel during the Crusades; it is somewhere to the left of the blue coat of arms.

2 The yellow shield is somewhere to the right of the one depicting an eagle, which can be seen alongside Lord Bertram's arms in the diagram.

3 The lion does not appear on Lord Mallender's coat of arms.

4 The background color of shield C is green.

5 Shield A is the coat of arms of Lord Liversedge.

Peers: Lord Bertram; Lord Liversedge; Lord Mallender; Lord Rackham

Devices: eagle; lion; stag; turkey

Colors: blue; green; red; yellow

Starting tip: Begin by working out the color of shield A.

A   **B**   **C**   **D**

Peer:	_____	_____	_____	_____
Device:	_____	_____	_____	_____
Color:	_____	_____	_____	_____

Answer on page 480

Can you tell which of the five shadows belongs to the puppy in the top left-hand corner?

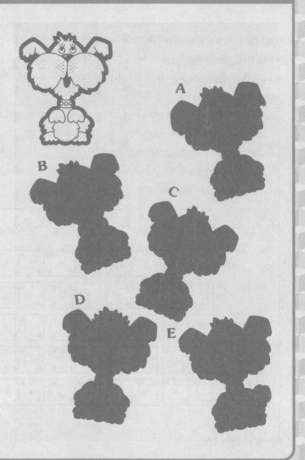

Answer on page 480

185 · BREAKTHROUGH

See how quickly you can break this grid down into the 28 dominoes from which it is formed.

0	5	6	3	2	5	4
0	5	6	2	2	1	5
2	0	0	6	5	2	1
1	5	5	3	3	2	3
5	1	4	2	3	2	6
4	0	4	3	4	4	4
0	6	1	3	0	1	6
6	6	1	1	3	4	0

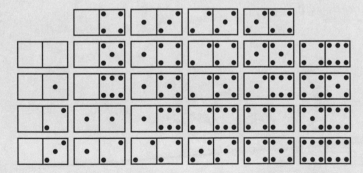

Answer on page 481

Follow the dots from 1 to 40 to reveal the hidden picture.

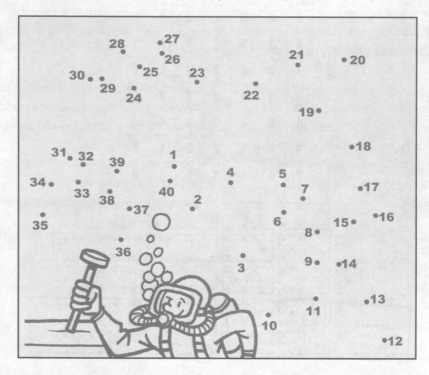

187 · KEEPING IN TOUCH

Diana was an inveterate letter writer, keeping in touch with all her former school friends on a regular basis. The other day she wrote four letters to friends in different parts of the country. From the clues given below, can you fill in the full names and the town that appeared on each envelope lying on the table in the positions numbered 1 to 4?

1 Betty's letter is immediately to the right of the one addressed to Ms. Hardy.

2 Letter 2 is about to wing its way to New York; it is not the one addressed to Ms. Riley.

3 Jenny's name appears on the envelope containing letter 3; she does not live in Hawaii.

4 The letter to California is somewhere on the table to the left of the one addressed to Sally.

5 Ms. Dukes is destined to receive letter 1.

First names: Betty; Jenny; Jill; Sally
Surnames: Dukes; Hardy; Markham; Riley
States: California; Hawaii; Idaho; New York

Starting tip: Start by working out which letter is addressed to Ms. Hardy.

Answer on page 481

188 · SNAPSHOT

Can you figure out which of nine photographs
is an exact replica of the model?

Answer on page 481

189 · LITTLE AND LARGE

In this puzzle, the little numbers are large and the large numbers are little! Each little number from 1 to 9 is to be placed into the boxes, one per box.

Each larger number in the boxes is the sum of the little number that goes in it plus the little number in each box with which it shares an edge.

So the corner squares have two neighbors, the rest along the sides have three, and the square in the middle has four. From the little larger numbers given and the large little numbers already placed, can you fill in the rest?

14 **7**	16	14
25	22	18
19	18	14 **2**

Answer on page 481

190 · CODE MASTER

Just follow the rules of the classic game of Mastermind to crack the color code. The first number tells you how many of the pegs are exactly correct—the right color in the right place (✓✓). The second number tells you how many pegs are the correct color but are not in the right place (✓). Colors may be repeated in the answer.

By comparing the information given by each line, can you work out which color goes in which place?

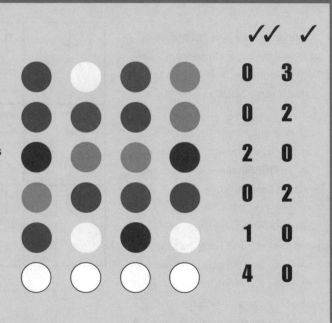

✓✓	✓
0	3
0	2
2	0
0	2
1	0
4	0

Answer on page 481

191 · CROSSNUMBER

Just like a crossword—but the answer to each clue is a number that is entered by putting one digit into each square. See if you can fill all these empty squares:

ACROSS

1. (7x8) − 9
3. (9x8) − 7
6. (3x3) x (3x3)
8. (4x5) x 6
10. 93 + 99
11. (2x2) x (2x3)
12. 96/6
14. 102 − 38
17. 97 − 59
19. 387 − 93
21. 18x20
23. 1986/3
24. (12x8) + 1

DOWN

2. 1000 − 211
4. (29x18) − 10
5. 200/4
7. 11 X 11
9. 71 + 82 + 93
10. 24 − 8
13. 101 − 38
15. 20 X 20
16. 14 x 14
18. 364 + 475
19. 52/2
20. 6x7
22. (3x9) + (5x8)

Answer on page 481

Can you see which two small rectangles contain the same four symbols?

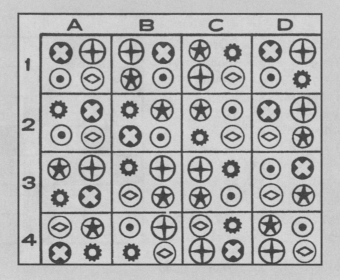

Answer on page 481

193 · PLUGGED IN

Which one of the four cords should the guitarist plug into the amplifier?

Answer on page 481

Five novels make up Letitia Perowne's *Malthouse Saga*, which tells the story of a landowning New England family from 1780 to 1977. From the clues below, can you figure out the period covered by each title and the first names of the family members who are the books' main male and female characters?

1 *Chronicle*, which deals with the life and adventures of Vaughan Malthouse and his headstrong wife, is not the novel covering the period 1938–1977, which features Claudia Malthouse as its heroine.

2 Joseph and Miriam appear first as childhood sweethearts, then lovers, and finally husband and wife.

3 *Birthright*, which begins on the eve of World War I, doesn't tell the story of Eugenie's rebellion against her overbearing husband.

4 Major Lambert Malthouse isn't the hero of *Testament*.

5 *Heritage*, the volume of the saga that features the tragic story of Rosalind Malthouse and her faithless husband, neither begins nor ends in 1830, the year of Samuel's birth.

6 Hannah Malthouse appears in a volume two earlier in the series than the one that details the life and mysterious death of Esmond.

Title	Period	Male character	Female character

Answer on page 481

	1780–1830	1830–1881	1881–1914	1914–1938	1938–1977	Esmond	Joseph	Lambert	Samuel	Vaughan	Claudia	Eugenie	Hannah	Miriam	Rosalind
Birthright															
Chronicle															
Domain															
Heritage															
Testament															
Claudia															
Eugenie															
Hannah															
Miriam															
Rosalind															
Esmond															
Joseph															
Lambert															
Samuel															
Vaughan															

Record in this grid all the information obtained from the clues, by using an X to indicate a definite "no" and a check mark to show a definite "yes". Transfer these to all sections of the grid thus eliminating all but one possibility, which must be the correct one.

195 · IT FIGURES

Place a number from 1 to 9 in each empty cell so that the sum of each vertical or horizontal block equals the number at the top or on the left of that block. Numbers may only be used once in each block.

Answer on page 481

196 · DOUBLE TROUBLE

Which of these two students are identical?

Answer on page 482

197 · SET SQUARE

All the digits from 1 to 9 are used in this grid, but only once. Can you work out their positions in the grid and make the totals work? We've given two numbers to start you off.

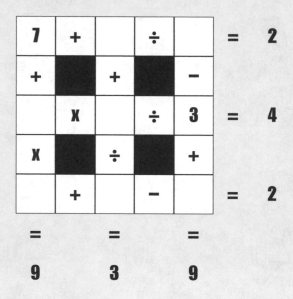

Answer on page 482

Which two numbers continue this sequence?

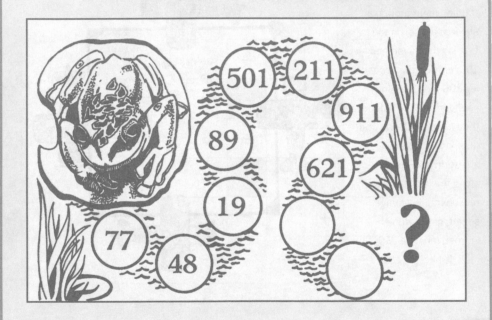

Answer on page 482

199 · ON THE FLY

One day, a flying instructor took Algy on a training flight around a square course. On the first leg they averaged 100 mph; on the second leg 200 mph. Gaining confidence, they did the third leg at 300 mph and finished with a strut-shattering 400 mph along the last leg. Algy reckons their average speed for the whole journey must be 250 mph. Is he right?

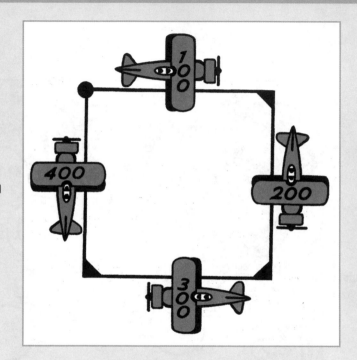

Answer on page 482

By packing numbers in the empty spaces, can you make the numbers in each of the 16 hexagons add up to 25? No two numbers in each hexagon may be the same, and you can't use zero. We've started you off.

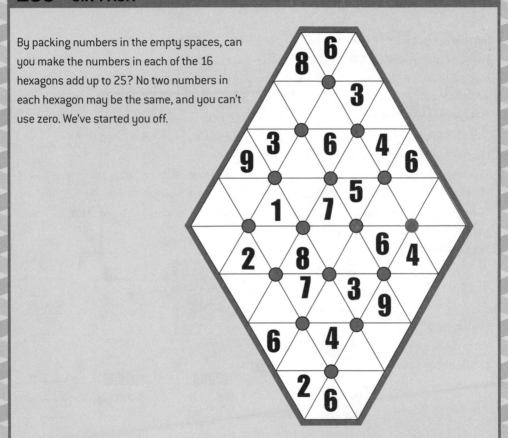

Answer on page 482

201 · GUYS IN THE BLACK HATS

The four posters on the wall of the Sheriff's office in the Wild West town of Redrock show the members of the notorious Black Hat Gang of train robbers. From the clues given below, can you fill in each outlaw's first name, nickname, and surname?

1 Herbert's picture is horizontally adjacent to that of "Butch" McColl.

2 Poster A shows Jacob, but Silvester Jaggard isn't depicted on poster C.

3 The poster with a picture of the man surnamed Wolf is horizontally adjacent to the one that shows the one nicknamed "Pony."

4 Churchman, who appears on poster D, isn't the outlaw nicknamed "Apache."

First names: Herbert; Jacob; Matthew; Silvester
Nicknames: "Apache"; "Butch"; "Pony"; "Rio"
Surnames: Churchman; Jaggard; McColl; Wolf

A
First name: _____
Nickname: _____
Surname: _____

B
_____
_____
_____

Starting tip: Figure out the first name of the baddie on poster C.

C
First name: _____
Nickname: _____
Surname: _____

D
_____
_____
_____

Answer on page 482

202 · KNOT SO

Which of the tangled ropes below will form a knot, and which will not?

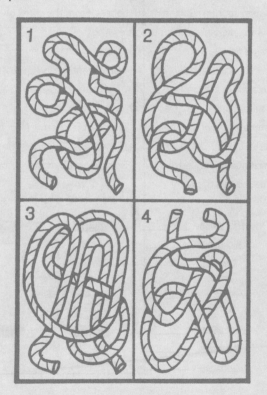

Answer on page 482

203 · CELL STRUCTURE

The object is to create white areas surrounded by black walls, so that:

- Each white area contains only one number.
- The number of cells in a white area is equal to the number in it.
- The white areas are separated from each other by a black wall.
- Cells containing numbers are not filled in.
- The black cells are linked into a continuous wall.
- Black cells do not form a square of 2 x 2 or larger.

4		6						3
					2			3
						2		
5							1	
	3			4				
1			2					
		3				3		4
4							4	
	2							
			3					
	3		4					
								2
4							3	
		1						
	1						4	

Answer on page 482

Can you spot which three squares are identical? Watch out—they may not be the same way up!

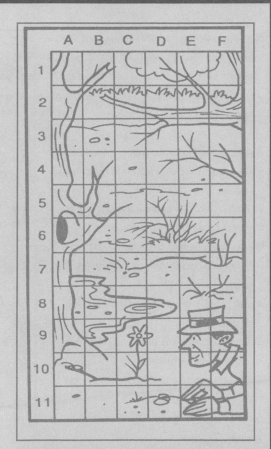

Answer on page 482

205 · CAROUSEL

The carousel is a popular ride with the toddlers at Orles Fair. There are eight different animals on it, and so that the children don't get bored with it, Sid Slick, the owner, changes the positions of the animals each day. With the position of the horse given and the knowledge that the animals face and move in a clockwise direction, see if you can use the clues to work out the positions of each animal and child on today's ride.

1 No child is next to or opposite another with the same number of letters in his or her name.

2 Both mythical animals have boys on them, and both birds have girls on them.

3 Bob is opposite the emu and two places behind Chloe, whose neighbors are both boys.

4 The zebra is two places in front of the dragon.

5 Sue is opposite the camel, and Alan is opposite the elephant.

6 David is two places in front of the horse but is not next to the emu.

7 There are also a unicorn and a peacock, and the other riders are Edward, Helen, and Joan.

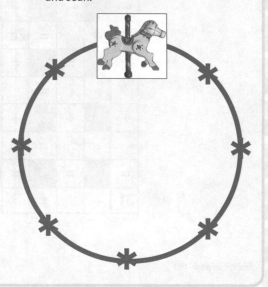

Answer on page 483

206 · NUMBER SQUARES

Can you complete the grids below with the aid of the numbers given, so that all sums, whether horizontal or vertical, are correct?

(Please note that each sum should be treated separately.)

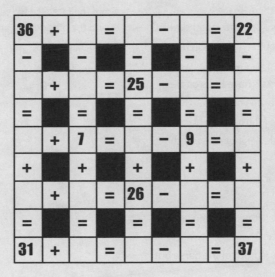

Answer on page 483

207 · MIXED PAIRS

For their annual lawn bowling tournament this year, the Tisbury club has arranged a novel competition. Four married couples who had fought their way through earlier rounds playing with their spouses now played three final rounds without them. In each round, nobody played with his or her spouse, and each partnered a different member of the opposite gender in each round. After the three rounds, each individual player counted up the points his or her pair had scored in each round. Each married couple then added their two totals together. The couple with the highest combined total score won the competition. From the facts shown on the master scoreboard, can you name each couple, give their occupations, and then name the eventual winners?

Answer on page 483

SHE	Round 1 SCORE	AND HE	SHE	Round 2 SCORE	AND HE	SHE	Round 3 SCORE	AND HE
Caterer's wife	15	Mr Kelly	Thelma	11	Director's husband	Mechanic's wife	17	Teacher's husband
	v			v			v	
Post-mistress	10	Butcher	Brenda	8	Sculptor's husband	Director	16	Mr. Watson
Ann	14	Pete	Clive's wife	12	Jack	Len's wife	14	Clive Dawson
	v			v			v	
Vet's wife	6	Len	Rose	5	Mechanic	Teacher	14	Mr. Morris

208 · THAT LITTLE BIT OF DIFFERENCE

There are eight differences between the two cartoons. Can you spot them?

Answer on page 483

209 · FOURSOME

This man would like to buy four identical vases. Which design will he choose?

Answer on page 483

210 · DARTING AROUND

A dart player scores 71 with three darts hitting a triple, a double, and a single. Given that the three numbers that he hits add up to 35 and that the difference between the largest and smallest numbers is 9, can you figure out how his score is made up?

Triple   Double   Single

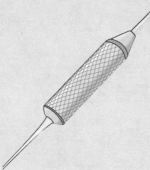

Answer on page 483

211 · DOT-TO-DOT

Follow the dots from 1 to 51 to reveal the hidden picture.

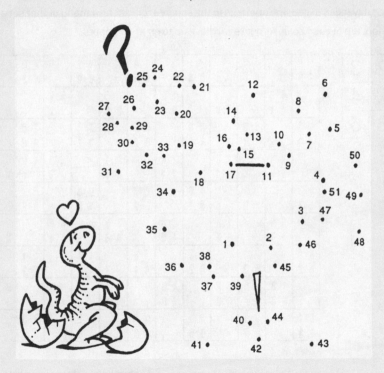

Answer on page 483

212 · QUILTESSENTIAL

In this patchwork quilt, squares of material have been sewn together—each square being either blue, green, lavender, or red. The numbers in the squares tell you how many of that square and its neighbors are of each color. A square can have up to eight neighbors:

1	2	3
8	x	4
7	6	5

3 0 1 0		4 0 0 2		1 1 0 4		1 4 0 1		4 2 0 0		4 0 0 2		0 1 0 3
	4 0 4 1		3 1 1 4		1 4 0 4		4 5 0 0		5 2 0 2		2 2 0 5	
1 0 4 1		4 0 4 1		2 3 1 3		4 3 0 2		4 3 1 1		2 0 3 4		0 3 1 2
	0 1 5 3		1 3 4 1		2 4 2 1		6 1 1 1		2 1 3 3		0 3 4 2	
0 3 1 2		0 1 3 5		0 5 3 1		2 2 3 2		3 0 1 5		0 1 6 2		0 4 2 0
	0 5 0 4		1 3 1 4		2 3 4 0		1 0 4 4		3 0 2 4		3 3 3 0	
0 4 0 2		2 4 0 3		4 3 0 2		1 3 4 1		1 0 4 4		5 1 2 1		4 2 0 0
	1 3 0 5		5 2 0 2		3 5 1 0		0 4 4 1		3 1 4 1		6 0 3 0	
0 1 0 3		3 1 0 2		3 3 0 0		0 5 1 0		0 2 4 0		2 0 4 0		2 0 2 0

Sadly, there is no pretty picture—just chunks of colors. Using brain power alone, can you work out the color of each patch?

Answer on page 483

213 · POSER

The artist has made five mistakes while trying to paint an exact portrait of the model. Can you spot the five errors?

Answer on page 483

214 · SAFE BET

This is a strange safe. Solve all the clues, and the combination appears in the shaded areas.

ACROSS

1 Reverse digits of 3 across
3 Square root of 1,745,041
5 Divide 8 down by 213,326
6 Multiply 29 across by 22 down
9 Divide 10 down by 29 across
11 Add 4,875 to 13 across
13 Multiply 29 across by 178
15 Cube of 3 down
19 Cube of 2 down
21 Multiply 29 across by 526
23 Subtract 1 down from 22 down, then add 10
25 Square root of 7,921
26 15 percent of 343,400
29 Cube root of 1,728
30 Multiply 1 down by 2
31 Add 6,000 to 24 down

Answer on page 484

DOWN

1 Multiply 5 across by 50
2 Half of 5 down
3 Half of 10 down
4 Anagram of digits of 3 across
5 Multiply 16 by 17
6 25 percent of 16,486,100
7 Add 3,925,005 to 8 down
8 Add 144,995 to 6 down
10 Multiply the last two digits of 24 down by 8
12 Add 9,809 to 23 across
14 Square 28 down
16 Next in series 614, 713, 812, . . .
17 Add 73 to 16 down
18 Add 2 down to 3 down
20 Add 27 down to 9 across
22 Square root of 15,225,604
24 Square root of 1,283,689
27 Multiply 5 across by 5
28 Divide 1,644 by 29 across

230

215 · WANTED!

The sheriff is sure that one of the ten men shown is the wanted outlaw in the poster in the top right-hand corner. Can you help identify the suspect?

Answer on page 484

Twenty-five of the numbers between 1 and 49 have been inserted in the grid. Clues to each of the answers in each row and column are given below, but we must add that the numbers in the long diagonal from top left to bottom right total 112 and the other long diagonal from top right to bottom left totals 137. No two consecutive numbers are in the same row, column, or diagonal. Using this information, can you complete the original grid?

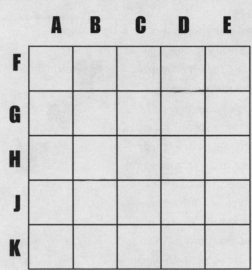

ACROSS

F: D equals twice E; D plus E equals twice A; B equals C plus 9

G: C plus E equals B plus D; total of entire row equals 116

H: B plus D equals E; only one odd number

J: A equals seven times C; E equals twice C

K: D equals three times B

Answer on page 484

COLUMN

A: G equals twice H

B: F plus K equals H plus J; total equals 123

C: F plus G equals J plus K; K is a cube number; total equals 84

D: K equals twice (F plus H); J is the second highest number

E: H equals three times F

217 · SMALL HOLDINGS

When Ivan the Not-too-bad-really decided to divide a spare kingdom between four faithful followers, he stipulated that each should hold an identically shaped chunk of territory the same size as every other. Each, of course, was to have just one castle and one farm. Can you show Ivan's real estate agent, Manfromm Prudential, how to achieve his master's wishes?

Answer on page 484

Each row and column originally contained one A, one B, one C, and two blank squares. Each letter and number refers to the first or second letter encountered when traveling in the direction of the arrow. Can you complete the original grid?

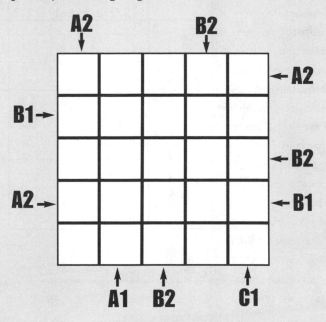

Answer on page 484

219 · HANJIE

The numbers alongside each row or column tell you how many blocks of black squares are in a line. For example: 2, 3, 5 tells you that from left to right (or top to bottom) there is a group of two black squares, then at least one white space, then a group of three black squares, then at least one white square, then a group of five black squares. Each block of black squares on the same line must have at least one white square between it and the next block of black squares. Sometimes it is possible to tell which squares are going to be black without reference to other lines or columns. In the example below, we can deduce that any block of six black squares must incorporate the two central squares.

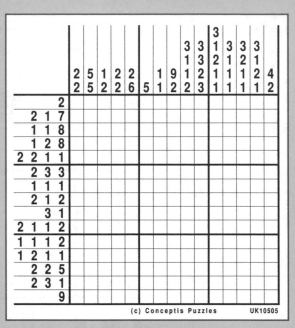

Can you complete this Hanjie puzzle to reveal the hidden pattern or picture?

Answer on page 484

220 · LOGI-5

Each line, across and down, is to have each of the letters A, B, C, D, and E, appearing once each. Also, every shape—shown by the thick lines—must also have each of the letters in it. Can you fill in the grid?

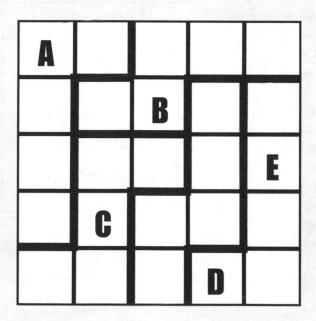

Answer on page 484

221 · WHERE THE L?

Twelve L shapes like the ones on the right have been fitted into a square grid. Each L has one hole, and there are three of each type in the square. No two pieces of the same type are adjacent, even at a corner. They fit together so well that the spaces between pieces do not show. From the locations of the holes, can you tell where each L is?

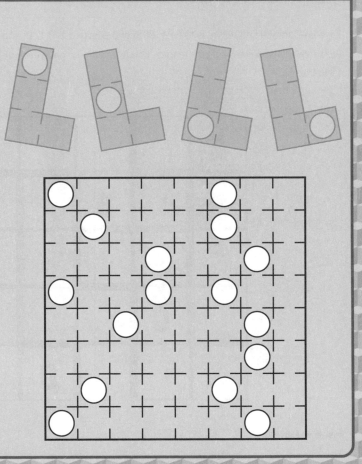

Answer on page 484

222 · CELL STRUCTURE

The object is to create white areas surrounded by black walls, so that:

- Each white area contains only one number.
- The number of cells in a white area is equal to the number in it.
- The white areas are separated from each other by a black wall.
- Cells containing numbers are not filled in.
- The black cells are linked into a continuous wall.
- Black cells do not form a square of 2 x 2 or larger.

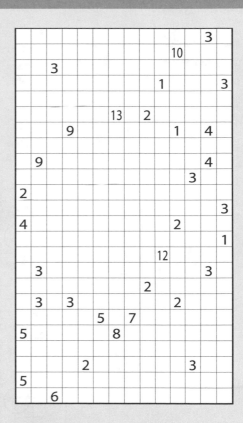

Answer on page 484

223 · TOGA PARTY

Each figure differs from the other three by one extra detail. Can you spot all four extra details?

Answer on page 485

224 · CODE MASTER

Just follow the rules of the classic game of Mastermind to crack the color code. The first number tells you how many of the pegs are exactly correct—the right color in the right place(✓✓). The second number tells you how many pegs are the correct color but are not in the right place(✓). Colors may be repeated in the answer. By comparing the information given by each line, can you figure out which color goes in which place?

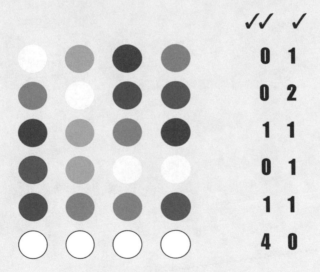

✓✓	✓
0	1
0	2
1	1
0	1
1	1
4	0

Answer on page 485

225 · CUT BACK

The first three pictures — A, B, C — form a sequence. Which of the pictures D, E, and F is the correct one to continue the pattern?

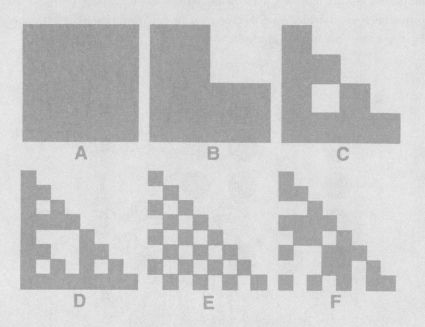

Answer on page 485

226 · SHORT ORDER

These six souls are happy couples—can you put a name to each and match up the pairs?

1 Art is heavier than Alice's date.
2 Bill's date is taller than Chuck's date.
3 Chuck is heavier than Beth's date.
4 Chuck's date is taller than Cathy.

Answer on page 485

227 · CELL STRUCTURE

The object is to create white areas surrounded by black walls, so that:

- Each white area contains only one number.
- The number of cells in a white area is equal to the number in it.
- The white areas are separated from each other by a black wall.
- Cells containing numbers are not filled in.
- The black cells are linked into a continuous wall.
- Black cells do not form a square of 2 x 2 or larger.

4		3						
						1		
			2					
					2		5		4
2			1					
4					1			
							2	
		5						1
	3							

Answer on page 485

228 · SET SQUARE

All the digits from 1 to 9 are used in this grid, but only once. Can you figure out their positions in the grid and make the totals work? We've given two numbers to start you off.

Answer on page 485

229 · HIGH CARDS

Five cards have been laid out; all are between ace and ten. All four suits are represented. No three of the cards form a consecutive sequence of numbers.

The total value of red cards is the same as the total value of black cards.
The total value of hearts is 12.
The even-value cards have a total four higher than the sum of the odd-value cards.
The club has a lower value than the spade. The lowest card is a diamond.

Which five cards have been dealt?

Answer on page 485

230 · NUMBER JIG

Fit the numbers into the grid. One has been done for you.

3 figures		62320
165	6912	68688
168	9553	71206
248	**5 figures**	71209
364	10211	71301
381	10860	78800
400	15131	80035
550	15771	83247
~~591~~	20185	89905
610	27761	91206
702	32198	91324
883	32909	98801
892	34848	
956	35016	**6 figures**
983	39246	280376
	40118	330514
4 figures	50106	483321
1336	50662	615229
5193	60345	861234

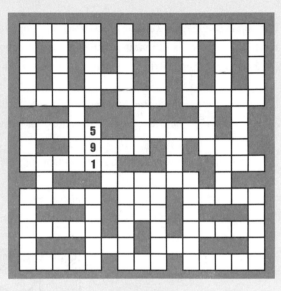

Answer on page 485

231 · SIX GEESE A-LAYING

Once upon a time there were six geese who lived happily with their owner Miss T Hyde. One morning, she discovered that they had begun laying eggs in their nests, numbered 1 to 6. From the clues below, can you figure out each bird's nest number and how many eggs they laid?

1 Only two of the birds laid the same number of eggs as the number of the box each was in.

2 Twenty-one eggs were laid altogether, no two birds laying the same number. No bird failed to lay any.

3 Clarissa, who was on one end, laid half as many eggs as were laid by both Brenda and the goose in box 5 added together.

4 Deirdre laid twice as many eggs as her box number. Her neighbor on one side, Felicity, laid two less eggs than Edwina, who was Deirdre's neighbor on the other side.

5 The goose to the right of Abigail, from our point of view, laid 3 eggs, which was less than were laid in box 1.

Answer on page 485

232 · ON THE SPOT

Can you place the dominoes into the grid so that the four vertical, four horizontal, and both diagonal rows each have a pip total of ten?

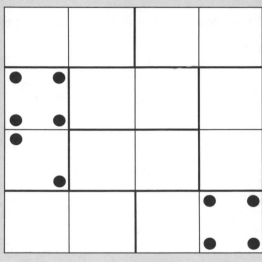

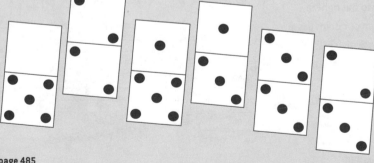

Answer on page 485

233 · FIT TOGETHER

Which are the only three pieces that will fit together perfectly to form a complete polygon?

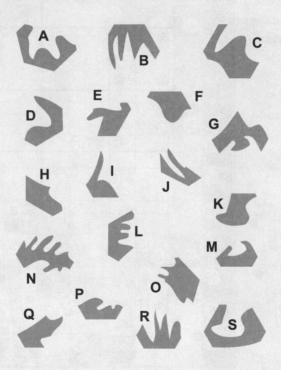

Answer on page 486

Place a number from 1 to 9 in each empty cell so that the sum of each vertical or horizontal block equals the number at the top or on the left of that block. Numbers may only be used once in each block.

Answer on page 486

235 · DOTTY DILEMMA

Connect adjacent dots with vertical or horizontal lines so that a single loop is formed with no crossings or branches. Each number indicates how many lines surround it, while empty cells may be surrounded by any number of lines.

Answer on page 486

Each row and column originally contained one A, one B, one C, and two blank squares. Each letter and number refers to the first or second letter encountered when traveling in the direction of the arrow. Can you complete the original grid?

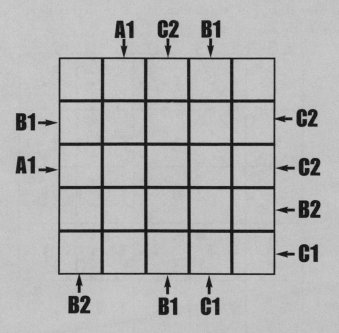

237 · IT'S MAGIC

This magic square can be completed using the numbers from 61 to 85 inclusive. To give you a start, in each square with a black corner dot, all the even digits have been entered. In a plain square, all the odd digits have been entered. Can you complete the square so that the five numbers in each row, column, and long diagonal add up to the magic total? The total—and close your eyes now if you don't want to be told—is 365.

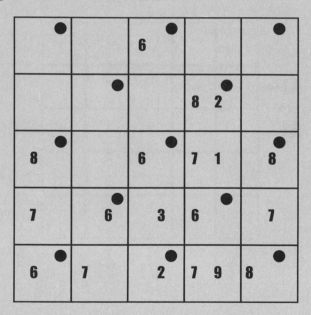

Answer on page 486

238 · DOMINO SEARCH

A set of dominoes has been laid out, using numbers instead of dots for clarity, but the lines that separate the dominoes have been left out. Can you, armed with a sharp pencil and keen brain, show where each domino in the set has been placed? You may find the check grid useful, because each domino is identified by its number pair and the appropriate box can be checked off when the domino has been located. To give you a start 2–9 is given.

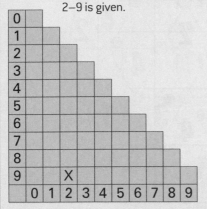

	4	7	2	9	9	2	5	6	3	7	2
	4	3	7	0	4	1	2	2	0	4	7
	0	9	8	5	9	9	3	8	3	1	9
	0	5	3	6	4	6	1	4	6	8	8
	6	6	3	0	7	7	5	5	2	6	0
	7	5	1	9	3	4	1	1	4	1	9
	9	0	6	6	1	0	0	1	5	8	3
	8	1	2	5	8	7	2	7	3	1	2
	4	0	8	5	9	4	5	2	7	8	6
	3	4	3	9	5	8	0	7	6	8	2

Check grid:

	0	1	2	3	4	5	6	7	8	9
0										
1										
2										
3										
4										
5										
6										
7										
8										
9			X							

Answer on page 486

239 · SIX-PACK

By packing numbers in the empty spaces, can you make the numbers in each of the sixteen hexagons add up to 25? No two numbers in each hexagon may be the same, and you can't use zero. We've started you off.

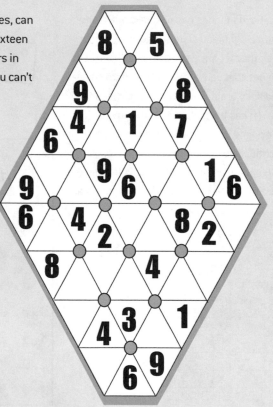

Answer on page 486

240 · OUT WEST

Toward the end of the last century in Wichita, Kansas, the main street was becoming quite well established, as our drawing of the first five buildings in that street shows. From the following clues, can you discover the name of each establishment and the name of the proprietor? By eliminating with an X any initial letter in the answer block that does not apply, you will eventually arrive at the full answer.

1 Frank Foster is at number 2, but he does not run the trading post.

2 Jesse Jones is not the proprietor of number 3.

3 The number of Jesse Jones's building is smaller than the number allocated to Chuck Carson's saloon, which is not number 5.

4 The bank is at number 4; the trading post is not number 1.

5 Rocky Rawlings is not the manager of the bank. The Wells Fargo office is not number. 2.

6 The jail is one of the buildings, but is Dave Dalton the sheriff?

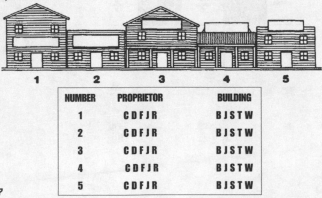

NUMBER	PROPRIETOR	BUILDING
1	C D F J R	B J S T W
2	C D F J R	B J S T W
3	C D F J R	B J S T W
4	C D F J R	B J S T W
5	C D F J R	B J S T W

Answer on page 487

All the digits from 1 to 9 are used in this grid, but only once. Can you work out their positions in the grid and make the totals work? We've given two numbers to start you off.

Answer on page 487

242 · NUMBER JIG

Fit the numbers into the grid.
One has been done for you.

3 figures	8243	403647
161	8313	409214
358	9054	524939
444		538018
~~483~~	**5 figures**	640882
560	27328	713648
809	39902	810123
942	48326	932100
	71166	
4 figures	73014	**7 figures**
1108		1638425
2921	**6 figures**	2152260
3250	103600	4236909
4230	175050	5990304
6307	235798	6539112
6323	326419	6603299
6519	384104	9013302

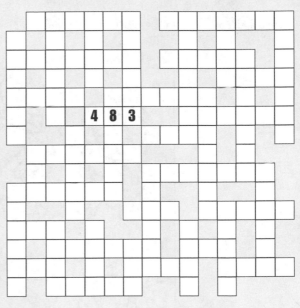

Answer on page 487

243 · KNOT SO

Can you figure out which tangles will form a knot and which will not?

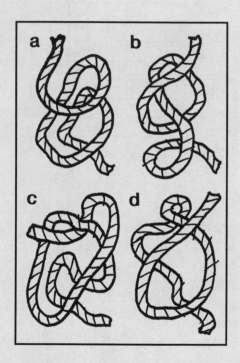

Answer on page 487

244 · HEDGE YOUR BETS

Can you draw the boundary lines on this subdivision so that each plot is the same size as each of the others and each contains a house, a cat, a dog, and a tree?

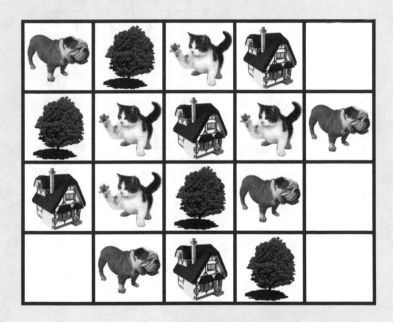

Answer on page 487

245 · PATTERN MAKER

Can you place the numbered blocks into the grid to form the pattern shown? The blocks may be placed horizontally or vertically and can be turned round.

Answer on page 487

246 · COG-ITATE

When the handle is turned in the direction shown, which two of the four weights will rise and which two will fall?

Answer on page 487

247 · CELL STRUCTURE

The object is to create white areas surrounded by black walls, so that:

- Each white area contains only one number.
- The number of cells in a white area is equal to the number in it.
- The white areas are separated from each other by a black wall.
- Cells containing numbers are not filled in.
- The black cells are linked into a continuous wall.
- Black cells do not form a square of 2 x 2 or larger.

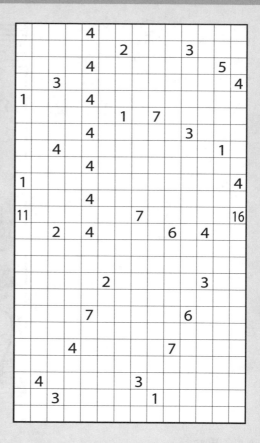

Answer on page 487

248 · STICKY TIME

These 13 sticks have been placed to form four squares. Can you remove three sticks then move two of those left to form just two squares?

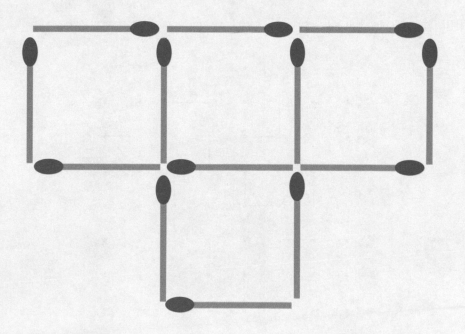

Answer on page 487

249 · ROUND TRIP

We have made a round trip through the dots in the grid, visiting each dot once and returning to the start. Part of our path is shown. Can you deduce the rest?

HINT: Once a dot has two lines leaving it, it can't have any more. You can show this with four Xs.

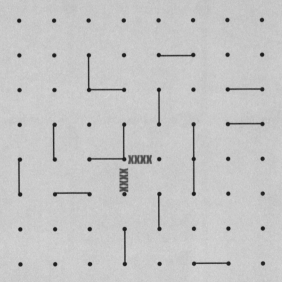

Answer on page 488

250 · SUDOKU

Place a number from 1 to 9 in each empty square so that each row, each column, and each 3 x 3 block contain all the numbers from 1 to 9.

							5	4
	5	4				6		
3			2			7		
			1	7			4	8
7	3			4	9			
		1			7			9
		5				3	2	
2	9							

Answer on page 488

251 · CUBE IT

Inside the circle are three views of the same cube. Which of the lettered shapes can be folded up to make this cube?

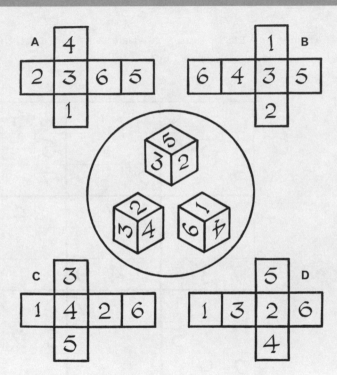

Answer on page 488

The cards eight to king of each suit, together with the ace of hearts, have been placed in a 5 x 5 square. Figures and letters showing the values 8, 9, T, J, Q, K and suits C, D, H, S have been placed at the end of each line across and down. With the ace in place and the fact that the two cards shown on the top left belong in the shaded squares, can you work out the unique place for each card?

		T T J J C D S S	8 9 J K A C D H S	8 J Q K C D H H	8 8 Q K C C H S	9 9 T Q C D H S
8 H	**J** H					
8 8 T K C D H S				▨		
8 J K Q C C S S			A H			
8 9 9 T K C D H S						
9 T Q Q K C D H S						
9 J J Q C D H H			▨			

Just fit these numbers into the grid.

3 figures	671
129	716
172	785
173	905
216	936
219	987
272	
273	**4 figures**
292	1107
334	3722
361	4171
362	7853
371	

611	**7 figures**	**9 figures**	419728652
619	1012392	182763544	612186177
620	2618282	273611773	
651	6661761	296724217	

Answer on page 488

254 · WEIGHED UP

How many cans are needed to make the third pair of scales balance?

Answer on page 488

Can you decide which three
objects do not make a pair?

Answer on page 488

256 · WELL SPOTTED

The number in each circle tells you how many of it and its touching neighbors are to be filled in.

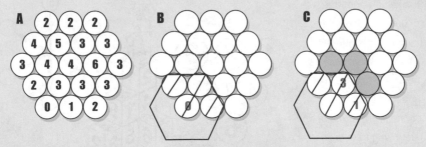

In our example, A, the zero gives a start — put lines through it and its neighbors (B). Three circles can now be filled (C) — lightly, though, so the numbers can still be read . . .

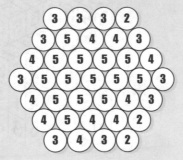

Answer on page 488

257 · MOUNT CUBIC

There are six possible directions that will take you from the center of one face across an edge to the next face on the mountain. Each direction has been given a number from 1 to 6. Can you figure out which direction has which number and so find your way from base to peak?

Answer on page 488

258 · THE CHAMPIONS CUP

Eight soccer teams all got through to the quarterfinal stage of this major cup competition, much to the delight of their numerous fans who had followed the progress of each team. From the clues given, can you work out the status of all the stages up to the final and the eventual winner? Chelsea, who played and beat Norwich, won one more game than Watford. Southampton lost to the team that played Everton in the semifinals. Arsenal won one more game than Liverpool. Everton, who won one more game than Arsenal, never met either Chelsea or Spurs.

Quarterfinals	Semifinals	Final	Winner

Answer on page 489

259 · FILLING IN

Each of the nine empty boxes contains a different digit from 1 to 9. Each calculation is to be treated sequentially rather than according to the "multiplication first" system. Can you fill in the empty boxes?

	+		−		= 9
÷		+		×	
	×		−		= 7
+		÷		÷	
	+		÷		= 4

= 7   = 2   = 3

Answer on page 489

Can you place the letters A, B, C, D, E, one to each square, so that every line across and down contains each letter once and every shape made from five squares also has each letter once?

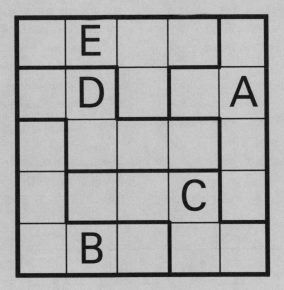

Answer on page 489

261 · THE SPECIAL FIVE

Although P. A. Lette, the Netherlipp artist, has sold or given away most of his paintings, he still keeps five, for various sentimental reasons, on one of his walls. From the clues below, can you indicate in the diagram the title and date of the picture in each position?

1 The picture painted in 1976 hangs directly next to and to the right of one of a building.

2 There is a larger gap in dates between the paintings in positions A and B than between those in positions D and E. The painting in position A is earlier than the one in B, and the painting in E is earlier than the one in D.

3 The picture entitled *Lower Woods* is directly next to and to the left of the one painted in 1988.

4 The date of the picture of St. Aidan's Church is immediately between that of the picture in position C. *Fiddler's Brook* is more than one place to the right of the picture of St. Aidan's Church.

5 *The Old Mill* was painted during the decade preceding that when Lette painted *Crane Bay*.

Titles: *Crane Bay*, *Fiddler's Brook*, *Lower Woods*, *St. Aidan's Church*, *The Old Mill*
Dates: 1964, 1976, 1981, 1988, 1992

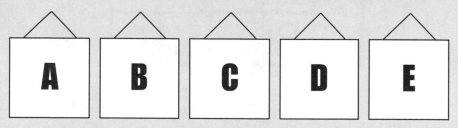

A B C D E

Answer on page 489

262 · DOMINO DEAL

A standard set of dominoes (0–0 to 6–6) is laid out below. Each domino is placed so the that the larger number will be on the bottom:

i.e.: 3   not   6
       6   3

Those top numbers show the four numbers that form the top half of each domino in that column. The bottom numbers, below the grid, give the four bottom numbers for that column. The seven numbers on the left show the numbers that belong in that row. Can you cross-reference the facts and deduce where each domino had been placed? 1–5 is given as a start.

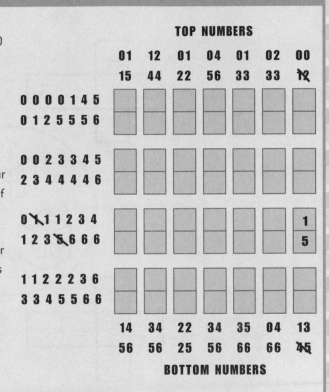

TOP NUMBERS

| 01 | 12 | 01 | 04 | 01 | 02 | 00 |
| 15 | 44 | 22 | 56 | 33 | 33 | 1̶2̶ |

0 0 0 0 1 4 5
0 1 2 5 5 5 6

0 0 2 3 3 4 5
2 3 4 4 4 4 6

0 ̶1̶ 1 1 2 3 4
1 2 3 ̶5̶ 6 6 6   1
                                    5

1 1 2 2 2 3 6
3 3 4 5 5 6 6

| 14 | 34 | 22 | 34 | 35 | 04 | 13 |
| 56 | 56 | 25 | 56 | 66 | 66 | 4̶5̶ |

BOTTOM NUMBERS

Answer on page 489

263 · CUBE IT

Inside the circle are three views of the same cube. Which of the lettered shapes can be folded up to make the cube?

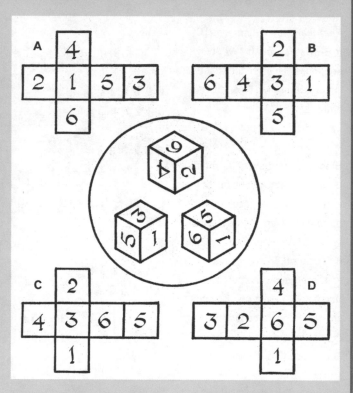

Answer on page 489

264 · OFF YOUR ROCKER

In a negative, everything that is really white appears black and everything that is really black appears white. Can you see which one of the four lettered rocking horses is shown as a negative in the top left-hand corner?

Answer on page 489

265 · WHERE THE L?

Sixteen L shapes like the ones below have been inserted into a square grid. Each L has one hole, and there are four of each type in the square. No two pieces of the same type are adjacent, even at a corner. They fit together so well that the spaces between pieces do not show. From the locations of the holes, can you tell where each L is?

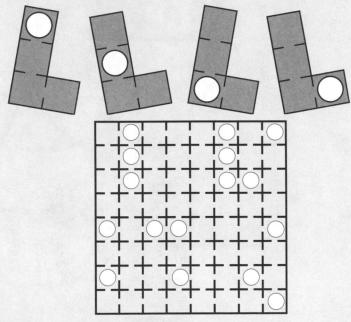

Answer on page 489

266 · COG-ITATE

Can you see which two weights will rise and which three will fall when the man releases the tension as shown?

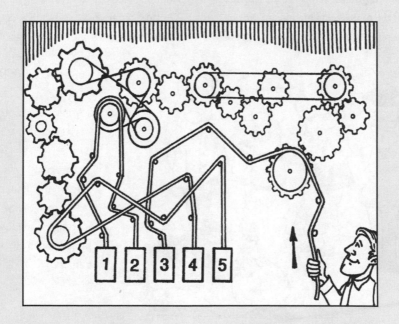

Answer on page 490

Each of the six persons mentioned has at least one sibling in the group and exactly one spouse in the group. Each person is a member of one of the professions mentioned. No one shares a profession with a sibling or a spouse.

Here are the names with some other facts:

1 Neither Alice nor Dave is a surgeon.
2 Betty's sister's husband is an accountant.
3 Carol's husband's brother is an accountant.
4 Ed's wife is a surgeon, and so is Ed's sibling's spouse.
5 Frank's wife's brother is a lawyer.

You are now invited to identify the premarriage family groups, the marriages, and the profession of each person.

Answer on page 490

Each row and column originally contained one A, one B, one C, and one D, and two blank squares.
Each letter and number refers to the first or second of the four letters encountered when
traveling in the direction of the arrow. Can you complete the original grid?

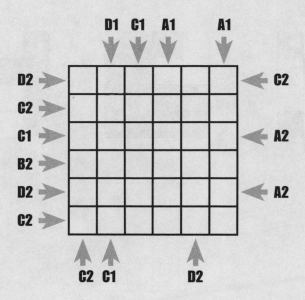

Answer on page 490

269 · LOGI-PICK

Following the first diagram, there is a logical rule that determines how the next block is to be filled in. Given these three blocks, can you color in the fourth?

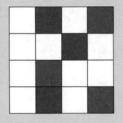

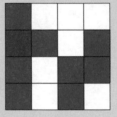

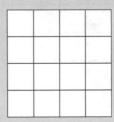

Answer on page 490

270 · EASY AS ABC

Each row and column originally contained one A, one B, one C, one D, and two blank squares. Each letter and number refers to the first or second of the four letters encountered when traveling in the direction of the arrow. Can you complete the original grid?

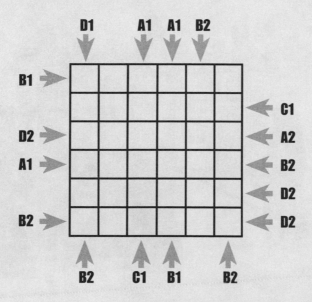

Answer on page 490

271 · OLD HAUNTS

Each of these five English ghosts, one of whom is supposedly Mr. Windham and another of whom is Blanche Legh, is reputed to haunt a notable property. Can you put a name to each apparition, say where it just may be seen, and what special feature distinguishes it from all the other unnerving manifestations found in museum houses?

Answer on page 490

1 It is a man who strolls around Claydon House looking for his hand — sent back there without the rest of him after being cut off in the battle of Edgehill.

2 Anne Boleyn is neither ghost A nor the lady who infests Lyme Park. The papers that one of the ghosts seeks were hidden in the wall at Ham House, which is not haunted by ghost E.

3 Take care when driving to Blickling Hall, because the ghost sits in a coach with her head in her lap — and the horses are headless, too. What state the coach driver is in, we shudder to think.

4 Ghost B is the one still searching for his favorite library books — perhaps because the fines due must now outweigh the national debt.

5 Ghost E is not that of Elizabeth Dysart or the ghost of Felbrigg.

6 Neither Sir Edmund Verney nor the lady in white who follows her husband's funeral procession is ghost B or C.

GHOST	OF	AT	FEATURE
A			
B			
C			
D			
E			

272 · SET SQUARE

All the digits from 1 to 9 are used in this grid, but only once. Can you work out their positions in the grid and make the totals work? We've given two numbers to start you off.

Answer on page 490

273 · SPOT THE DIFFERENCES

Can you spot the ten differences between these two pictures?

Answer on page 490

274 · BATTLESHIPS

Do you remember the old game of battleships? These puzzles are based on that idea. Your task is to find the vessels in the diagram. Some parts of boats or sea squares have already been filled in, and a number next to a row or column refers to the number of occupied squares in that row or column. The boats may be positioned horizontally or vertically, but no two boats or parts of boats are in adjacent squares — horizontally, vertically, or diagonally.

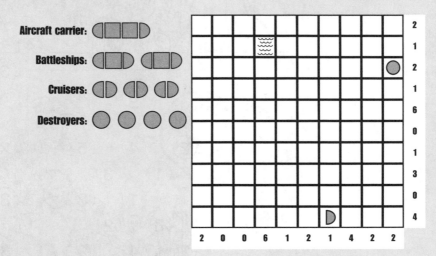

Aircraft carrier:

Battleships:

Cruisers:

Destroyers:

Answer on page 491

275 · BRIDGES

Each circle containing a number represents an island. The object is to connect each island with vertical or horizontal bridges so that:

- The number of bridges is the same as the number inside the island.
- There are no more than two bridges between two islands.
- Bridges do not cross islands or other bridges.
- There is a continuous path connecting all the islands.

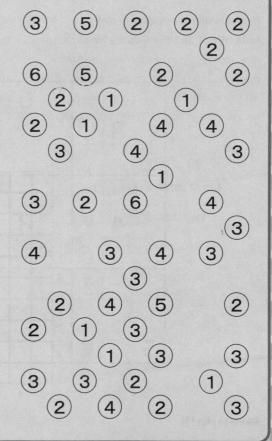

Answer on page 491

276 · SUDOKU

Place a number from 1 to 9 in each empty square so that each row, each column, and each 3 x 3 block contain all the numbers from 1 to 9.

				6	9			4
	8				4			
2						8		
						3	2	
	4			8			5	
	9	6						
		3						9
			5				6	
5			2	7				

Answer on page 491

277 · NUMBER KROSS

See how quickly you can fit all these numbers into the grid. We've filled one figure in to start you off.

3 figures	8326	73346
217	9083	84168
226	9447	89224
304		90718
421	**5 figures**	97179
572	10439	
815	14756	**6 figures**
874	24514	107989
907	27190	134871
	30947	172351
4 figures	46023	212806
1740	55326	213071

1783	57147	316293	572215	713954
6137	60175	341268	581941	819201
7576	61513	453527	661630	971329
7657	67329	551108	676869	

Answer on page 491

An architect and four of his friends swim in the same pool. Mark and the dentist both swim laps in the morning. Karl and Mr. Harkness sometimes dive together in the afternoons. Mr. Jones recently considered the idea of making up a swimming team using the five of them. He observed that:

- In the 100-meter freestyle, both Mr. Harkness and Mr. Gainor are slower than Mark.

- Both Mr. Harkness and Otto are faster than the economist.

- In the backstroke, only Neil is willing to swim more than 50 meters, and Karl will not compete at all.

- In the 50-meter backstroke, Mr. Ives is faster than Mark. Mark, Otto, and Luke are all slower than the barber. Mark is faster than the critic.

- In the breaststroke, the critic, the dentist, and the economist are all slower than Mr. Franklin. Luke is faster than Mr. Ives.

- As to springboard diving, Mr. Franklin, Mark, and Karl are the three best divers.

Can you identify all five men, giving names and occupations?

Answer on page 491

279 · ACE IN PLACE

The cards eight to king of each suit, together with the ace of hearts, have been placed in a 5 x 5 square. Figures and letters of the values 8, 9, T, J, Q, K and suits C, D, H, S have been placed at the end of each line across and down. With the ace in place and the fact that the two cards shown at the top left belong in the shaded squares, can you figure out the unique place for each card?

K S	K D	9 K K Q / C D H S	8 T Q / A C H H S	8 T T J / C H H S	9 J Q K / D S S S	8 J J Q / C D D H
9 T T Q Q / C H S H S						
9 T J J K / C C C S						
8 J J K / 9 K D D H S						
8 Q Q K / 9 K D H S S						
8 K / T A 8 / C H / H D H			A H			

280 · CODE MASTER

Just follow the rules of the classic game of Mastermind to crack the number code. The first number tells you how many of the digits are exactly correct — the right digit in the right place (✓✓). The second number tells you how many digits are the correct number but are not in the right place (✓). By comparing the information given by each line, can you work out which number goes in which place?

					✓✓	✓
2	4	3	1	5	0	2
8	2	1	3	4	2	0
1	9	6	2	7	1	3
6	4	1	7	9	0	4
7	5	9	6	8	1	2

Answer on page 491

281 · IT FIGURES

Place a number from 1 to 9 in each empty cell so that the sum of each vertical or horizontal block equals the number at the top or on the left of that block. Numbers may only be used once in each block.

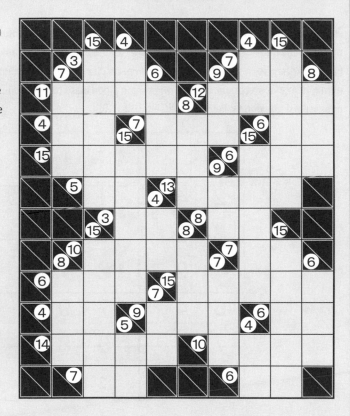

Answer on page 491

282 · IT'S MAGIC

This magic square can be completed using the numbers from 32 to 56 inclusive. To give you a start, the first row has all its even digits entered, the second row all its odd digits, the third row even again, the fourth odd, and the fifth even. Can you complete the square so that the five numbers in each row, column, and long diagonal add up to the magic total? The total—close your eyes if you don't want to be told—is 220.

2		4 6	4 8	
5 1	5 3	3 5	3 7	
4 0	4 2	4	6	
5	3	3	5	7
4	0	2	4 4	

Answer on page 491

283 · TRILINES

Can you draw three straight lines, each one drawn from one edge to another, so that they divide the box into five sections each containing a cup and a saucer?

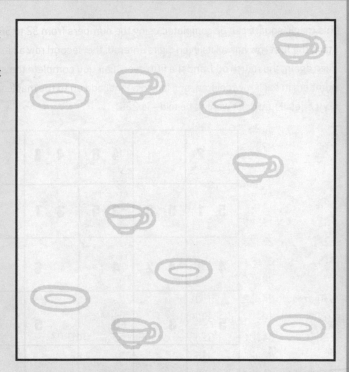

Answer on page 492

284 · NUMBER KROSS

See how quickly you can fit all these numbers into the grid. We've filled one figure in to start you off.

3 figures	7042	75740
209	8406	83992
314	9758	87437
504		93620
526	**5 figures**	94339
620	13129	
731	15521	**6 figures**
832	23328	140415
915	27138	180356
	34005	283913
4 figures	34452	294897
1971	40226	345950

5863	75233	566157	678565	
4981	64894	494874	636031	984942
3640	60926	453124	587001	860221
2295	54501	394352	568265	841807

Answer on page 492

285 · NUMBER TREE

Sixteen leaves are on the eight branches of the tree, and each contains a different number from 1 to 16. Using the following clues, can you determine which number is on which leaf? All the totals of two leaves at the same height are different (leaf 2 is at the same height as leaf 9, 3 is the same as 10, and so on). Four of the totals of the leaves on each branch are unique, but the other two totals each appear twice. No number is the same as the leaf that it is on, and no two consecutive numbers are on the same branch or at the same height. The seven prime numbers, including 1, are all on leaves that have prime numbers. 2 and 14 are on the same branch, and the number on leaf 14 is a multiple of that on 12. A leaf containing a square number is immediately above another with a square number, neither of the square numbers being 9. Number 7 is higher than number 9, which is higher than number 10, which is immediately below number 1. The total of leaf 9 (which does not contain 15) and leaf 11 is the same as the total of the numbers on leaves 5 and 7. Number 13 is at the same height as number 4, which is somewhere higher than number 16. Number 1 is immediately below an odd number. Only two branches contain two odd numbers, and the total of the numbers on leaves 6 and 8 is a prime number, which is also the same as the total of one of the branches. Number 3 is somewhere below number 11.

Answer on page 492

The twins would like to buy matching belts. Which two will they choose?

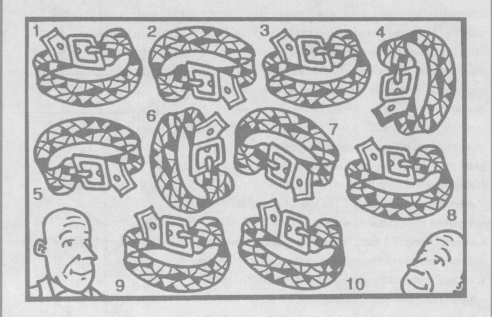

Answer on page 492

287 · ALL SQUARE

Each of the 16 small squares making up the large square in the diagram contains either one of the numbers 1–8 or the square of one of these numbers. From the clues given below, can you place the correct number in each square?
Note: The numbers 1 and 4 will, of course, each appear twice.

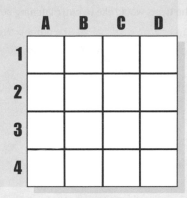

1. The numbers in the four corner squares, which are all different, total 21 when added together.
2. 16 is immediately to the right of 64, and immediately below 49.
3. The 9 and 6 are both in column A.
4. Squares B2 and C4 both contain single-digit numbers, the former being an even number.
5. The total of the four numbers in row 1 is one higher than the number in square A2.
6. The number in square D2 is twice the one in C1.
7. The number in square B3 is the square of the one in D1.

Answer on page 492

8. The 25 and the 8 are on the same horizontal row of squares.
9. One of the 1s is in column B.
10. The number in C4 is the square root of one of the other numbers in column C.

Numbers: 1; 1; 2; 3; 4; 4; 5; 6; 7; 8; 9; 16; 25; 36; 49; 64

Starting tip: Begin by figuring out where to put the 16.

288 · TROUBLESOME TRIANGLE

The numbers 1–15 are to be inserted into the grid. No two consecutive numbers are in the same row or arrowed diagonal. The numbers on the left show the total in the horizontal row, and those below show the total of the diagonal.

If squares 5 and 8 total 16, and in the diagonal totaling 27 only one square contains an even number, can you complete the grid?

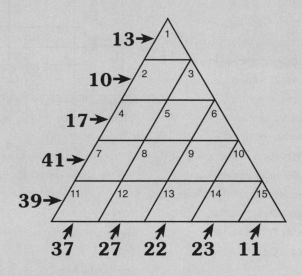

Answer on page 492

289 · RED, WHITE, AND BLUE

Each of the squares numbered 1 to 13 is colored red, white, or blue, one color being represented five times and the other two colors four times each. From the clues given below, can you insert the correct color in each of the squares?

1 No two adjacent squares vertically or horizontally are the same color.
2 There is a white square directly to the left of a blue square in the middle horizontal row, which has no other white squares.
3 None of the four isolated squares (numbers 1, 5, 9, and 13) is blue.
4 Two of the four squares denoted by a double-digit number are red.
5 There is just one red square in the horizontal row numbered from 2 to 4.
6 Central square number 7 is red.
7 Squares 1 and 12 are the same color.
8 One white square has a number that is twice that of a red square.

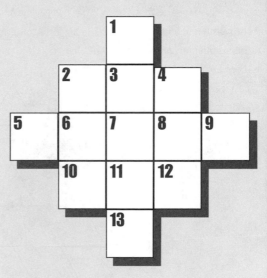

Starting tip: Begin by identifying the blue squares.

Answer on page 492

Each circle containing a number represents an island. The object is to connect each island with vertical or horizontal bridges so that:

- The number of bridges is the same as the number inside the island.
- There are no more than two bridges between two islands.
- Bridges do not cross islands or other bridges.
- There is a continuous path connecting all the islands.

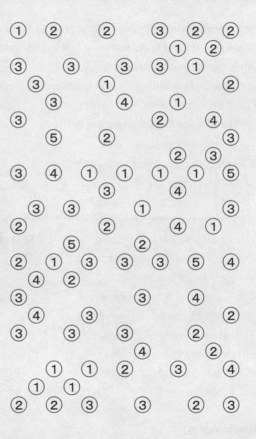

Answer on page 493

291 · CARDS ON THE TABLE

The 13 cards of a suit are shuffled and dealt out in a row, and it is found that none is in its correct numerical position (ace left, king right) and the face cards are not at either end or adjacent to each other. The ace is between 9 (left) and 8, the 4 between queen (left) and jack, the 2 two places left of 10, the 7 two places left of 3, the left-hand card one higher than the right-hand card, and the king is left of the queen. The ninth and tenth cards from the left total 9, the ninth being of lower value. Can you locate each card?

Answer on page 493

Follow the dots from 1 to 37 to reveal the hidden picture.

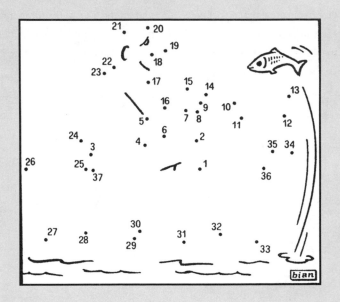

Answer on page 493

293 · SET SQUARE

All the digits from 1 to 9 are used in this grid, but only once. Can you work out their positions in the grid and make the totals work? We've given two numbers to start you off.

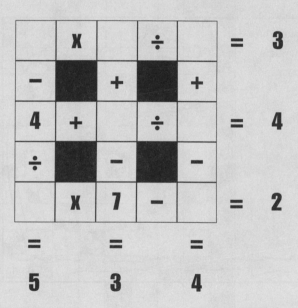

Answer on page 493

294 · IT FIGURES

Place a number from 1 to 9 in each empty cell so that the sum of each vertical or horizontal block equals the number at the top or on the left of that block. Numbers may only be used once in each block.

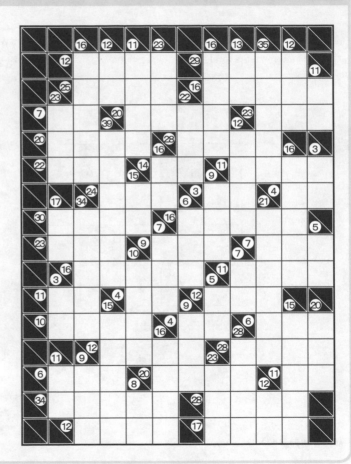

Answer on page 493

295 · TRIO

Which three vases are identical?

Answer on page 493

296 · COFFIN'S CANOE

This extraordinary little puzzle was made by Stuart Coffin—a world-renowned puzzle craftsman.

The "canoe" has two recesses, one at each end, into which the balls will fit. A divider separates the two balls. If you think that the problem of rolling balls into the holes is just too easy, let us point out that you must pop them into place simultaneously! Now that might seem impossible—but it can be done. How?

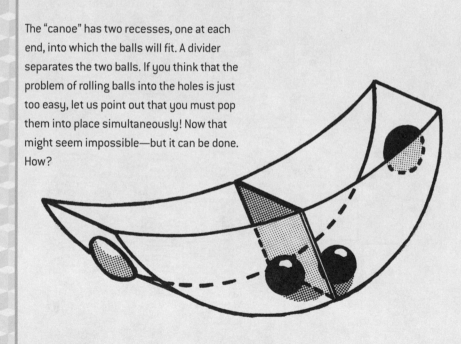

Answer on page 494

297 · DICEY BUSINESS

In order to answer that all-important social question — how many are out to lunch? — four dice are thrown. The answers to the first two throws are given. So what is the answer for the third throw?

= 3

= 30

= ?

Answer on page 494

298 · DARTING AROUND

A dart player scores 66 with three darts hitting a triple, a double, and a single. Given that the three numbers that he hits add up to 31 and that the difference between the largest and smallest numbers is 10, can you figure out how his score is made up?

Triple   **Double**   **Single**

Answer on page 494

299 · NUMBER SQUARES

Can you complete the grid below with the aid of the numbers given, so that all sums, whether horizontal or vertical, are correct? (Please note that each subtotal should be treated separately.)

48	÷		=		+		=	44
−		+		×		÷		−
	÷	4	=		÷		=	
=		=		=		=		=
	+		=	32	+		=	
×		+		+		+		+
	+		=		+	1	=	
=		=		=		=		=
64	−		=		+		=	53

Answer on page 494

300 · QUEENS HIGH

If you can rustle up eight tiny coinlike items, you could use our chessboard to try an old puzzle. Place the eight counters so that no two are in the same line across or down or diagonally. If you choose, say, A3, then you could not put a mark in any other square in column A or in row 3 nor in squares like C1 and D6, which are in a diagonal line from A3. The real puzzle, though, is to choose your eight squares, according to the rule, so that the total of the eight numbers you mark is as high as possible. Just how many can you score with your eight tiny queens on each of these chessboards?

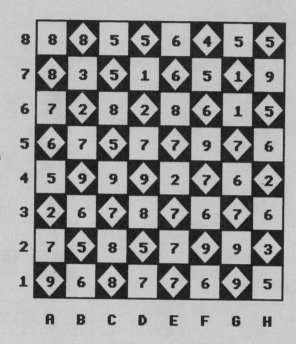

Answer on page 494

In the following problem, the digits 0 to 9 are represented by letters. Within each separate puzzle, the same letter always represents the same digit. Can you find the correct values each time so that all totals, both horizontal and vertical, are correct?

With each separate puzzle, there is a clue to help start you off.

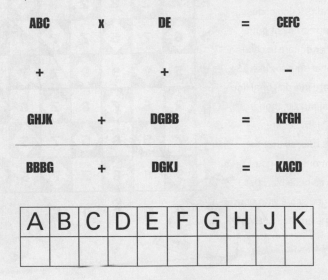

	ABC	x	DE	=	CEFC
	+		+		−
	GHJK	+	DGBB	=	KFGH
	BBBG	+	DGKJ	=	KACD

A	B	C	D	E	F	G	H	J	K

Clue: BG + KE = HC

Answer on page 494

302 · TENTACKLE

Eight children are camping, two to each tent, and some have given us a couple of clues as to how to find them. The trouble is their senses of direction are as bad as their cooking, and in each case only one direction is true while the other is an exact opposite, so that east should read west, etc. Directions are not necessarily exact, so north could be north, northeast, or northwest. To help you, one child is already tucked into a sleeping bag.

Alice says: "I'm north of Fiona and west of Beth."

Carol says: "I'm south of Helen and east of Gina."

Fiona says: "I'm north of Gina and east of Carol."

Helen says: "I'm south of Daisy and west of Enid."

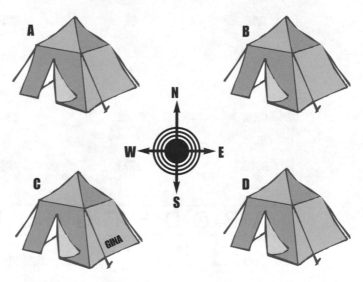

Answer on page 494

303 · ARROW PUZZLE

Can you help the ship reach the Americas
by following the arrows, being careful not
to land on Australia by mistake?

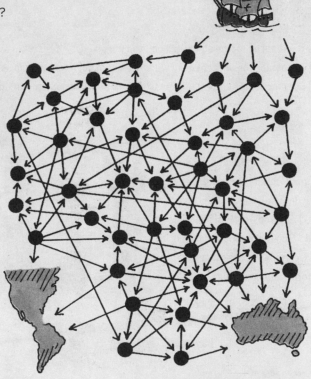

Answer on page 494

304 · PILE UP

These piles of blocks aren't the random results of a child playing but clues to a final, at present blank, pile on the right. Like the rest, that one has six blocks each with a different one of the six letters.

The numbers below the stacks tell you two things:

(a) The number of adjacent pairs of blocks in that column that also appear adjacent in the final pile.

(b) The number of adjacent pairs of blocks that make a correct pair but the wrong way up.

So: would score one in the "Correct" row if the final stack had an A directly above a C and one in the "Reversed" row if the final heap had a C on top of an A. From all of this, can you create the tower before it finally topples?

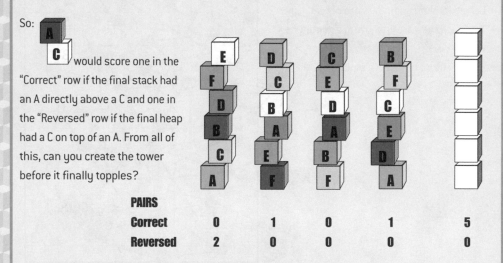

PAIRS					
Correct	0	1	0	1	5
Reversed	2	0	0	0	0

Answer on page 494

305 · CELL STRUCTURE

The object is to create white areas surrounded by black walls, so that:

- Each white area contains only one number
- The number of cells in a white area is equal to the number in it.
- The white areas are separated from each other by a black wall.
- Cells containing numbers are not filled in.
- The black cells are linked into a continuous wall.
- Black cells do not form a square of 2 x 2 or larger.

7				3			5					
6				5			1					
6				2			8					
			3		2			2				
			1		4			5				
			7		1			8				
		8		7		3						
		2		3		2						
		7		3		3						
			2			7					3	
			2			5					1	
			7			4					3	

Answer on page 494

306 · LETTER MAZE

The object is to pass through the maze and reach the exit at the top. No diamond may be passed through more than once in any one move, nor may you leave a diamond the same way you came in. You must not enter diamonds that contain the letters you are told to avoid.

1 Move 4 diamonds. Avoid A, C, and F.
2 Move 3 diamonds. Avoid C, E, and G.
3 Move 5 diamonds. Avoid A and E.
4 Move 3 diamonds. Avoid C.
5 Move 4 diamonds. Avoid C, D, and E.
6 Move 5 diamonds. Avoid B and F.
7 Move 5 diamonds. Avoid C and G.
8 Move 2 diamonds. Avoid B.
9 Move 2 diamonds. Avoid A, C, and G.
10 Move 3 diamonds. Avoid A, B, and E.

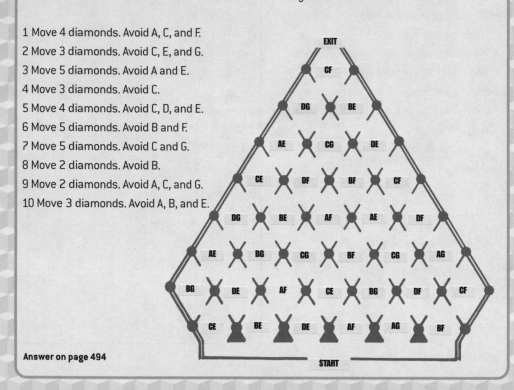

Answer on page 494

307 · DOMINO DEAL

A standard set of dominoes (0–0 to 6–6) is laid out below. Each domino is placed so that the larger number will be on the bottom:

i.e.:   3   not   6
         6   3

Those top numbers show the four numbers that form the top half of each domino in that column. The bottom numbers, below the grid, give the four bottom numbers for that column. The seven numbers on the left show the numbers that belong in that row. Can you cross-reference the facts and deduce where each domino has been placed? 3–6 is given as a start.

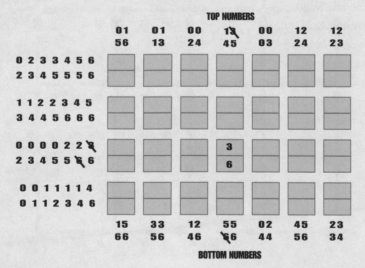

308 · STICKY TIME

There are 30 squares here of various sizes. Remove nine matchsticks, so that no squares exist at all.

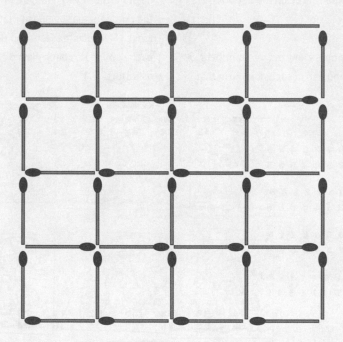

Answer on page 495

Which one of the
numbered prints did
the stamp create?

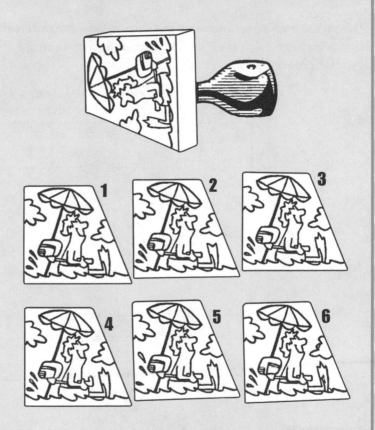

Answer on page 495

310 · TRILINES

Can you divide this square into six sections, each containing three pairs of different symbols, by drawing three straight lines? The lines must run from one reference number to another on the other side of the square.

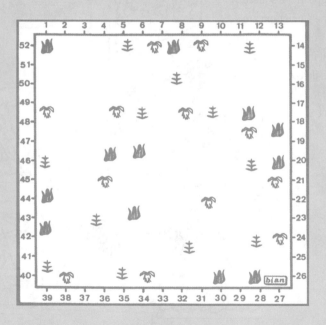

Answer on page 495

311 · WHERE THE L?

Twelve L shapes like the ones below have been fitted into a square grid. Each L has one hole, and there are three of each type in the square. No two pieces of the same type are adjacent, even at a corner. They fit together so well that the spaces between pieces do not show. From the locations of the holes, can you tell where each L is?

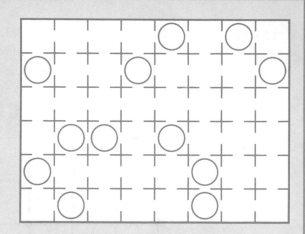

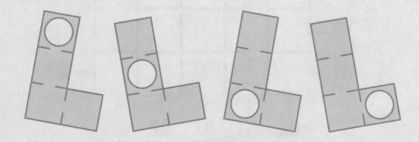

Answer on page 495

312 · EASY AS ABC

Each row and column originally contained one A, one B, one C, and two blank squares. Each letter and number refers to the first or second of the four letters encountered when traveling in the direction of the arrow. Can you complete the original grid?

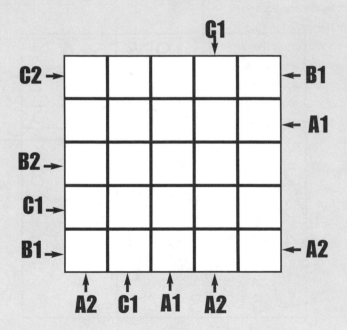

Answer on page 495

313 · SUDOKU

Place a number from 1 to 9 in each empty square so that each row, each column, and each 3 x 3 block contain all the numbers from 1 to 9.

				9	5	6	4	
			6				8	2
			8		4	9		5
	4	6	1		3	5		7
2				5				8
3		5	7		9	2	6	
4		8	9		7			
1	2				8			
	6	7	3	4				

Answer on page 495

314 · NUMBER SQUARES

Find the following numbers in the grid in a square formation. The first set has been found for you. Take care: some digits may be mixed up within the square.

4	2	0	4	3	9	3	1	3	8
8	3	5	8	5	1	2	4	0	4
9	1	4	6	1	8	2	0	5	7
2	7	3	7	0	3	8	9	3	9
5	0	9	6	8	2	4	2	1	4
9	7	2	1	7	5	3	6	5	8
3	1	4	9	2	8	0	2	3	2

3159   2890   6523   9713

4531   7681   0483

315 · DOUBLE DUTCH

Theo Versteylan, a tulip grower from Zuidelijk, was found murdered. He had been hit on the head with one of his own clogs. Commissaris Van Drijver of the Amsterdam police was dispatched to investigate. Five suspects were discovered, but they all claimed alibis. The facts listed may sound like double Dutch, but from them Van Drijver was able to deduce that one suspect did not have an alibi. Can you?

1 Hein was not with Roel or Rudig unless Jan was with Wouter.

2 Jan was not with Roel or Wouter unless Hein was with Rudig.

3 Roel was not with Jan or Rudig unless Hein was with Wouter.

4 Rudig was not with Jan or Wouter unless Hein was with Roel.

5 Wouter was not with Hein or Roel unless Jan was with Rudig.

Answer on page 495

316 · PUPPY POWER

When the dog pulls the
rope, which weights will
go down and which will
go up?

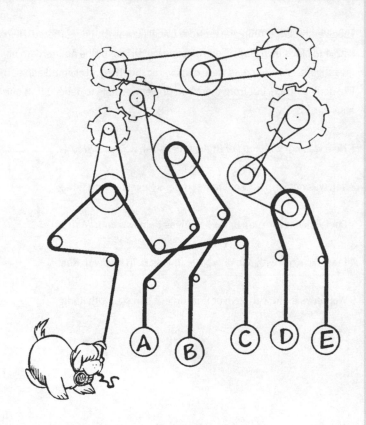

Answer on page 495

Can you place the numbered blocks into the grid to form the pattern shown? The blocks may be placed horizontally or vertically and may be turned around.

0	1	3	2
1	2	3	2
2	2	0	0
1	1	1	0
3	3	0	3

0	1

0	3

2	2

1	3

3	3

0	2

1	2

0	0

1	1

3	2

Answer on page 495

Each row and column originally contained one A, one B, one C, one D, and two blank squares. Each letter and number refers to the first or second of the four letters encountered when traveling in the direction of the arrow. Can you complete the original grid?

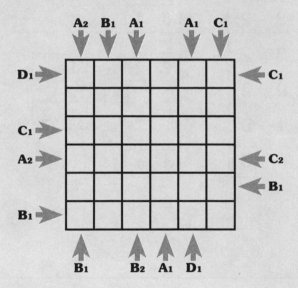

Answer on page 496

319 · TOP APARTMENT

The brass number plate for the apartments in Leakey Towers was bought at the Nutting-Fitz Hardware Store, which never has exactly what anyone wants, so the locals have to make do with what they get. Young vandals have already ensured that one apartment number needs replacing. What should it be?

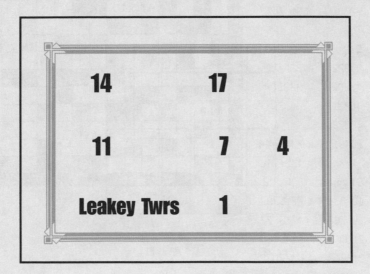

Answer on page 496

320 · NUMBER JIG

Fit the numbers into the grid. We have done one for you.

3 figures
214
311
362
401 ~~401~~
421
637
729

4 figures
1714
1762
2773
3018
3707
3979
4233

6913
7326
9032

5 figures
37022
48206
48221
48872
79491

6 figures
102331
193767
212669
312943
404331

466278
476236
618243
721426
739998
760636
920307
943201

7 figures
1382916
2361712
2719383
4216072
5173484
6377028
8920973

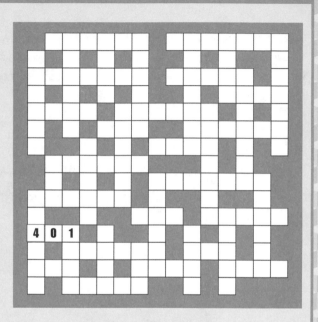

Answer on page 496

321 · END OF THE LINE

There are eight differences between these two pictures—can you find them all?

Answer on page 496

322 · FLOWER POWER

Patriotic Pete sells bunches of red, white, and blue flowers in the market. Some bunches have just a single color, some two, and some a mixture of all three. If he brings along a total of 80 bunches, can you work out how many bunches have flowers of all three colors?

The number of bunches with both red and blue flowers but no white is the same as the number with red only, and the number of bunches with both blue and white but no red is the same as the number with blue only and this is equal to the total number of bunches with red only and with both red and white but no blue. Three times as many bunches have white flowers only as have all three colors. Twenty-nine bunches contain red flowers, and 41 bunches contain blue.

Answer on page 496

323 · WELL SPOTTED

The number in each circle tells you how many of it and its touching neighbors are to be filled in.

In our example, A, the zero gives a start — put lines through it and its neighbors (B). Three circles can now be filled (C) — lightly, though so the numbers can still be read . . .

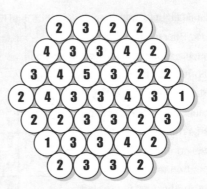

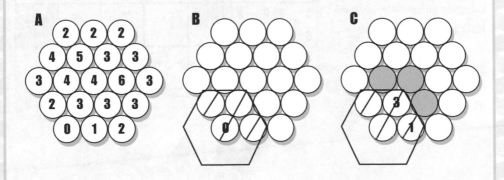

Answer on page 496

324 · ACE IN PLACE

The cards eight to king of each suit, together with the ace of hearts, have been placed in a five-by-five square. Figures and letters of the values 8, 9, T, Q, K and suits C, D, H, S have been placed at the end of each line across and down. With the ace in place and the fact that the two cards shown at the top left belong in the shaded squares, can you figure out the unique place for each card?

Answer on page 496

Connect adjacent dots with vertical or horizontal lines so that a single loop is formed with no crossings or branches. Each number indicates how many lines surround it, while empty cells may be surrounded by any number of lines.

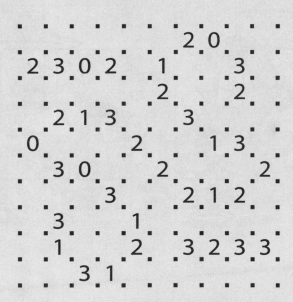

There are six differences in the pictures below.
Can you spot them?

Answer on page 497

Connect adjacent dots with vertical or horizontal lines so that a single loop is formed with no crossings or branches. Each number indicates how many lines surround it, while empty cells may be surrounded by any number of lines.

328 · STRAPPED

The six straps leading from the central hexagon each contain three different instances of the numbers 1 to 18. From the clues given below, can you place each number in the correct position on the correct strap?

1 The six innermost numbers total 64.
2 The single-digit middle number on strap A minus the number outside it produces the outermost number on strap F.
3 There are just two even numbers, one of which is the outermost one, on strap E, but only one on strap F.
4 The 5 is the innermost number on strap D; the 7 is not on the strap directly opposite.
5 The 17 and 12 are separated by the 1 on one of the straps.
6 The 10 on one strap, which is immediately next to the 16, is in the same relative position as the 3 on another; the 6 is farther

away from the center than the 15 on an adjacent strap.
7 Strap C, which has only one two-digit number on it, does not contain the 1 or 2, the latter of which corresponds in its position with the 13 on another strap.
8 The largest of the three numbers on strap B is not its innermost one; the outermost one is a lower number than the innermost number of the strap opposite, which is ten higher than the corresponding number on strap F.

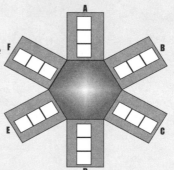

Starting tip: Start by working out which is the strap referred to in clue 5.

Answer on page 497

329 · IT FIGURES

Place a number from 1 to 9 in each empty cell so that the sum of each vertical or horizontal block equals the number at the top or on the left of that block. Numbers may only be used once in each block.

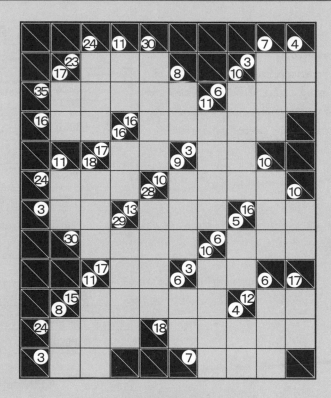

Answer on page 498

Four celebrity panelists, aided and abetted by that helpful host, Robin Robertson, have guessed the jobs of four guests. Can you sign in, please, with each guest's full job title and the name of the celebrity who revealed all?

GERTA

~~ANN~~	~~CONNIE~~
~~ENA~~	KEN
~~CRIMPER'S~~	FLEDGER'S
GRUTTLER'S	TADDLER'S
CRINGE	~~HOOKER~~
POSSET	SLANT

NOAH

ANN	CONNIE
ENA	~~KEN~~
CRIMPER'S	FLEDGER'S
GRUTTLER'S	TADDLER'S
CRINGE	HOCKER
POSSET	SLANT

Answer on page 498

348

MILES

ANN	CONNIE
ENA	~~KEN~~
CRIMPER'S	FLEDGER'S
GRUTTLER'S	TADDLER'S
CRINGE	HOCKER
POSSET	SLANT

WANDA

ANN	CONNIE
ENA	~~KEN~~
CRIMPER'S	FLEDGER'S
GRUTTLER'S	TADDLER'S
CRINGE	HOCKER
POSSET	SLANT

1 Ken's occupation was guessed by Gerta and he is neither the Hocker nor the Crimper's. No one was a Crimper's Hocker.

2 Miles did not realize Ann was a Slant. Wanda guessed the Posset, which was not Connie's occupation.

3 One occupation was Fledger's Cringe.

4 A lady panelist guessed Taddler's.

Clue 1 has been entered for you.

331 · SILHOUETTE

Shade all the shapes that contain a dot to reveal a hidden picture.

Answer on page 498

332 · CIRCLE OF DIGITS

The figure below consists of three concentric circles divided into eight sectors; the three single-digit numbers in each sector add up to 15. The circles will be referred to as outer, middle, and inner; one number in the inner has been inserted to give you a start. From the clues given, can you insert all the other numbers?

1 The only 0 appears in the outer circle, where there is no 1 or 3; there is no 9 in the middle, and no number is repeated in any sector or circle.

2 All the numbers in sectors A and B are odd; B outer is one more than C inner and one less than H middle, which is one more than H inner; B inner is one less than G outer.

3 The 6 in the outer circle is diagonally opposite the 6 in the inner.

4 C inner is twice D inner, while D outer is twice D middle; F outer is twice F middle, which is twice G middle and the same as C outer; E outer is the same as A middle.

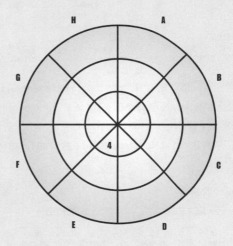

Starting tip: Figure out the number in C inner.

Answer on page 498

333 · DVD RENTAL

Will nothing stop the DVD boom? These four shops have just opened, to add to the dozen already cluttering Lampwick's side streets. Can you record a summary as to the customer at each shop and the film being rented?

1 D. Cryer is at Rent 'N' Rave but is not renting *Gosh!* or *Whew!*
2 Just Flicks are not renting out to A. Blinkon, whose choice is *Wow!*
3 B. Dee-High is not the one choosing *Gosh!*
4 C. Nitt is not at More Movies, who are not renting out *Wow!*

JUST FLICKS

A. BLINKON	B. DEE-HIGH
C. NITT	D. ~~CRYER~~
GOSH!	HEY!
WHEW!	WOW!

MORE MOVIES

A. BLINKON	B. DEE-HIGH
C. NITT	D. ~~CRYER~~
GOSH!	HEY!
WHEW!	WOW!

NITE RATES

A. BLINKON	B. DEE-HIGH
C. NITT	D. ~~CRYER~~
GOSH!	HEY!
WHEW!	WOW!

RENT 'N' RAVE

A. ~~BLINKON~~	B. ~~DEE-HIGH~~
C. ~~NITT~~	D. CRYER
~~GOSH!~~	HEY!
~~WHEW!~~	WOW!

Answer on page 498

334 · DOGGY DUOS

Can you put these dogs into four identical pairs?

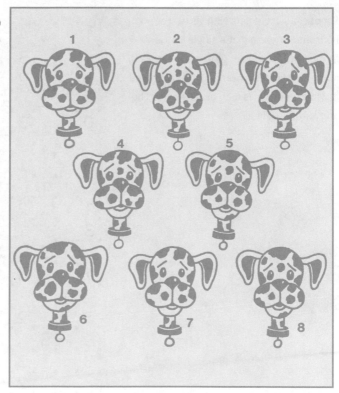

Answer on page 498

Connect adjacent dots with vertical or horizontal lines so that a single loop is formed with no crossings or branches. Each number indicates how many lines surround it, while empty cells may be surrounded by any number of lines.

```
1    3    1 2    3    0
        3      1
3    2      1      2
    2   0 3    1
0    3      1      2
  1              1
3      1      3      1
    1    1 2    2
1      2      3      3
3      1      0      1
    3    2 1    3
1      3      0      0
  1              1
3      2      3      1
    3    2 2    2
3      3      2      1
        2      2
3    1    0 2    3    3
```

336 · COURT ORDER

Of the eight kings and queens in a pack of cards, four are lined up here.
In these clues TO THE RIGHT or LEFT means NEXT DOOR and not anywhere beyond.

There's a king to the right of a king.

There's a king to the left of a queen.

There's a queen to the left of a king.

There's a queen to the right of a spade.

There's a spade next to a spade.

There's a club to the left of a heart.

There's a club to the right of a spade.

Can you identify each card?

Answer on page 499

337 · BRIDGES

Each circle containing a number represents an island. The object is to connect each island with vertical or horizontal bridges so that:
* The number of bridges is the same as the number inside the island.
* There are no more than two bridges between two islands.
* Bridges do not cross islands or other bridges.
* There is a continuous path connecting all the islands.

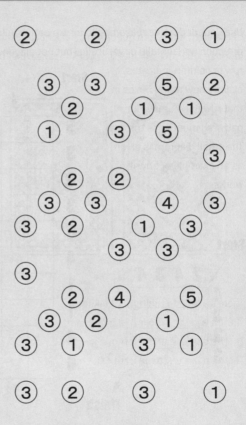

Answer on page 499

338 · LOGI-PATH

Use your deductive reasoning to form a pathway from START to FINISH moving in either direction horizontally or vertically (but not diagonally). The number at the beginning of every row or column indicates exactly how many boxes in that row or column your pathway must pass through. The small diagram is given as an example of how it works.

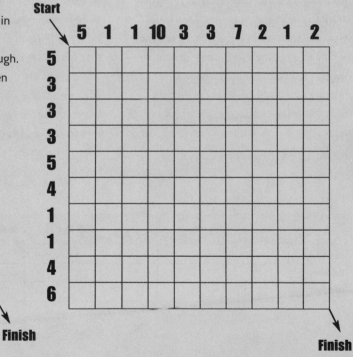

339 · TEE TIME

Those three old-timers are back for their weekly game of golf on the Golden Lawns 18-hole, par 72, course. Each score at every hole falls into one of five categories. Each golfer gets a different result in each category. Also, no category has the same result for another player, i.e., if a player has two eagles, he has a different number in the other four and no other player has two eagles. With the score details below and the information given, can you fill in their card?

Parnell, who did not get the fewest pars, got one more eagle than bogey, and the two added up to his number of birdies. This number was the same as Barry's pars, which were two fewer than his birdies and two more than his double bogeys. Nick got twice as many pars as birdies and twice as many birdies as double bogeys, of which he had the same number as Barry's eagles. This number was one more than Barry's number of bogeys, which was two less than his double bogeys.

	Eagle −2	Birdie −1	Par 0	Bogey +1	Double Bogey +2	FINAL SCORE
Parnell Darma						
Nick Jackliss						
Barry Clayer						

Answer on page 499

340 · STICKY TIME

Move two matches only so that you end up with the cherry outside the glass.

Answer on page 499

341 · DOMINO SEARCH

A standard set of dominoes has been laid out, using numbers instead of dots for clarity. Using a sharp pencil and a keen brain, can you draw in the lines to show where each domino has been placed? You may find the check grid useful—crossing off each domino as you find it.

2	6	1	4	4	3	0	3
2	3	5	5	6	6	4	2
0	1	0	2	1	1	1	4
5	3	0	0	5	3	0	5
0	6	1	2	1	6	4	1
4	3	3	4	0	5	5	6
2	4	6	3	2	2	6	5

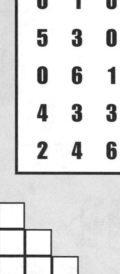

Answer on page 499

Which two of the numbered pieces will fit together to make cube A?

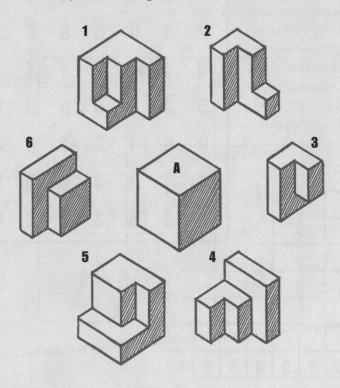

Answer on page 499

343 · SUDOKU

Place a number from 1 to 9 in each empty square so that each row, each column, and each 3 x 3 block contain all the numbers from 1 to 9.

		5			1	9		
	4			2			7	
1			8					3
		9	2					6
	1			5			8	
4					9	5		
5					6			7
	9			3			1	
		1	7			6		

Answer on page 500

344 · ANTIPATHETIC

A reluctant ant, not wanting to be sent out on yet another food gathering journey, decided to take the longest route back to the nest. Such is its tiny brain, though, that it will only go along the edges of the patio tiles and will not go over any part of its path more than once. What was the longest way home?

START

FINISH

Answer on page 500

345 · TOTTERING TOWERS

These piles of blocks aren't the random results of a child playing but clues to a final, at present blank, pile on the right. Like the rest, that one has six blocks each with a different one of the six colors.

The numbers below the stacks tell you two things:

(a) The number of adjacent pairs of blocks in that column that also appear adjacent in the final pile.

(b) The number of adjacent pairs of blocks that make a correct pair but the wrong way up.

So:

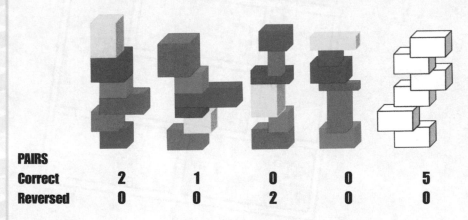

would score one in the "Correct" row if the final stack had green directly above yellow and one in the "Reversed" row if the final heap had yellow on top of green. From all of this, can you create the tower before it finally topples?

PAIRS					
Correct	2	1	0	0	5
Reversed	0	0	2	0	0

Answer on page 500

346 · DRUM ROLL

In a negative, everything that is really black appears white and everything that is really white appears black. Can you tell which one of the seven kettledrums is shown as a negative in the top left-hand corner?

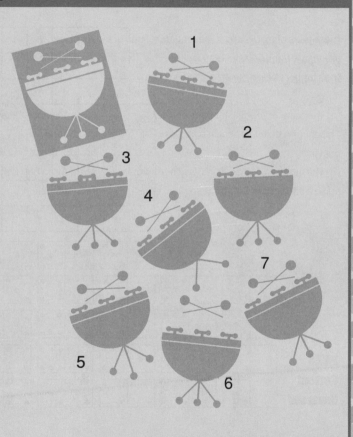

Answer on page 500

347 · BREAKTHROUGH

See how quickly you can break this grid down into the 28 dominoes from which it was formed.

2	6	0	6	0	5	3
3	3	3	5	5	6	5
6	2	0	4	1	6	6
3	2	1	4	4	3	4
5	2	4	1	1	1	6
2	3	0	2	3	2	4
5	4	1	0	0	1	6
5	0	1	0	4	5	2

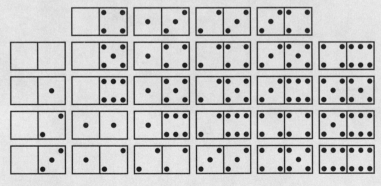

Answer on page 500

348 · LOGIMAZE

The grid is a symbol maze through which you must find a route by moving from one symbol to another according to the progression of the code sequence indicated in figure A. You can start anywhere on the edge of the grid, but you must start on a Santa, proceed to the opposite side of the grid (repeating the sequence as often as necessary), and end on a stocking. You can move up, down, left, or right, but not diagonally.

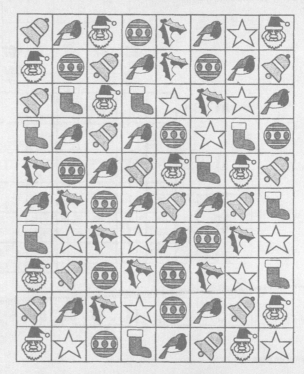

Answer on page 500

349 · EASY AS ABC

Each row and column originally contained one A, one B, one C, one D, and two blank squares. Each letter and number refers to the first or second of the four letters encountered when traveling in the direction of the arrow. Can you complete the original grid?

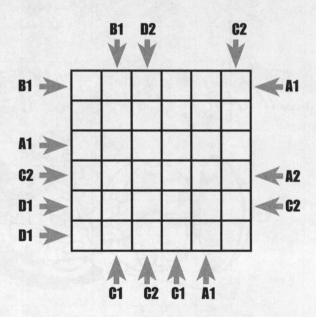

Answer on page 500

350 · PLUMB BLUFF!

Which of the numbered boilers belongs in the plumbing system shown?

Answer on page 500

351 · UPSTAIRS, DOWNSTAIRS

A group of eight people are playing Hide and Seek, and each has hidden in a separate room. Your job is to find them. You are looking at the house from the side, and the front and back are as shown. Adjacent rooms share a wall on the same floor. To help you on your way, one person has already been found.

1 Fred is not adjacent to Enid.
2 Hank is directly above Bess.
3 Alan is not directly above Gina.
4 Dave is not adjacent to Enid.
5 Fred is in a back room.
6 Enid is directly below Cary.
7 Dave is on the same side as Gina.

Answer on page 500

352 · NUMBER KROSS

See how quickly you can fit all these numbers into the grid. We've filled one figure in to start you off.

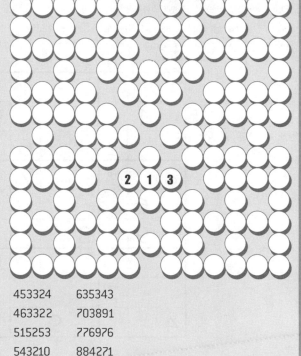

3 figures
213
412
547
623
721
736
837
941

4 figures
3552
4174
5342
6219

7280
7475
8749
9293

5 figures
10679
19658
20184
29017
33401
35709
40233
43581
49832

57689
69177
71705
78905
81507
87174
91370

6 figures
100200
121314
212223
243444
312111
344071

453324
463322
515253
543210
624896

635343
703891
776976
884271
921404

Answer on page 500

Place a number from 1 to 9 in each empty square so that each row, each column, and each 3 x 3 block contain all the numbers from 1 to 9.

				5				3
	1					9		
		2			6			
8					7		5	
	6						1	
	9		3					4
			1			8		
		7					2	
4				9				

Answer on page 501

354 · BACK TO SCHOOL

Four school friends are off to different universities to take different courses. Can you complete the enrollment form with each girl's full name, subject, and destination?

1 Barbara, who is not Moore, is studying physics but not at Princeton.
2 Diana is not Jones, who is neither the student going to Harvard nor the one studying chemistry.
3 The student majoring in math at Yale is not Moore.
4 Clare Taylor is at MIT but is not the student studying biology, who is not Brown, nor is either of these Anna.

FIRST NAME	SURNAME	SUBJECT	UNIVERSITY

Answer on page 501

355 · LOGI-5

Each line, across and down, is to have each of the five colors appearing once each. Each color must also appear just once in each shape, shown by thick lines. Can you color in this crazy quilt or mark each square with its correct letter B, G, R, V, or Y?

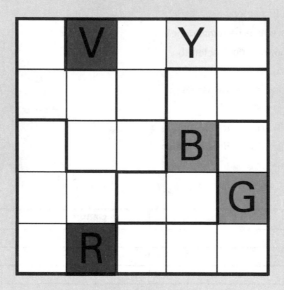

Answer on page 501

356 · MISMATCHES

The numbers 1–10 are to be entered in the top row of boxes so that none is in its correct numerical position, counting from left to right, and no two consecutive numbers are adjacent to each other. The letters A–J are to be entered in the bottom row, so that none is in its correct alphabetical position, left to right, none is below its correct number (A=1, B=2, etc.), and no two consecutive letters, and no vowels, are adjacent. The number 1 is not with letter I; the letter below 9 is one place earlier in the alphabet than that below 8. The second number from the left is three higher than the number of the letter below it; the eighth number from the left is two lower than the number of its letter. The left-hand number is two lower than the right-hand number; the left-hand letter is three later in the alphabet than the right-hand letter. The fourth and seventh from the left are vowels—the numbers above them total 10. The 10 is somewhere left of A; 8 is somewhere left of D; 2 is somewhere right of E, and 4 is somewhere right of C. The third letter from the left is three earlier in the alphabet than the sixth. There is one box between 4 (left) and D, and one between A (left) and 7. Can you match numbers and letters?

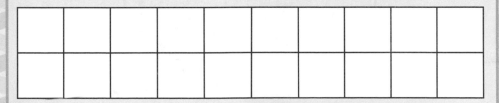

Answer on page 501

357 · DOTTY DILEMMA

Connect adjacent dots with vertical or horizontal lines so that a single loop is formed with no crossings or branches. Each number indicates how many lines surround it, while empty cells may be surrounded by any number of lines.

```
.  .0 .  .  .  .  .3 .  .  .  .3 .
.1.2 .  .3 .3 .  .3 .  .2.0 .
.  .  .  .3 .  .0 .3 .  .  .  .
.  .  .  .3 .1 .  .1 .  .  .  .
.  .3.1.3 .  .  .3 .  .1.0.3 .
.  .  .  .  .1 .  .  .  .  .  .
.0 .  .  .2 .  .1 .2 .  .  .  .
.2 .  .3.2 .3 .  .0.2 .  .0 .
.  .2 .  .0 .  .  .3 .  .1 .
.  .1 .  .1 .3.3 .2 .  .3 .
.  .  .2 .  .  .  .  .  .2 .  .
.0 .  .3 .1 .  .2 .1 .  .3 .
.1 .  .2 .1 .  .2 .1 .  .2 .
.  .  .3 .  .  .  .  .2 .  .
.  .3 .  .1 .3.3 .2 .  .3 .
.  .2 .  .3 .  .  .3 .  .1 .
.3 .  .1.2 .  .1 .0.3 .  .0 .
.1 .  .  .3 .3 .  .2 .  .  .1 .
.  .  .  .  .  .3 .  .  .  .  .
.  .2.3.2 .  .1 .  .  .2.1.3 .
.  .  .  .3 .  .2 .2 .  .  .  .
.  .  .  .0 .3 .  .1 .  .  .  .
.2.0 .  .3 .  .1 .3 .  .3.3 .
.  .3 .  .  .  .1 .  .  .0 .  .
```

Answer on page 501

358 · SUDOKU

Place a number from 1 to 9 in each empty square so that each row, each column, and each 3 x 3 block contain all the numbers from 1 to 9.

				2	3	4	9	
1				6	8			
2								
5	8							
9	4			7			6	3
							2	5
								1
			9	4				7
	6	3	2	5				

Answer on page 501

359 · IT FIGURES

Place a number from 1 to 9 in each empty cell so that the sum of each vertical or horizontal block equals the number at the top or on the left of that block. Numbers may only be used once in each block.

Answer on page 501

Not for the first time, the Engagements column of the South Fork Gazette has upset the parents of several brides-to-be. After the computer threw a fit, attempts by Herbert, the new copy boy, just added to the confusion. The result was that, when the printed version hit the newsstands, no name in each announcement actually belonged with any of the other three. Can you name the now not-so-happy couples?

ENGAGEMENTS

The engagement is announced between:

Ann Chovies & Ed Lynes.
Ann Noble & Frank Copes.
Bella Daball & Frank Stamps.
Cher Chovies & Horace Stamps.
Cher Noble & Gary Baldy.
Bella Brakes & Ed Baldy.
Dawn Brakes & Horace Copes.
Cher Brakes & Frank Lynes.

Answer on page 501

361 · NINE-CARD TRICK

Cards numbered from 2 to 10, the latter of which is not in the right-hand column, are set out as shown in the diagram with one card face up.

The numbers on any three cards in a line, vertically, horizontally, or diagonally, add up to the same total. No card shares an edge with one of its own color or a corner with one of its own suit; there are more diamonds than hearts.

Can you correctly identify the other eight cards?

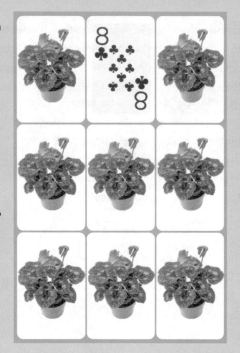

Answer on page 502

362 · TENTACKLE

Eight children are camping, two to each tent, and some have given us a couple of clues as to how to find them. The trouble is their senses of direction are as bad as their cooking, and in each case only one direction is true while the other is an exact opposite, so that east should read west, etc. Directions are not necessarily exact, so north could be north, northeast, or northwest. To help you, one child is already tucked into a sleeping bag.

Alvin says: "I'm east of Harvey and south of Dexter."

Dexter says: "I'm west of Frank and north of Elmer."

Frank says: "I'm west of Conrad and north of Brad."

Gary says: "I'm west of Elmer and south of Harvey."

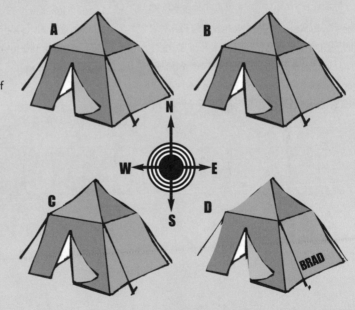

Answer on page 502

363 · CARDS ON THE TABLE

The 13 cards of a suit plus 2 jokers are shuffled and dealt in a line. No two consecutive cards are adjacent, no joker or face card is at either end, and no two face cards are adjacent.

Ace is two places left of queen, 2 is two places left of 8, one joker two left of 3, the other joker somewhere left of both and between 6 (left) and 10. The 7 is two left of 4, jack two right of king, 5 somewhere right of 9, which is somewhere right of 7, which is somewhere right of 10. Ace is left of 7.

The seventh and tenth cards from the left are even (ace = 1, king = 13, queen = 12, jack = 11, and a joker is neither odd nor even). The queen is left of the king. The third and tenth cards from the left total 12, as do the eighth and fifteenth. Can you locate each card?

Answer on page 502

Each row and column originally contained one A, one B, one C, one D, and two blank squares. Each letter and number refers to the first or second of the four letters encountered when traveling in the direction of the arrow. Can you complete the original grid?

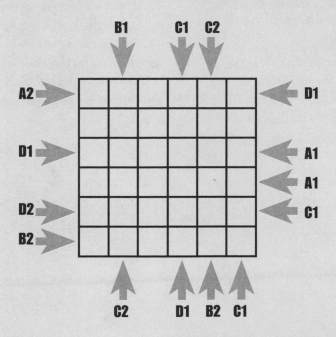

Connect adjacent dots with vertical or horizontal lines so that a single loop is formed with no crossings or branches. Each number indicates how many lines surround it, while empty cells may be surrounded by any number of lines.

```
  . .   . 3 . 2 . 3 .   . . 1 . 2 . 3 .   . . 1 . 2 .
  . 2 . . . . . . . . . 0 . . . . . 1 . 1 . . . . .
  . 0 . . . . . . . 2 . . . . . . . . . . . 3 . . .
  . . 1 . . . 3 . 0 . . . . . . 2 . . . 3 . . . . .
  . . 1 . . . . . 1 . 0 . . 0 . . . . 2 . . . . . .
  . . 3 . . . 0 . 1 . . . . . 3 . . . . . . . . . .
  . . . 1 . . . . . 1 . . . 1 . . . 1 . 1 . 3 . . .
  . . . 0 . . . . 2 . . . 3 . . . . . . . . . . . .
  . 0 . . 3 . 3 . 3 . . . . . 2 . . . . 2 . . . . .
  . 1 . . 2 . . . . . 2 . 2 . . . . 2 . . 0 . . . .
  . 2 . . . 3 . . . . . . . 3 . . 1 . 3 . . . . . .
  . . . . . . 3 . . . 3 . 2 . . 2 . . . . . . . . .
  . . . . 2 . 1 . 3 . . . . . 1 . . . . . . . . . .
  . 3 . 1 . 3 . . . . . . 2 . . . . 1 . . . . . . .
  . 1 . . 2 . . . 1 . 3 . . . . . 3 . . 1 . . . . .
  . 1 . . . 2 . . . . . 1 . 0 . . 1 . 0 . . . . . .
  . . . . . 2 . . . 1 . . . . 2 . . . . . . . . . .
  1 . 3 . 2 . . 2 . . . 2 . . . 3 . . . 2 . . . . .
  . . . . . . 1 . . . 3 . 2 . . . . 2 . . . . . . .
  . . 3 . . 0 . 1 . 2 . . . . . 1 . . . . . . . . .
  . . 3 . . 3 . . . . . 0 . 2 . . . 2 . . . . . . .
  . . 3 . . . . . . 2 . . . . . . . . . . . 2 . . .
  . . 1 . 1 . . . . . 1 . . . . . . . . . . . 0 . .
  1 . 0 . . . 1 . 3 . 2 . . . 0 . 2 . 3 . . . . . .
```

Siren screaming, Frank Drabin pulled his squad car onto the side of the road, demolishing three trash cans and a pizza stand. He raced into the building, gun drawn, took the stairs three at a time, and gave them back two at a time. Finally he turned into a square hallway and crouched down behind an aspidistra.

"What have we got, Ed?"

A nearby rubber plant shook its leaves.

"We got a gunman or gunmen, Frank. We also have one informer who tipped us off."

"Where are they?"

"We're not sure—but somewhere in the five rooms leading off this landing."

"Well, just open 'em up one at a time and go in blasting."

"No can do, Frank. We've almost used our quota of bullets for the month, and we don't want to hit the informer."

"I see someone's been playing games and put notices on the doors."

"Yeah—before we got here. They're trying to confuse us. Each stuck a note on his door and maybe on an empty door as well. The notice on the informer's door is entirely true. The notice on any gunman's door is completely false."

"And the empty rooms?"

"The notice may be either entirely true or entirely false."

"So where's the gunman/men?"

Answer on page 502

367 · NETWORK

The letters A–P are to be arranged in the diagram, with one letter allocated to each point, so that no two consecutive letters are connected by any direct line, e.g., 1–15 or 7–10. F is to the left of and in the same horizontal line as I, which is above C. H and D are both somewhere left of B though not necessarily in the same line. P is somewhere higher than J, O somewhere higher than F, H somewhere higher than M, and L somewhere higher than E but not necessarily in the same line.

B is diagonally adjacent to G, and A is diagonally adjacent to C. N is the greatest distance possible from O.

L is immediately left of I, G immediately left of K, J immediately left of C, and D immediately left of O.

If the positions of the letters E and F add up to 17, can you place each letter in its correct position?

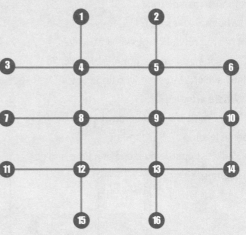

Answer on page 502

Can you see which of these five balloons contains two of each of the different symbols?

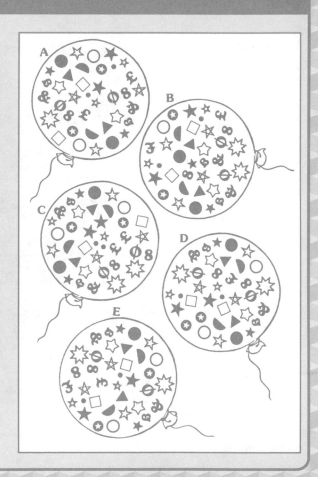

Answer on page 502

369 · CROSSNUMBER QUICKIE

1A = 122 x 5A
5A is a prime number
6A = 101 x 4A
1D = 101 x 5D
2D is a square number
3D = 4A x 2D
7, 8, and 9 do not appear
in the solution.
A is across, D is down.

Historical clue: Death of
Shakespeare. The year
can be read in the lightly
shaded squares.

Answer on page 502

370 · CODE MASTER

Just follow the rules of the classic game of Mastermind to crack the number code. The first number tells you how many of the digits are exactly correct—the right digit in the right place (✓✓). The second number tells you how many digits are the correct number but are not in the right place (✓). By comparing the information given by each line, can you work out which number goes in which place?

					✓✓	✓
4	5	2	8	9	1	1
1	2	6	4	3	2	2
7	0	1	4	9	1	1
8	5	2	0	1	1	1
2	0	4	5	8	0	3
5	8	2	3	6	1	2

Answer on page 502

371 · ACTION STATIONS

A city's subway system consists of four lines, one running north to south, one east to west, and two crossing these diagonally, all passing through the central interchange station at Nelson Square. From the clues given below, can you work out the color in which lines 1 to 4 are depicted on the map posted at every station and name the terminals on each line, entering your answers in the spaces provided? Note: The terms western and eastern apply to any of the three terminals in each of those directions.

1 One of the diagonal lines runs from The Unicorn to Gradwell, which is the next terminal clockwise from Wallgate.

2 The blue line forms a right angle at Nelson Square with the one whose western terminal is Molton Park.

3 The red line bears a number two higher than the one whose eastern terminal is Riverhead.

4 Potterfield is indicated on the map by a letter two farther down the alphabet than Lampwick.

5 Castlebridge is not on the green line.

6 The two terminals on the blue line do not have names containing the same number of letters.

Starting tip: Begin by figuring out which station is Riverhead.

Answer on page 502

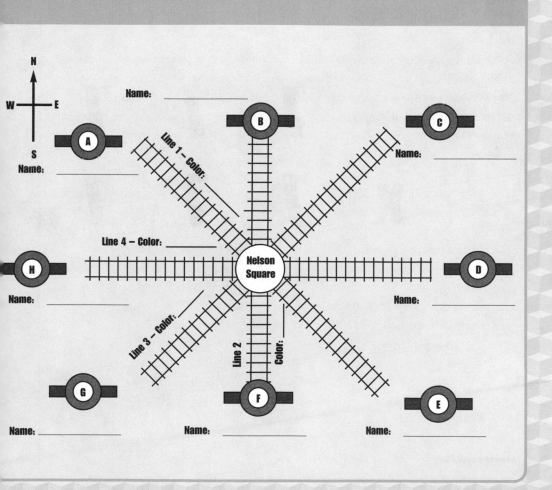

N

W — E

S

Name: _____

Name: _____

Name: _____

Line 1 – Color: _____

Line 4 – Color: _____

Nelson Square

Line 3 – Color: _____

Line 2

Color: _____

A

B

C

H

D

G

F

E

Name: _____

Name: _____

Name: _____

Name: _____

Name: _____

372 · SEVEN ALL

7 x 7 is 49.

So, without using a calculator, just how quickly can you find the answer to:

$$7 \quad 7 \quad 7$$
$$\times \quad 7 \quad 7 \quad 7$$

Answer on page 503

373 · SUDOKU

Place a number from 1 to 9 in each empty square so that each row, each column, and each 3 x 3 block contain all the numbers from 1 to 9.

3						5		
		9	6	8				
	1			4				7
	6		2					
	7	5				1	3	
					9		4	
2				3			8	
				1	7	9		
		4						6

Answer on page 503

Which one of the numbered prints was made from the stamp?

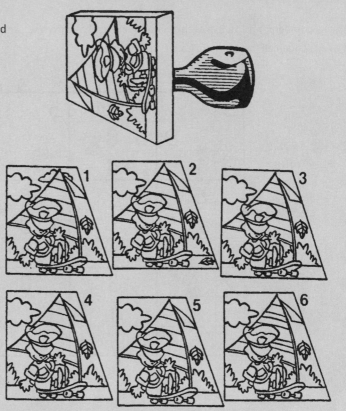

Answer on page 503

375 · NUMBER KROSS

See how quickly you can fit all these numbers into the grid. We've filled one figure in to start you off.

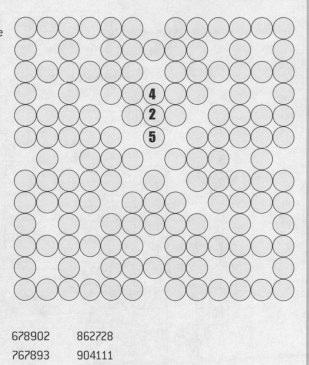

3 figures	6122	73842
142	7901	74256
216	8234	83445
425		88640
511	**5 figures**	96780
635	16539	
732	17822	**6 figures**
848	27383	120816
920	29743	134565
	34551	206317
4 figures	37894	241327
1968	42345	367687
2075	43049	423458	678902	862728
3545	57182	454288	767893	904111
4656	66278	519619	775406	941157
5483	66978	637452	822538	

Answer on page 503

Which of the four plugs is connected to the chainsaw?

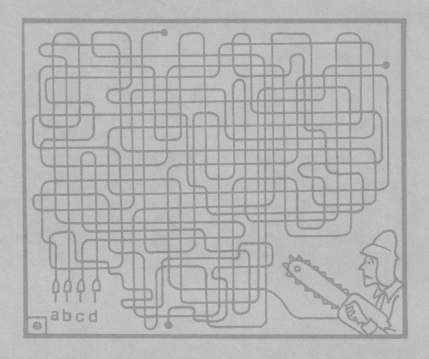

abcd

Answer on page 503

377 · SQUARED AWAY

In how many different ways can these three pieces be arranged to form unique 3 x 3 squares? The pieces are numbered on the front and the back, so they can be turned over. Rotations and reflections of the final numbered square are not counted as different.

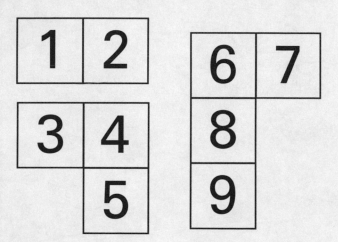

Answer on page 503

Follow the dots from 1 to 33 to reveal the hidden picture.

Answer on page 503

379 · MASTERMIND BANDITS

The one-armed bandits in the puzzle-mad land of Enigmatica are different from those we might be familiar with in amusement arcades and on seaside piers. To play this version of the game, gamblers pull the handle and the four rollers spin and stop to reveal four fruits. The window next to the rollers then lights up to reveal how well that spin matches up with the jackpot line hidden by a shield at the bottom of the fruit machine. An X in the results window indicates that one roller is exactly correct, that is, a right fruit on the right roller. An O indicates that one fruit is correct in that it appears in the winning combination, but is on the wrong roller. Enigmaticans are given four pulls of the handle and then have to deduce the winning jackpot combination. Below is a machine at that final stage of the game after the four pulls of the handle. Can you emulate the good people of Enigmatica and work out the details of the winning line hidden beneath the jackpot shield?

Symbols:

Cherry		Grapefruit	
Orange		Banana	
Lemon		Pear	

Answer on page 504

380 · NUMBER KROSS

See how quickly you can fit all these numbers into the grid. We've filled one figure in to start you off.

3 figures
110
228
342
534
618
720
840
935

4 figures
1948
2587
3118

4419
6720
7732
8313
9821

5 figures
16334
16422
22212
25719
32023
35081
49887

50450
54578
63958
70598
76756
82759
85177
92056
96145

6 figures
156414
246647
272674

309220
402631
471017
520293
588289
630580
640658
731290
772042
834015
897613
900510
913097

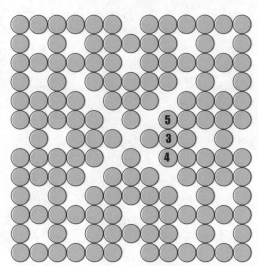

Answer on page 504

381 · TWINNED-UP

This boy would like to buy a spinning top identical to the one he's holding. Which one will he choose?

Answer on page 504

382 · IT FIGURES

Place a number from 1 to 9 in each empty cell so that the sum of each vertical or horizontal block equals the number at the top or on the left of that block. Numbers may only be used once in each block.

Answer on page 504

383 · CODE MASTER

Just follow the rules of the classic game off Mastermind to crack the color code. The first number tells you how many of the pegs are exactly correct—the right color in the right place (✓✓). The second number tells you how many pegs are the correct color but are not in the right place (✓). Colors may be repeated in the answer. By comparing the information given by each line, can you figure out which color goes in which place?

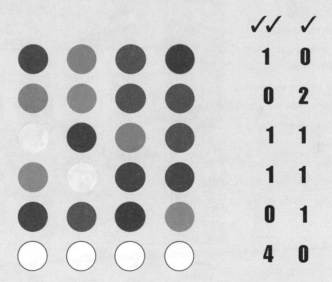

✓✓	✓
1	0
0	2
1	1
1	1
0	1
4	0

Answer on page 504

Mr. Prendergast, who teaches math at Netherlipp High, always has four colored pens in his top pocket. A pupil, whose mind kept drifting away from considering the implications of Pythagoras, noticed that each day this week up to Thursday no pen stayed in the same position. His observations are embodied in the clues that should enable you to work out the position of each pen on each day.

Starting tip: Figure out the color of pen D on Thursday.

1 On Monday the blue was just to the left of the red, but on Thursday the red was just to the left of the blue.

2 The green was in the same place on Monday as the red on Wednesday and in the same place on Tuesday as the black on Wednesday.

3 The green was one place farther left on Wednesday than on Tuesday and one place farther left on Thursday than on Monday.

4 On Tuesday the red was third from the left.

Colors: black; blue; green; red

Answer on page 504

Monday: _____ _____ _____ _____
Tuesday: _____ _____ _____ _____
Wednesday: _____ _____ _____ _____
Thursday: _____ _____ _____ _____

Place a number from 1 to 9 in each empty square so that each row, each column, and each 3 x 3 block contain all the numbers from 1 to 9.

	8		1		7		4	
6		7				3		5
	2		8	5	6		1	
2		8		6		5		3
		6	5		3	8		
1		3		9		4		6
	6		7	1	2		3	
7		2				1		4
	3		6		9		5	

Answer on page 504

386 · NUMBER KROSS

See how quickly you can fit all these numbers into the grid. We've filled one figure in to start you off.

3 figures	6125	71827
147	7409	80724
257	8422	82133
348		93009
439	**5 figures**	94345
527	14214	
731	17012	**6 figures**
823	21234	101723
950	27893	107028
	30514	201034
4 figures	39130	279469
1735	43297	304050
2007	50781	317029	575859	809010
3976	54829	417924	610778	817345
4041	69483	450353	721707	971872
5923	71335	557894	771644

Answer on page 504

387 · ON SITE

Four couples are spending their vacations in their trailers at a popular seaside site. From the clues given below, can you name the couple in each of the trailers numbered 1 to 4 and say where each pair is from?

1 Paul's trailer is somewhere to the right of the one being used by Alicia, from Cardiff, and her partner.

2 Esme and her partner are separated from Desmond and his partner only by the couple from Boston.

3 Sebastian and Zoe have a lower-numbered trailer than the couple from L. A.

4 Miranda is staying in trailer 3 but not with Luther.

Males: Desmond; Luther; Paul; Sebastian
Females: Alicia; Esme; Miranda; Zoe
Cities: Boston; Cardiff; El Paso; L. A

Starting tip: Start by naming the woman in trailer 4.

	1	**2**	**3**	**4**
Male:				
Female:				
City:				

Answer on page 505

388 · MODERN ART

Having bought one of the abstract paintings, the art lover can't remember which one it is or which way up it should go. Can you help him?

Answer on page 505

389 · SQUARE NUMBERS

The numbers 1–25 are entered randomly in a 5 x 5 square so that no two consecutive numbers are adjacent in any direction, or included in any row, column, or long diagonal. The four corner numbers are all two-digit prime numbers increasing each time clockwise starting from one of the corners. E4 is twice that in C1 but only half B3. D5 is twice C5 but only half A2. A4 is twice D3 but only half B2. B1 and D4 are both prime, the latter being five higher than D5; C1 and C4 total 25; E2 plus E3 equals C1, the former being less than the latter. B1 plus B5 equals D2. Can you locate each number?

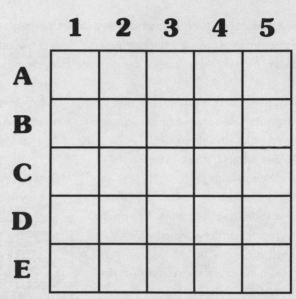

Answer on page 505

390 · TROPHIES

Karen Mills is 17 and a talented athlete. On the mantelpiece of her parents' home are displayed the three trophies she's won this year. From the clues below, can you fill in on the diagram the details of each trophy: her placing, the event, the competition, and the month?

1 The 1,500 meters trophy was won the month after she received the third-place award, which isn't Trophy A.

2 Her discus trophy stands to the left of the one she won in July.

3 Trophy B was won at the County Amateur Athletics Association meeting, for a placing one higher than she achieved in the high jump.

4 It was in the annual town competition that she took a first place.

Placings: First; second; third
Events: Discus; 1,500 meters; high jump
Meetings: County; interscholastic; town
Months: May; June; July

Starting tip: Work out for which place Trophy B was awarded.

Placing:	_____	_____	_____
Event:	_____	_____	_____
Meeting:	_____	_____	_____
Month:	_____	_____	_____

Answer on page 505

391 · FIGURE WORK

Each figure contains a detail that is not present in the other three. Can you spot all four details?

Answer on page 505

392 · BOTTLED UP

Can you help the shop assistant find four identical bottles?

Answer on page 505

393 · NUMBER KROSS

See how quickly you can fit all these numbers into the grid. We've filled one figure in to start you off.

3 figures	6786	70310
103	7998	79287
208	8112	84332
321		88017
435	**5 figures**	90021
530	10549	
645	19353	**6 figures**
847	20291	160056
923	32433	176802
	37064	246795
4 figures	41183	263857
1707	47890	302960
2067	55213	381526
3214	56658	410430
4134	64755	423557
5670	64980	504879

520128	842710
614809	~~951671~~
690560	982912
746740	

Answer on page 506

In the five puzzles A, B, C, D, and E, can you replace each ? with the right number that fits the pattern?

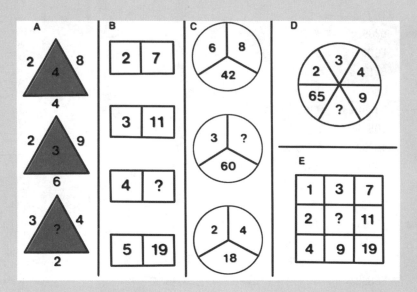

Answer on page 506

Can you spot the eight differences between these two pictures?

Answer on page 506

396 · FIGURE IT OUT

Each figure from 1–9 appears four times in the square, no two similar digits being diagonally adjacent. Where the same digit appears more than once in any row or column, this is stated. Can you complete the square?

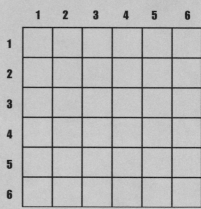

Row

1 Two 4s and two 9s alternating; total 34
2 One even, two odd, two even, one odd digit, from left to right; lowest is 2; total 37
3 Two 1s separated by an 8; two 5s but no 4s
4 Two adjacent 6s with an odd digit and two 8s
5 Two 3s separated by a 6; highest is a 7; total 22
6 Two adjacent 7s; total 24

Column

1 Two 8s separated by an odd digit; total 29
2 Two adjacent 9s; the other digits also total 18
3 Two adjacent 2s; total 27

4 Two 9s separated by two digits; total 31
5 Two 6s separated by two digits, all bracketed by two odd digits
6 Total 22

Answer on page 506

416

397 · BARGAIN BRIC-A-BRAC

The diagram shows four neighboring booths at a flea market each selling an assortment of bric-a-brac. From the clues given below, can you identify the person in charge of each of the booths lettered A to D and say which customer was buying which item from which booth at the particular moment in question?

1 Lesley bought something from Ken, whose booth was separated by just one from the one where the fire irons were offered for sale.
2 The vase was sold at booth B.
3 Norman, who did not buy the paperback books, was the customer at booth C, which was not run by Ted.

4 Elsie's booth is lettered A in the diagram; her customer was not Ray.

Booth-holders: Elsie; Ken; Mary; Ted
Customers: Lesley; Norman; Penny; Ray
Items bought: books; fire irons; radio; vase

Starting tip: Begin by figuring out which booth sold the fire irons.

Seller:

Customer:
Purchase:

Answer on page 506

The diagram shows four straight lines whose extremities are numbered I to VIII. Each of the arms has two circles, the inner of which should contain a different one of the numerals 1 to 8 and the outer of which should contain a different one of the letters A to H. From the clues given can you fill in all the numbers and letters correctly?

1 The word HAG can be read counterclockwise on the outer ring; all of its letters are accompanied by even digits on the inner ring.

2 The 8 and the 7 are on the same straight line that bears even Roman numerals at each end, the 8 end having a higher numeral than the 7 end.

3 The letter in position III is the B.

4 The numeral on arm V and the one on the arm directly opposite the one bearing the A total the number on arm IV.

5 The 5 is on the arm numbered I in the diagram.

6 The letter in position VI is a vowel.

7 The 1, which is not on the same straight line as the 6, is on an arm numbered two higher than the one occupied by the C.

8 The letter on arm IV has an earlier position in the alphabet than the one on arm II but does not come immediately before it.

Answer on page 506

Letters: A; B; C; D; E; F; G; H
Numerals: 1; 2; 3; 4; 5; 6; 7; 8

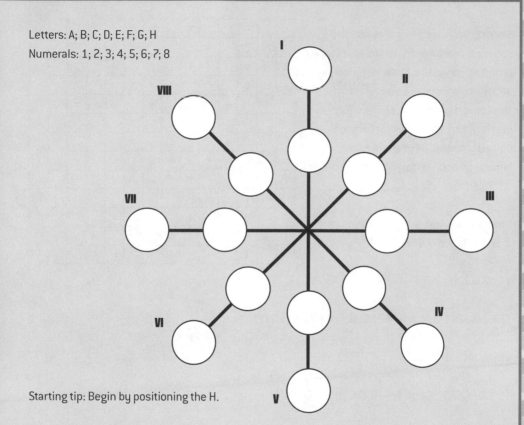

Starting tip: Begin by positioning the H.

399 · SKELETON SUMS

Insert the following numbers into the spaces on each horizontal line so as to form thirteen valid equations, treating each calculation sequentially rather than according to the "multiplication first" system. When the numbers are correctly placed, the digits in each vertical column will total 45.

				×		=					
			+				=				
2		+		+				=			
		×					=				
	+		+		+		−		÷		=
					=			+			
		×				÷		=			
	−		−			+		÷			=
	×						=				
				−				=			
		+				+				=	
		−					−			=	
		×			−				=		

2 2 3 4 5 5 6 7 7 7 8 9 9 9

14 18 18 19 24 25 30 36 39 42 45 90 96

168 200 249 397 439 439 566 574 622 675 700

1089 1425 1711 2323 2587 2889 9991

10009 11545 36218 42546 69270 85092

Answer on page 507

420

400 · PAIRED UP

Can you spot which three rabbits are gnawing identical carrots?

Answer on page 507

401 · FIGURE IT OUT

The digits 1–9 each appear four times in the grid, and no two squares that are adjacent horizontally or vertically contain the same digit. Each instance of a digit occurring more than once in a row or column is mentioned in the clues.

	1	2	3	4	5	6
1						
2						
3						
4						
5						
6						

ACROSS
1 A pair of 6s, but no 9; the sum is 36
2 A pair of 1s; 7 is the second highest number; the sum is 23
3 A pair of 5s, but no 7s; the sum is 34
4 A pair of 2s, but no 7s; the sum is 28
5 A pair of 8s; the sum is 36
6 A pair of 1s; 9 is the highest number

DOWN
1 A pair of 6s; the sum is 41
2 A pair of 5s enclosing a 1
3 A pair of 7s; the sum is 35
4 A pair of 6s and a pair of 4s; the sum is 25
5 A pair of 9s; the sum is 39
6 A pair of 1s; the sum is 16

Answer on page 507

402 · LENGTH IS STRENGTH

Four bridge players, seated in the traditional positions north, south, east, and west (the two former being partners against the two latter), each picked up a hand with a different long suit and a different length in each case. From the clues given below, can you name the player in each seat, match him with his long suit, and say how many cards of that suit he held?

1 Ruff had more of his suit than his partner had in clubs, which was his long suit.

2 Trumpet had a suit longer than that of the player who held the long diamonds.

3 South's long suit had only five cards in it.

4 East's suit was hearts.

5 Pass was the player in the north seat.

6 It was Bidding's partner at the table who had the longest suit of all.

Names: Bidding; Pass; Ruff; Trumpet
Suits: Clubs; diamonds; hearts; spades
Length: 5; 6; 7; 8

Answer on page 507

Name: _____
Suit: _____
Length: _____

Name: _____
Suit: _____
Length: _____

N

W   E

S

Name: _____
Suit: _____
Length: _____

Name: _____
Suit: _____
Length: _____

403 · CAN YOU DIGIT?

ACROSS

1 Add 1 to the square of (6 across + 7 across +
   2 down + 11 down)
6 Subtract (4 down plus 1) from 7 across
7 Multiply 2 down's second digit by 19
8 Cube (11 down minus 1)
9 First two digits of 8 across
11 Add 3 to the square of 4 down's first digit
12 Square (11 across + 2 down)

DOWN

1 Square (7 across + 4 down + 10 down)
2 Reverse (7 across reversed minus 1)
3 Cube 11 down
4 Reverse (7 across plus 1)
5 Square (7 across + 11 across + 10 down +
   11 down)
10 Third and fourth digits of 3 down
11 Subtract 2 from 11 across

1	2	3	4	5
6			7	
8				
9	10		11	
12				

Answer on page 508

404 · IT FIGURES

Place a number from 1 to 9 in each empty cell so that the sum of each vertical or horizontal block equals the number at the top or on the left of that block. Numbers may only be used once in each block.

Answer on page 508

405 · NUMBER HEX

What number belongs in the hexagon marked "?"?

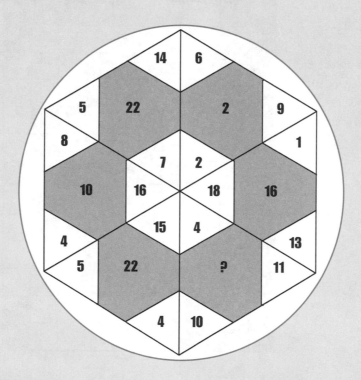

Answer on page 508

406 · SHADOWS

There's nothing a dragon likes better than a mug of cocoa to round off a meal of tasty McKnight burger! Can you tell which one of the numbered shadows has been cast by this dragon?

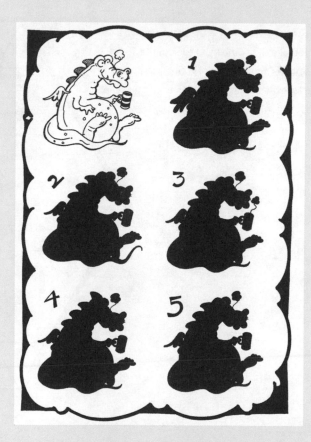

Answer on page 508

407 · SIX-PACK

By packing numbers in the empty spaces, can you make the numbers in each of the 16 hexagons add up to 25? No two numbers in each hexagon may be the same, and you can't use zero. We've started you off.

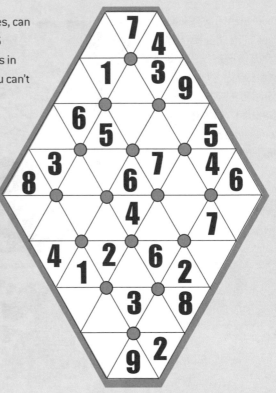

Answer on page 508

408 · LET'S FACE IT

Four children were each given a picture of a man's face and invited to adorn it in a different manner. From the clues given below, can you figure out the name and age of the child who was given each of pictures 1 to 4, and complete them by drawing in the missing detail in each picture?

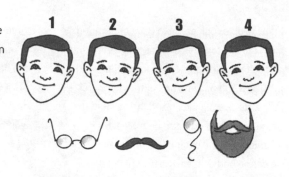

Name: _____ _____ _____ _____

Age: _____ _____ _____ _____

Feature: _____ _____ _____ _____

1 Picture 2, which is clean-shaven, was produced by the artist a year older than Mary.

2 The oldest child produced picture 1.

3 Silas gave his character a monocle; this picture is somewhere to the right of the one produced by the artist aged 8.

4 Alistair is 9; his picture is not immediately to the right of the one with a moustache.

Names: Alistair; Jennifer; Mary; Silas
Ages: 8; 9; 10; 11
Features: beard; monocle; moustache; spectacles

Starting tip: Begin by naming the child aged 11.

Answer on page 508

409 · GOLF LINK

Eight people took part in a golf competition. Each person took his or her turn by standing on the tee at the center of a large circle and putting a golf ball into one of the numbered holes. No two people putted the ball into the same hole, and each person took a different number of shots to sink the ball into the hole he or she had chosen, the number of shots ranging from one to eight. In no case did the number of shots taken by a person match the number of the hole into which he or she putted the ball. Each person won a different prize.

Gemma, who won the gym vouchers, putted the ball into a hole that was two counterclockwise of the hole at which the parasol was won. At the latter hole, two more shots were taken than at the former hole.

Seven shots were taken to win the sombrero at a hole that was two clockwise of the hole at which John won his prize. Four shots were taken at a hole that was diametrically opposite the hole at which Jane won her prize. The hole at which the swimsuit was won was diametrically opposite the hole at which Mary won her prize. At the latter hole, six more shots were taken than at the former hole.

The greatest number of shots were taken to win the beach ball, at a hole just counterclockwise of the hole at which Edward won his prize. The number of shots taken to win the deck chair was more than the number of shots taken at the hole just counterclockwise of the hole at which the deck chair was won. Carol's hole had a higher number than Mike's. Donald won his prize at a hole whose number was half the number of the hole at which the beach towel (which was

Answer on page 509

not Mike's prize) was won. One of the prizes won was a pair of sunglasses, and hole 8 was selected by a man.

Can you determine which person putted the ball into each hole, the prize each won, and the number of shots taken by each?

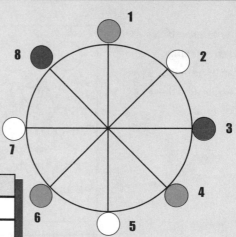

No.	Name	Shots	Prize
1			
2			
3			
4			
5			
6			
7			
8			

The numbered pictures each differ from picture A in three unique ways. Can you find these differences?

Answer on page 509

411 · TROMBONES

Which one of the numbered pictures has been developed from the negative of this trombone? Remember, in a negative, any area that is really white appears black and any area that is really black appears white!

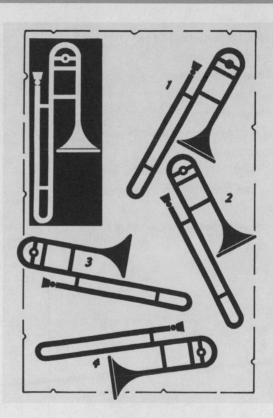

Answer on page 509

412 · CELL STRUCTURE

The object is to create white areas surrounded by black walls, so that:

- Each white area contains only one number.
- The number of cells in a white area is equal to the number in it.
- The white areas are separated from each other by a black wall.
- Cells containing numbers are not filled in.
- The black cells are linked into a continuous wall.
- Black cells do not form a square of 2 x 2 or larger.

9		3				5			
						6			
5									
3				4		3			
							1		4
3		1							
			4		5				9
									7
		7							
		3				2		1	

Answer on page 509

413 · BRIDGES

Each circle containing a number represents an island. The object is to connect each island with vertical or horizontal bridges so that:

- The number of bridges is the same as the number inside the island.
- There are no more than two bridges between two islands.
- Bridges do not cross islands or other bridges.
- There is a continuous path connecting all the islands.

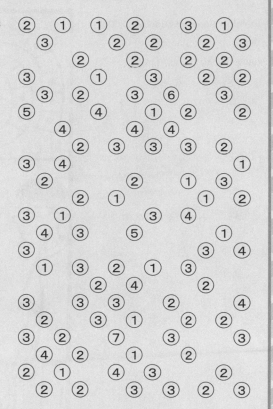

Answer on page 509

414 · STRIP TRICK

In what order must the five pieces below be arranged to form the complete strip shown above?

Answer on page 509

Can you complete this Magic Square so that every row, column, and diagonal adds up to the magic total of 185? To help you, we have placed figures above 5 in rows 1, 3, and 5 and figures below 5 in rows 2 and 4.

HINT: Every row has units 1, 3, 5, 7, and 9 once.

13	15	17	19	21
23	25	27	29	31
33	35	37	39	41
43	45	47	49	51
53	55	57	59	61

9		7 6		
	2 1	2	3	4 3
	9		7	
1 3	2	4 1	4	
		9		7

Answer on page 509

437

416 · DON'T PAY THE PIPER . . .

The diagram shows the Pied Piper leading away the children of Hamelin after the town refused to pay him for ridding it of rats. From the clues given below, can you name the first four children in the line, work out their ages, and say what work their father does in the town?

1 The cowherd's child is directly behind six-year-old Gretchen as they follow the Piper.

2 Hans is younger than Johann.

3 The boy who leads the line is not immediately followed by the butcher's child.

4 The child aged seven is number 3 in the line.

5 Maria, whose father is an apothecary, is younger than the child in position 2.

Names: Gretchen; Hans; Johann; Maria
Ages: 5; 6; 7; 8
Fathers: apothecary; butcher; cowherd; woodcutter

Starting tip: Start by placing Gretchen.

Answer on page 509

Pied Piper

1   2   3   4

Name: _____ _____ _____ _____

Age: _____ _____ _____ _____

Father's occupation: _____ _____ _____ _____

417 · HOUSE THAT AGAIN?

To the untutored eye, the houses on the Merryview estate look pretty much alike. Which is why Don, a trainee realtor's assistant, made plenty of notes on his few excursions.

1 Houses with double-glazing have central heating.
2 Houses with red roofs have front gardens.
3 Odd-numbered houses have green doors.
4 Houses with iron gates have fierce dogs.
5 Houses with green doors have red roofs.
6 Houses with few visitors have white paintwork.
7 Houses without chimneys have leaded windows.
8 Houses with fierce dogs have few visitors.
9 Houses with plastic gnomes have double-glazing.
10 Detached houses have iron gates.
11 Houses with central heating do not have chimneys.

12 Houses with front gardens have plastic gnomes.
13 Even-numbered houses are detached.

When asked by a prospective client what sort of house number 51 was, the only reply received was an "umm," an "agh," and a quick, nervous wipe round the inside of a hot collar. How much of a description can you give from this informative set of notes?

Answer on page 510

418 · TRYING TIMES

Substitute each letter with a digit (0–9) so that this long multiplication problem works out correctly.

```
     ABCD
x    FEFE
    GEDFF
   EHBGE
  GEDFF
 EHBGE
EAECJKJF
```

Answer on page 510

419 · STRESSED MANAGEMENT

Four stressed executives have each taken up a relaxation system with an Eastern flavor. If it is not too much of a strain, can you figure out the name of each tense soul, the company each suffers at, and the method being tried?

1 Dee rolls Chinese iron balls in his hand and is known around his office as "Captain Queeg," but he is not Nathan, who works for Just Loans.

2 Poppin can, appropriately, be found looking like a sick hedgehog with acupuncture needles sticking out in all directions. She is not the one with the first name of Ellis.

3 Elsa does not work for J. C. Nutts, and neither of these two is the one who listens to sitar music all day.

4 The employee at U. B. Loopy does yoga and can be found upside down in front of her monitor most afternoons. She is not Tewitt. Val Heegham does not work for Hi-Fi Nants.

Answer on page 510

ACUPUNCTURE

ELLIS	ELSA	**FIRST NAME**
NATHAN	VAL	
~~DEE~~	HEEGHAM	**SURNAME**
POPPIN	TEWITT	
HI-FI NANTS	J. C. NUTTS	**COMPANY**
JUST LOANS	U. B. LOOPY	

CHINESE BALLS

ELLIS	~~ELSA~~
~~NATHAN~~	VAL
(DEE)	~~HEEGHAM~~
~~POPPIN~~	~~TEWITT~~
HI-FI NANTS	J. C. NUTTS
~~JUST LOANS~~	U. B. LOOPY

FIRST NAME

SURNAME

COMPANY

SITAR MUSIC

ELLIS	ELSA
NATHAN	VAL
~~DEE~~	HEEGHAM
POPPIN	TEWITT
HI-FI NANTS	J. C. NUTTS
JUST LOANS	U. B. LOOPY

YOGA

ELLIS	ELSA
NATHAN	VAL
~~DEE~~	HEEGHAM
POPPIN	TEWITT
HI-FI NANTS	JC NUTTS
JUST LOANS	U B LOOPY

420 · HIDE 'N' SEEK

Four of the six objects shown at the top can be found hidden in the picture. Can you see which ones and where they are?

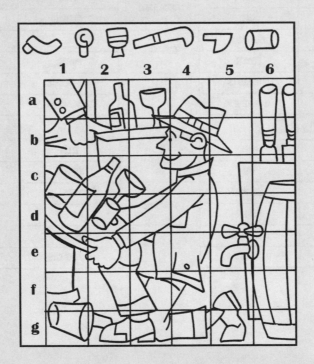

Answer on page 510

421 · PIECES OF EIGHT

Which pieces (four red and four yellow) can be used to make a square, where all four sides are of equal length? Any piece may be rotated but not flipped over.

Answer on page 510

422 · FITBITS

Can you identify the two fragments on the left that form part of the main picture?

Answer on page 510

423 · GARDENER'S WORLD

The large picture has been reproduced in twelve pieces. However, three of the pieces contain an extra detail, while four pieces have a detail missing. Can you spot all the extra and missing details?

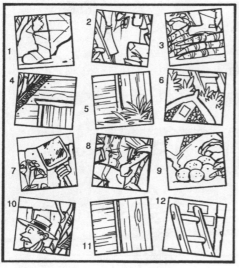

Answer on page 510

424 · LOGIQUATIONS

In the following problem, the digits 0–9 are represented by letters. Within each separate puzzle, the same letter always represents the same digit. Can you find the correct values each time so that all sums, both horizontal and vertical, are correct?

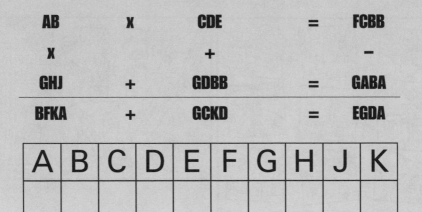

AB	x	CDE	=	FCBB
x		+		–
GHJ	+	GDBB	=	GABA
BFKA	+	GCKD	=	EGDA

A	B	C	D	E	F	G	H	J	K

Answer on page 510

425 · TAKE ONE

Remove just one letter and leave all 26 letters of the alphabet...

X	J	N	D	O	
K	G	W	P	L	
S	C	Q	V	H	
R	B	Z	F	T	
E	Y	M	U	I	A

Answer on page 510

426 · 2 X 6 X 6

All the clues lead to single or two-digit answers to be filled into the main grid. You must also complete the crossword grid, which will help you complete the main grid. Where there are two single-digit answers, they are not adjacent in that row or column. The clues are in no particular order for the indicated row or column. For example, a clue that reads "12 squared; cube of 27" might be entered as "3144" or "1443." The digit zero only appears in the main grid. Good luck!

COLUMN

A Square root of 2 down; first two digits of 1 across; 9 across, which is twice 11 down; one less than the other single digit.

B Two-digit cube number; two consecutive digits multiplied together; 11 down, which is a prime number; all digits are different.

C Half of 12 across; half of 14 across; two more than 5 across; all digits are different.

D Half of 12 across; first digit is three times the second; five times the first two digits of column A.

E (3 across reversed) minus one; 6 down; total of the other two answers.

F One-eighth of 7 across; two consecutive ascending digits; 8 down, which is three times a prime number.

Answer on page 510

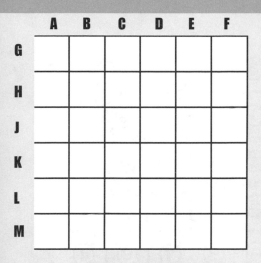

	A	B	C	D	E	F
G						
H						
J						
K						
L						
M						

ROW

G Three times 3 across; square root of 1 across; two single digits that are consecutive numbers.

H Half of 4 down; quarter of 1 down; two single digits that total 5.

J Cube number that is also one-quarter of 7 across; prime number that is two more than 11 down; cube number.

K 8 down plus 13 down, which is also two consecutive numbers multiplied together; three times a cube number; two consecutive numbers multiplied together.

L Half a square number; 6 down; square number.

M 15 across; four times 15 across; 5 across.

In this tangle of numbers, can you find a path that passes through all the numbers from 1 to 10? The numbers must run consecutively.

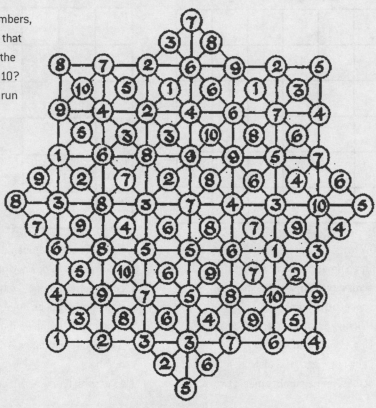

Answer on page 511

428 · TAKE NOTE

Something's gone wrong with Tony's saxophone. He wants to play a tune but can't produce a note. Can you find ten musical notes hidden somewhere in this picture so that Tony can start to play?

Answer on page 511

Can you help this
long-distance
runner find his
way to the flag?

Answer on page 511

430 · FACE VALUES

There are three faces hidden somewhere in this picture—can you find them?

Answer on page 511

431 · BEARED RIDDEN

Goldie Locks was not alone in wreaking havoc at the Bears' duplex in Dingley Dell. Four companions helped her cause devastation by sampling a different cereal each, breaking an item of furniture, and crashing in each of the family's beds. Goldie Locks was not the one who broke the table and slept in Papa Bear's bed; nor did Cilla Field, who ate Bran Bits. The one who broke the chair ate Chafflakes, but neither she nor Cilla slept in Fred Bear's bed, which was claimed by the one who smashed the sideboard. Cher Noble slept in Mama Bear's bed but is not the one who flattened the desk. Wyn Frith did not eat the Ricypops, but Dawn Ray did try the Weetybricks. Neither slept in Teddy Bear's bed. The one who ate Muesli Munch broke the bookcase but did not sleep in Carmen Bear's cot or Teddy Bear's bed.

Who slept in each bed, what did she eat for breakfast, and what did she break?

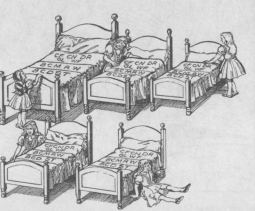

Answer on page 511

432 · DOUBLE DUCKS

Can you spot three pairs of identical ducks and say which two are totally different from the others?

Answer on page 511

1

2

3

4

Pictures 3 and 4 are the same. Picture 1 has an extra leaf, and picture 2 is missing a flower petal.

5

5	3	8	2	9	4	1	6	7
7	2	4	1	6	8	5	3	9
9	6	1	7	5	3	2	8	4
6	9	3	4	2	5	8	7	1
8	5	2	9	7	1	3	4	6
1	4	7	8	3	6	9	5	2
3	7	6	5	1	9	4	2	8
2	8	9	3	4	7	6	1	5
4	1	5	6	8	2	7	9	3

6

21	25	18	5	9
8	2	22	16	14
24	10	20	3	11
19	1	7	23	13
15	4	12	17	6

7

A, Maria, heraldic dragon, 1825
B, William V, shield, 1745
C, Karl II, crossed swords, 1865
D, Josef III, wreath of laurels, 1785

8

Oxford.

9

D and J.

10

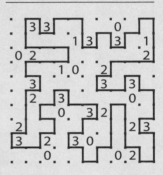

11

2	1	1	3
3	5	2	2
3	3	5	2
1	2	5	5
5	1	1	3

12

(grid puzzle with circles)

13

Hiatus could not have served for twelve years (clue 4). Nor could this have been Blunderbuss or Rictus (clue 1), so the man with that length of service must have been Voluminus. He could not have been from Syria (clue 2) or Germania (clue 4), and the man from Africa had 11 years' service, so Voluminus must have been from Gallia and must therefore have been stationed on the west wall (clue 3). Blunderbuss must therefore have been on the east wall (clue 1). The man on the north wall had served for nine years in the legion (clue 3). He could not have been Hiatus (clue 4) so must have been Rictus, and Hiatus must consequently have been on the south wall, and, from clue 4, the man from Germania must have been Blunderbuss on the east wall. By elimination, he must have served for ten years. Finally, Rictus, with his nine years' service, cannot have been

from Africa (clue 3), so he must have been from Syria, leaving Hiatus on the south wall as the African with eleven years of service.

In summary:
North, Rictus, Syria, nine years.
East, Blunderbuss, Germania, ten years.
South, Hiatus, Africa, eleven years.
West, Voluminus, Gallia, twelve years.

14

```
3 4 1 7 1 2   5 2 7 3 5   5 9
8   3   7 2       4   7       1
6 1 5 7 2 4 8   2 8 1 3 5     0
2   1   6   4       2   1 6 2 2
5 9 2 1   6 3 7 9 0 1     1   6
6   7   9 4 3       7 2 9 3 6 2
1     1   3     8 2 7 3     9   6
  3 1 4 5 1 7         0     8
  9   6   1     9 9 2 1 3 4 9
4 1 0 3 5 5     5     7       1
6     0     1 5 0     2 7 4 0 3
7 8 2   5       9   9   8       2
1     1 8 7 3 3 2     8 8 8     6
6 2 9   6     4 5 7 0     3 1 6 0
9 · 1 3 8 0 4         1   6
```

15

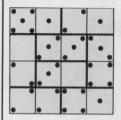

16

A is 35, B is 40, C is 25, and D is 20.

17

2	1	1	3	5	7	4	7
1	6	3	4	7	5	2	6
4	1	2	3	2	6	1	6
6	3	5	7	2	3	3	7
1	4	4	1	4	3	6	6
5	7	4	5	3	6	5	7
5	1	2	2	4	5	2	7

18

1 Crazy Carvellos
2 Fred the Fire-eater
3 Madame Poll's Parrots
4 Clever Clowns
5 Jim the Juggler
6 Señor Pedro's Poodles
7 Flying Fortresses
8 Agilles Acrobats

19

20

21

1	x	4	÷	2	=	2
+		x		x		
9	÷	3	+	7	=	10
÷		÷		−		
5	+	6	−	8	=	3
=		=		=		
2		2		6		

22

6	8	9	4	2	1	5	3	7
7	2	3	6	8	5	4	9	1
4	1	5	9	7	3	8	6	2
1	3	8	5	4	6	7	2	9
5	7	4	1	9	2	3	8	6
9	6	2	8	3	7	1	4	5
3	4	1	2	5	9	6	7	8
2	5	7	3	6	8	9	1	4
8	9	6	7	1	4	2	5	3

23

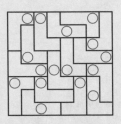

24

25

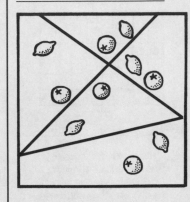

26

T / C	9 / H	K / C	J / S	8 / H
T / D	8 / D	Q / C	9 / S	Q / D
8 / C	8 / S	K / H	Q / S	A / H
T / H	K / S	J / H	J / C	J / D
Q / H	9 / C	T / S	9 / D	K / D

27

Weights 2, 3, and 4 will rise, and weights 1 and 5 will fall.

28

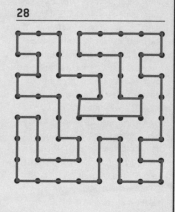

29

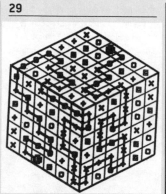

30

7	+	8	−	9	=	6
−		−		−		
4	+	5	−	6	=	3
÷		+		÷		
1	×	2	×	3	=	6
=		=		=		
3		5		1		

31

Monsters 3 and 5 are the same.

32

	3	6	8	7	0	1	5	2	5	9	8
9		8	8	9		7		2	6	0		4
6	6	3		1		0		4		7	9	1
7	2	0	5	0	3		1	5	4	5	6	4
6	4	8	2		8	8	4		9	9	7	7
2	1		6	3	5	7	6	5	5		7	9
4	1	6	7	0	7		9	1	9	3	5	0
5	4		4	6	2	9	3	9	0		3	3
8	2	1	8		9	5	5		1	2	7	6
8	9	6	9	5	2		3	3	8	0	8	5
1	8	6		3		2		0		4	0	2
3		5	4	8		2		9	1	7		5
	7	0	2	6	4	2	9	3	0	6	1

33

34

The actor sitting in seat D could not have been Lime (clue 1), Pitt (clue 2), Lynes (clue 4), or Green (clue 5), so must have been Flood. The one in B could not have been Lime (clue 1), Pitt (clue 2), or Green (clue 5), so must have been Lynes. Therefore the one who wanted to play Bottom must have been in C and the one who was cast as Quince in F (clue 4). So, from clue 5, Green's position was not F and must have been either C or E. From clue 3, the man cast as Oberon was not in F, so he must have been in D (clue 5), with Green therefore at C. Now, from clue 5, the actor cast as Bottom must have sat in B, while the place of the man chosen to be Demetrius must have been C (clue 3). By elimination, the one selected for

the role of Lysander must have been in E, and Pitt's place must accordingly have been F (clue 2). By elimination, Lime must have sat in seat E. The would-be Lysander was opposite Pitt (clue 2), so must have been Lynes, and the would-be Oberon must have been Lime (clue 3). From clue 4, Green in C must have hankered after the part of Bottom. Finally, Flood must have yearned to be Quince (clue 5) and, by elimination, Pitt must have wanted the role of Demetrius.

In summary:
(hoped-for parts are in parentheses)
B, Lynes, Bottom, (Lysander)
C, Green, Demetrius, (Bottom)
D, Flood, Oberon, (Quince)
E, Lime, Lysander, (Oberon)
F, Pitt, Quince (Demetrius)

35

Green, green, blue, red

36

Take the third price (40 cents) away from the first (80 cents), and you have the price of two chocolate bars. So one costs 20 cents. So, from the middle price, a cone and two scoops costs 75 cents; therefore, using the third price, a scoop costs 35 cents.

37

6	4	3	1	4	6	5
1	2	1	1	2	0	6
3	6	1	3	5	1	0
6	4	1	3	2	6	0
6	6	5	2	3	0	4
5	0	5	5	3	0	3
0	2	4	3	4	1	2
2	2	4	5	4	5	0

38

Since the only letter in row B is not a vowel (clue 1), from clue 5, the U in question cannot be in row A or row B and must be in row C, which places the J as the letter in row B. Similarly, from clues 1 and 3, the A must be in row C and the 7 in row B, so the S must be in row A. This cannot be in A4 (clue 3) or A2 (clue 6). If it was in A1, the A would be in C2 (clue 3), and the only positions for the U and the 1 would be C3 and C4. But C4 contains a letter (clue 6). Therefore the S must be in A3, and, from clue 3, B4 must contain a 7 and C4 the A. We know the J is the only letter in row B, so, from clue 4, the L must be in row A. We know it is not in A3, and the fact that the S is there also rules out the L for

A2 (clue 4). Since we know a 7 is in B4, the L cannot be in A4 (clue 4), so it must be in A1 and the 6 in B1 (clue 4). Clue 5 now places the J in B2, a U in C2, and the 1 in C3. We have now placed three of the five numbers, leaving a 7 and a 4, one of which must be in B3 (clue 1). This cannot be the 7 (clue 2), so it must be the 4. So, from clue 4, the number in A2 must be the second 7. Clue 2 now rules out the second U for C1, so it must be in A4, leaving the Y in C1.

In summary:

	1	2	3	4
A	L	7	S	U
B	6	J	4	7
C	Y	U	1	A

39

(grid puzzle)

40

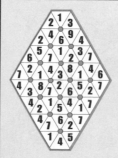

41

From the top: orange, red, green, blue, yellow, lavender.

42

1	+	2	+	4	=	7
+		X		+		
8	+	7	÷	5	=	3
÷		−		÷		
3	X	6	÷	9	=	2
=		=		=		
3		8		1		

43

Ramona, green, Phil Marvin.
Remus, red, George Krag.
Richard, silver, Claudia Score.
Romulus, blue, Selena Link.
Roxanne, yellow, Gregory Jenkins.

44

Wednesday. Each answer has the same vowels as the day with which it is associated.

45

8, 2, 7, 6, 3, 1, 0, 9, 4, 5

46

47

Bird 4.

48

22 hats.

49

50

51

52

53

The four shapes appear in squares 1b, 2f, 6b, and 7e.

54

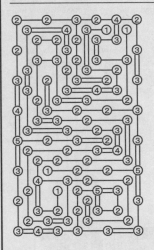

55

1 Cookies 2 Cakes 3 Tea/Coffee
4 Bread 5 Pet food 6 Soap Powder
7 Cleaning fluids 8 Kitchenware
9 Canned fruit 10 Candy 11 Canned
vegetables 12 Canned meat 13 Baking
14 Fruit juices 15 Frozen meat
16 Frozen vegetables

56

57

58

3	2	1	4	7	5	6
4	3	2	5	6	7	1
2	7	5	6	1	3	4
6	1	3	2	5	4	7
7	4	6	1	3	2	5
1	5	7	3	4	6	2
5	6	4	7	2	1	3

59

7	+	**1**	÷	**4**	=	**2**
+		+		x		
9	−	**6**	x	**3**	=	**9**
÷		−		−		
8	+	**2**	−	**5**	=	**5**
=		=		=		
2		**5**		**7**		

60

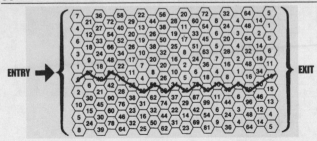

ENTRY → → EXIT

61

Ellen, 1R, 4B, 3Y, 2V.
Geoff, 1R, 5G, 4V.
Percy, 2R, 4B, 3Y, 1V.
Rosie, 4R, 3G, 2Y, 1V.

62

4	6	7	2	1	3	5
1	2	5	7	3	6	4
6	4	3	5	7	1	2
5	1	4	3	6	2	7
2	3	1	4	5	7	6
3	7	2	6	4	5	1
7	5	6	1	2	4	3

63

64

65

	19	35	13		19	11		37	8	13
7	2	1	4	15	7	8	20/11	8	5	7
21	8	4	9	24/15	9	3	2	4	1	5
15	9	6	10/10	7	3	20/20	8	9	2	1
10/9	7	2	1	12/9	8	1	3	6	11
27	4	9	8	2	1	3	9	6	1	2
13	5	8	22	5	8	9	21	7	5	9

66

(grid of mirror-reversed letters)

67

R. These are the letters of the alphabet, in order, that have just one enclosed area inside the letter.

68

From the top: D, B, A, E, C, F

69

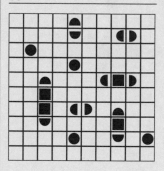

70

From	Al	Bob	Chris	Don	Ed
Al Harkness		2	4	1	3
Bob Jarrett	3		2	4	1
Chris Farley	1	3		2	4
Don Insley	4	1	3		2
Ed Gainor	2	4	1	3	

71

72

13 red, 3 yellow, 3 brown, 3 blue, 4 pink.

73

76

The cactus in the top right corner was left.
The purchases were:

Madge	Kim	Laura	Jackie	Cactus
Laura	Laura given	Kim	Madge	Jackie
Jackie	Laura	Jackie given	Kim	Madge
Kim	Jackie	Madge	Kim given	Laura
Madge given	Madge	Jackie	Laura	Kim

74

Pictures 3 and 5.

75

3	0	1	0	1	4	6
4	1	5	6	3	4	6
5	3	2	2	3	1	2
5	5	2	3	6	2	5
5	0	1	2	2	0	3
6	5	6	6	4	2	3
1	1	0	4	0	4	0
4	1	3	6	0	5	4

77

```
5 2 1 0 4    3    2    3 2 1 9 4
3   3    8    1 2 6 6 3    9    0
6 0    1    0    2    0 3    1
0   0    8 7 6    0    6    0    3
6 2 2 7 1    9 3 5    2 9 9 9 4
      7         2         7   2
6 5 0 1 8    5 0 2 4 2    1
7      2 0 3 9 3    1    5 8 8
1 1 0 3 7 5    9    4 6 3
  9         4 5 2 7 0 6    9
9 1 2 0 3    4 1 9    8 3 1 1 8
3      1    6 9 0    0      9
9 3 6 6 1    3    0    9 0 4 6 0
0      5 0 7    2 3 3       3
6 0 8 8 5    1 3 0    5 0 5 5 1
```

78

5	6	3	7	9	2	4	1	8
4	9	1	5	6	8	3	2	7
8	7	2	1	4	3	9	5	6
9	8	7	6	2	5	1	4	3
1	5	6	9	3	4	8	7	2
3	2	4	8	1	7	6	9	5
7	3	9	2	8	1	5	6	4
6	4	5	3	7	9	2	8	1
2	1	8	4	5	6	7	3	9

79

6	1	0	3	4	3	4	1
1	6	6	3	6	5	2	2
2	0	3	1	2	3	5	1
1	3	4	2	6	1	1	0
5	4	2	6	0	5	2	5
3	0	4	0	4	6	4	4
0	3	6	0	2	5	5	5

80

81

One of the green books is missing.

82

83

Girls 4 and 6.

84

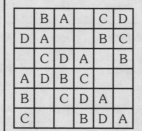

	B	A		C	D
D	A			B	C
	C	D	A		B
A	D	B	C		
B		C	D	A	
C			B	D	A

85

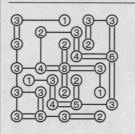

86

14 reds, 4 yellows, 3 greens, 2 blues, 5 pinks.

87

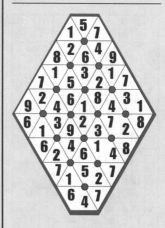

88

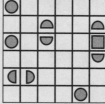

89

E and G.

90

```
2 9 3 0 6   4   9   7 2 4 3 1
6   0   7   2 9 3 1 7   8   4
8   1   1   6   7   2   8   7
1   1   5 4 1   7   1   8   1
7 3 5 3 8   8 2 0   3 9 7 9 2
    9       9       9   2
7 5 3 6 8   3 7 3 0 4   0
0     1 1 9 0 3   4   3 6 6
7 6 3 0 8 1     6     5 5 2
  2       4 9 3 9 1 8   1
5 2 7 8 9   4 1 3   7 2 4 2 2
0     3   6 7 3   6     1
4 0 0 1 3   1   0   4 9 9 8 0
6     7 4 5   1 7 2     1
8 6 2 6 1   2 9 6   1 5 7 0 4
```

91

92

Picture 4.

93

	Eagle	Birdie	Par	Bogey	Double Bogey	FINAL SCORE
PARNELL DARMA	4	1	6	5	2	72
NICK JACKLISS	3	5	7	2	1	65
BARRY CLAYER	1	8	2	3	4	73

94

95

Ten bunches have all three colors.

96

1–D, 2–B, 3–A, 4–C

97

Albert, 1R, 3B, 6V
Anne, 4B, 3G, 1Y, 2V
Barbara, 4R, 5G, 1Y
George, 3R, 1B, 6Y

98

2	4	3	3	0	3	3	1
4	1	1	6	1	6	4	3
5	2	4	5	4	4	1	5
4	2	0	1	5	3	5	2
3	6	2	0	4	6	0	1
3	2	1	0	0	5	5	2
6	6	2	6	5	0	6	0

99

2	7	3	5	8	4	9	1	6
6	8	5	1	3	9	2	7	4
4	1	9	7	6	2	3	8	5
3	5	4	9	7	6	1	2	8
9	6	8	2	5	1	4	3	7
1	2	7	8	4	3	6	5	9
8	3	2	4	9	7	5	6	1
7	9	6	3	1	5	8	4	2
5	4	1	6	2	8	7	9	3

101

F, J, C, I, A, H, B, G, E, L, D, K

102

Johnny is number 3 (clue 3). Number 1 cannot be Darren Poole (clue 2) or Shaun (clue 1), so he must be Garry. So, from clue 4, boy number 2 must have green boots. Those of boy number 4 cannot be red (clue 1) or brown (clue 2), so they must be black. So, from clue 4, Johnny, in position 3, must be Waters. Shaun's surname is not Brook (clue 1), so it must be Burne, leaving Garry's as Brook. So Shaun is not in position 2 (clue 3) and must be boy 4, wearing the black boots. By elimination, this leaves boy 2, in the green boots, as Darren Poole. So, from clue 2, the brown boots must belong to the boy in position 1, Garry, leaving Johnny Waters wearing the red boots.

In summary:
1, Garry Brook, brown.
2, Darren Poole, green.
3, Johnny Waters, red.
4, Shaun Burne, black.

103

5	8				2	5		
3	9	1		2	1	3	5	
2	5	4	1	3		2	1	5
1	7		4	1	3		3	1
		6	2		1	3	4	2
	7	9				1	2	
7	5	8	9		8	2		
9	6		8	9	7		5	3
8	9	7		8	9	5	7	6
	8	9	5	7		1	8	9
		6	3				9	7

104

Number 1.

105

Apart from the nine smaller squares, there is a tenth to be seen in 1/2/4/5, an eleventh in 2/3/5/6, a twelfth in 4/5/7/8, a thirteenth in 5/6/8/9, and one large square made up of all nine smaller squares.

106

Arthur, 2 begonias, 3 cyclamen, 1 gardenia, and 4 jasmines.
Barry, 1 African violet, 4 cyclamen, 3 gardenias, and 2 jasmines.
Connie, 6 African violets, 3 begonias, and 1 cyclamen.
Debbie, 1 African violet, 3 begonias, 4 gardenias, and 2 jasmines.

107

29.

108

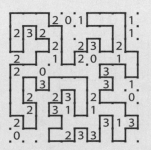

109

110

111

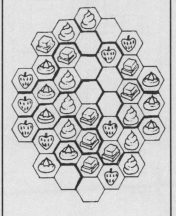

112

J	W	G	Z	U	P	E
B	R	N	P	X	H	U
D		Y	K	S	F	M
V	F	D	M	I	Y	S
L		A	R	E		W
G		K	I	O	T	C
Q	B	V	X	Z	J	O
N	T	Q	C	A	L	H

113

Billiard room, Lance O'Boyle;
Lounge, Wicklow, the maid;
Card room, Hon. Reginald Ackney;
Morning room, Reverend Rash;
Cloakroom, Lady Mole;
Study, Spott, the butler;
Library, Miss Felicity Bytes, the murderer.

114

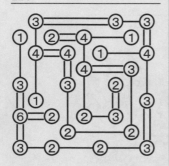

115

A, Kate and Naomi
B, Jenny and Lisa
C, Megan and Sally
D, Paula and Rita

116

C		B		A	D
D			C	B	A
	B	A	D		C
A	C		B	D	
	A	D		C	B
B	D	C	A		

117

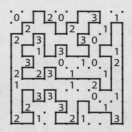

118

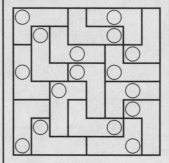

119

2 and 5.

120

121

5	5	7	5	6	5	7	5
3	3	3	1	1	2	1	2
3	4	6	2	6	7	3	1
6	1	5	7	1	1	7	7
2	7	7	4	4	2	6	1
5	4	4	2	3	2	4	6
3	6	4	1	2	1	3	6

122

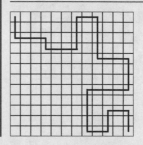

123

124

7	6	8	3	4	1	2	9	5
9	3	2	8	6	5	7	4	1
5	1	4	9	2	7	6	8	3
2	8	9	1	5	3	4	7	6
3	5	7	4	9	6	1	2	8
1	4	6	7	8	2	5	3	9
6	7	5	2	3	9	8	1	4
8	2	3	6	1	4	9	5	7
4	9	1	5	7	8	3	6	2

125

From the top: A, C, E, B, D, F

126

Piece 8.

127

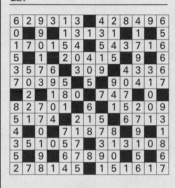

6	2	9	3	1	3	■	4	2	8	4	9	6
0	■	9	■	1	3	1	3	1	■	1	■	5
1	7	0	1	5	4	■	5	4	3	7	1	6
5	■	1	■	2	0	4	1	5	■	9	■	6
3	5	7	6	■	3	0	9	■	4	3	3	6
7	0	3	9	5	■	5	■	9	0	4	1	7
■	2	■	1	8	0	■	7	4	7	■	0	■
8	2	7	0	1	■	6	■	1	5	2	0	9
5	1	7	4	■	2	1	5	■	6	7	1	3
4	■	0	■	7	1	8	7	8	■	9	■	1
3	5	1	0	5	7	■	3	1	3	1	0	8
5	■	9	■	6	7	8	9	0	■	5	■	6
2	7	8	1	4	5	■	1	5	1	6	1	7

128

129

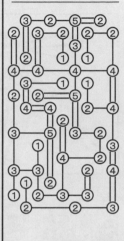

130

4	3	9	2	5
6	8	1	5	3
7	2	5	8	1
3	4	6	1	9
3	6	2	7	5

131

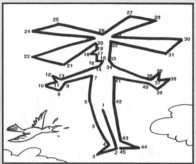

132

9	7		2	3		2	9		1	3
6	8	9	7	5		4	8	7	6	9
8	9	7		2	4	1	5	6	3	
	6	4	3	1	2		7	9		
	8	4			7	6	8	9		
	1	6	2		1	9		8	9	
3	4		1	2	4	8	3		6	7
1	2			3	2		1	2	7	
	3	2	5	1			2	4		
	1	2		8	9	7	6	4		
	8	5	4	6	9	7		3	1	2
4	6	3	1	2		5	3	1	2	4
1	9		3	1		8	2		3	1

133

134

Mia's sister is 2, Judy; Gill's sister is 1, Kylie; Kay's sister is 3, Mel; Jane's sister is 4, Linda.

135

136

Enrico Leone was in compartment 1 (clue 4). As "Sir Percival Gascoyne" was in compartment 2 (clue 3), Franz Schmidt cannot have been in compartment 4 (clue 5), nor was Boris Zugov (clue 2), so Maxwell Van Skyler must have been, and "Professor Nils Knudsen" therefore in compartment 3 (clue 1). Van Skyler was not posing as Prince Karim Al-Aziz (clue 2), so he must have called himself the "Duc de Chomette," and therefore Franz Schmidt was in compartment 2 (clue 5), posing as Sir Percival Gascoyne. By elimination, "Professor Knudsen," in compartment 3, must really have been Boris Zugov, and Enrico Leone in compartment 1 must have been posing as Prince Karim Al-Aziz.

In summary:
Compartment 1, "Prince Karim Al-Aziz," Enrico Leone;
Compartment 2, "Sir Percival Gascoyne," Franz Schmidt;
Compartment 3, "Professor Nils Knudsen," Boris Zugov;
Compartment 4, "Duc de Chomette," Maxwell Van Skyler.

137

3	8	15	6
12	5	1	10
9	16	7	13
14	2	11	4

138

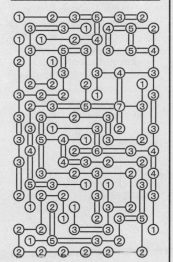

139

140

FORD	Sp	Se	suv
Red	J	A	R
Green	R	G	K
Blue	J	A	R
Silver	G	K	J
LINCOLN	Sp	Se	suv
Red	G	J	R
Green	J	A	K
Blue	G	K	G
Silver	A	R	A
CHEVROLET	Sp	Se	suv
Red	A	R	G
Green	K	J	A
Blue	*	K	G
Silver	R	J	K

The card Richard failed to declare was the blue Ford SUV. The 36th card featured a blue Chevrolet sports car.

141

6	11	2	8
9	13	5	15
4	16	10	12
14	1	7	3

142

143

67	31	35	49	53
45	59	63	27	41
23	37	51	55	69
61	65	29	33	47
39	43	57	71	25

144

8	x	1	÷	2	=	4
−		+		x		
7	+	9	÷	4	=	4
+		−		−		
3	+	6	−	5	=	4
=		=		=		
4		4		3		

145

Keith's wife is Angela (clue 2), and Lance is Gail's father (clue 4), so, from clue 5, Violet, whose daughter is Fiona and whose husband is not Perry, must be the wife of Chris. So their son is Garry (clue 4). We know Darren is not Violet's son, nor is he Angela's (clue 2). Since his surname is Morris (clue 2), he cannot be the son of Judy Langton (clue 3), so, by elimination, his mother must be Bridget. So they went to Majorca (clue 6). Violet is not Mrs. Chadwick, whose holiday location was Crete (clue 5), so, by elimination, she must be Mrs. Durham, leaving Mrs. Chadwick as Angela. We now know Judy Langton's holiday was not in Crete or Majorca, nor was it in Cyprus (clue 3), so she must have visited the Canaries, and, by elimination, the Durhams' island must have been Cyprus. Now, from clue 4, Lance's wife is not Judy Langton, who had the vacation in the Canaries, so she must be Bridget, and he is therefore Mr. Morris. Now, by elimination, Perry must be Mr. Langton, Judy's husband. Their son is not Ian (clue 3), so he must be Charles, and their daughter is therefore Rebecca (clue 1). So, by elimination, Keith and Angela Chadwick's children must be Ian and Janet.

In summary:
Chris and Violet Durham, Garry and Fiona, Cyprus. Keith and Angela Chadwick, Ian and Janet, Crete. Lance and Bridget Morris, Darren and Gail, Majorca. Perry and Judy Langton, Charles and Rebecca, Canaries.

146

147

From the top: F, D, B, C, A, E

148

Number 4.

149

15 and 13.
Each new number is the sum of the digits in the previous two circles; thus 3 + 7 = 10, 7 + 1 + 0 = 8, 8 + 1 + 0 = 9, 8 + 9 = 17, 9 + 1 + 7 = 17, and 1 + 7 + 1 + 7 = 16—so the sequence continues: 1 + 7 + 1 + 6 = 15 and 1 + 6 + 1 + 5 = 13.

150

The blue box contains 58 items (clue 2), and the green box contains the screws (clue 3), so the 43 nails, which are not in the brown box (clue 1), must be in the red one. We know the green box does not contain 43 or 58 items, and clue 3 rules out 65, so it must contain 39 screws. So, by elimination, the contents of the brown box must be 65 items. These are not washers (clue 3), so they must be carpet tacks, and they are in box C (clue 4), which leaves the blue box containing 58 washers. The green box cannot be box D (clue 3), since it has two neighbors, so that clue places it as box B, and the blue box containing the washers must be box A (also clue 3), leaving the red box as box D.

In summary:
A, blue, 58 washers.
B, green, 39 screws.
C, brown, 65 carpet tacks.
D, red, 43 nails.

151

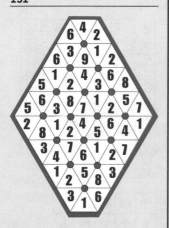

152

MERCHANT	CUSTOMER	ITEM	JOB
BRICKSRUS	T. BRAKES	SAND	GARAGE
HIRAN HIRE	CY BERMAN	STONE	BUNGALOW
HODSUP	ALF PRYCE	CEMENT	WALL
JUST SLATES	VAL NEEGHAM	WOOD	CONSERV.
MORTAR MART	A. COWERBOY	BALLAST	PATH

153

12. Count the pips you can see that are placed around a central pip. Thus 3 is worth 2 and 5 is worth 4. The other pips 2, 4, and 6 are worth nothing — they do not surround a central pip. One is just a grease spot with nothing around it.

154

1 and 8, 2 and 7, 3 and 4, 5 and 6 are pairs; 9 is the odd one out.

155

156

23. Four spoons balance 26 forks, so two spoons balance 13 forks; thus one knife balances five forks, so two knives balance 10 forks.

157

7	16	11	22	13
19	5	25	2	8
14	1	21	10	18
12	9	4	15	23
17	24	6	20	3

158

159

	11	19	17		6	18	21	16	11	8
14	2	8	4	39	5	4	9	8	7	6
24	8	9	7	23 / 13	1	3	8	5	4	2
15	1	2	3	9	7 / 18	1	4	2	20	6
	10	22 / 20	1	4	9	8	8 / 22	1	4	3
18	7	9	2	8 / 10	1	2	5	11 / 12	9	2
4	1	3	14 / 9	6	8	18 / 11	8	2	7	1
18	2	8	5	3	21 / 14	5	9	7	10	17
	12	11 / 23	3	1	5	2	15 / 16	3	5	7
9	2	6	1	10 / 16	1	4	5	12 / 29	3	9
10	1	9	12 / 21	4	8	13 / 9	7	3	2	1
30	9	8	7	6	9 / 17	3	4	2	19	11
	10	12 / 7	2	1	3	6	13 / 5	7	5	1
33	7	6	8	3	9	18	1	8	6	3
15	3	1	4	2	5	28	4	9	8	7

160

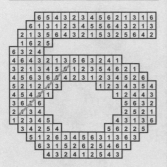

161

PERSON	JOB	FEATURE
ALF	BLACKSMITH	MONOCLE
FRED	LAWYER	PANAMA
GEORGE	MAILMAN	BEARD
TOM	DOCTOR	CRAVAT

162

163

A	B	C	D
FELIX	ISAAC	KEITH	CLIVE
E	F	G	H
LYDIA	HENRY	AGNES	DAVID
I	J	K	L
GRACE	JOYCE	BERYL	EMILY

164

Boot C.

165

0	0	1	5	4	5	2	6
1	0	5	3	6	1	4	2
3	5	0	4	5	3	4	1
2	5	6	5	6	1	3	6
2	3	2	3	2	4	3	6
0	0	5	0	2	1	0	6
4	3	6	1	1	4	2	4

166

```
  7 2 6 4 9 3   5 2 4 6 3 1 9
7   1     0   2     1   1     3
8 3 0 2 2 6 9   5 1 9 9 5   7
3   1   6   4     7   5 3 0 2
9 3 0 3   8 0 3 1 0 3   6   6
1   1   3 9 6     5 2 5 0 0 8
4     7   5   3 3 5 4   2   8
  9 3 8 1 1 8     8   4
  5   1   0   1 4 3 8 1 1 6
4 0 3 6 2 5   0     1     0
1   3     5 8 6   3 2 1 6 5
1 2 8   1     3   2   5 3
0   1 2 2 5 8 9   2 8 5   4
7 9 3   1   6 2 3 3   1 8 0 9
4   9 2 8 5 1     7   0
```

167

2	6	7	4	9	3	8	5	1
9	5	1	2	8	6	4	3	7
4	8	3	7	5	1	9	6	2
1	7	6	3	2	8	5	4	9
3	9	5	1	4	7	2	8	6
8	4	2	9	6	5	7	1	3
7	1	8	5	3	2	6	9	4
6	2	4	8	1	9	3	7	5
5	3	9	6	7	4	1	2	8

168

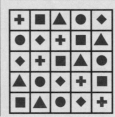

169

Seven bunches have all three colors.

170

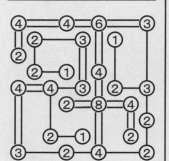

171

9	+	4	−	7	=	6
−		+		+		
5	+	6	−	3	=	8
+		−		−		
2	+	8	−	1	=	9
=		=		=		
6		2		9		

172

1	8	5	7	3	9	4	6	2
6	7	9	2	8	4	5	1	3
3	4	2	1	5	6	7	9	8
2	1	3	6	9	5	8	7	4
5	9	4	8	2	7	1	3	6
8	6	7	4	1	3	9	2	5
4	3	1	9	6	8	2	5	7
9	5	8	3	7	2	6	4	1
7	2	6	5	4	1	3	8	9

173

	Table 1	Table 2	Table 3	Table 4
N	Harry	Babs	Tessa (dummy)	Fred
E	Susie (dummy)	Kate	Connie	Lola
S	Jane	Roger (dummy)	Dot	Gordon
W	Peter	Alan	Michael	Eddie (dummy)
Contract	2 diamonds	4 spades	1 heart	3 clubs

174

175

1 Señor Pedro's Poodles
2 Fred the Fire-eater
3 Crazy Carvellos
4 Clever Clowns
5 Jim the Juggler
6 Flying Fortresses
7 Agilles Acrobats
8 Madame Poll's Parrots

176

0	0	3	6	4	2	3
3	4	4	4	4	5	2
0	5	5	0	5	5	6
4	3	3	6	6	6	2
4	5	3	0	5	1	3
6	2	2	0	1	1	1
1	5	2	0	2	4	1
1	3	6	6	2	1	0

177

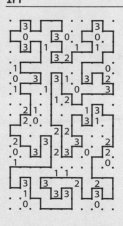

178

There are 54 missing bricks.

179

7	9		1	3	6		8	6
9	8		2	1	4		9	8
8	6	7	3		8	6	7	9
		9	6		7	9		
9	7	8	4		9	8	7	5
8	2						3	1
7	1	2	3		2	1	9	3
		4	8		9	7		
3	5	1	2		1	3	2	6
2	9		1	7	3		1	8
1	8		4	9	8		3	9

180

N	F	Y	K	C
Q	J	W	H	T
G	U	R	B	M
A	L	D	V	O
X	P	I	S	E

181

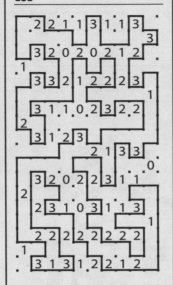

182

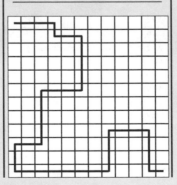

183

Shield C is green (clue 4). Shield A cannot be blue (clue 1) or yellow (clue 2), so it must be red. Since the owner of this shield is Lord Liversedge (clue 5), from clue 1, the blue shield cannot be shield B, so, by elimination, it must be shield D, leaving shield B as the yellow one. Therefore, from clue 2, the eagle is the device on Lord Liversedge's red shield in position A. Now, from clue 2, shield B must belong to Lord Bertram. Lord Rackham's shield bearing a turkey cannot be in position D (clue 1), so it must be shield C. This leaves shield D as Lord Mallender's. Its device is not the lion (clue 3), so it must be the stag, leaving the lion as the device on Lord Bertram's yellow coat of arms.

In summary:
A, Lord Liversedge, eagle, red.
B, Lord Bertram, lion, yellow.
C, Lord Rackham, turkey, green.
D, Lord Mallender, stag, blue.

184

Shadow C.

185

0	5	6	3	2	5	4
0	5	6	2	2	1	5
2	0	0	6	5	2	1
1	5	5	3	3	2	3
5	1	4	2	3	2	6
4	0	4	3	4	4	4
0	6	1	3	0	1	6
6	6	1	1	3	4	0

186

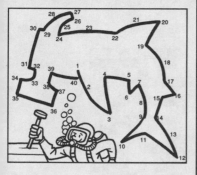

187

Letter 1, Jill Dukes, California.
Letter 2, Sally Markham, New York.
Letter 3, Jenny Hardy, Idaho.
Letter 4, Betty Riley, Hawaii.

188

Photograph H is the exact replica.

189

14 **7**	16 **1**	14 **5**
25 **6**	22 **3**	18 **8**
19 **9**	18 **4**	14 **2**

190

Lavender, green, orange, yellow.

191

4	7			6	5		5
	8	1			1	2	0
1	9	2			2	4	
6			1	6		6	4
	1		3	8			0
2	9	4			3	6	0
6	6	2			9	7	

192

1–C and 3–B.

193

Lead B.

194

Birthright, 1914–1938, Joseph, Miriam.
Chronicle, 1780–1830, Vaughan, Hannah.
Domain, 1938–1977, Lambert, Claudia.
Heritage, 1881–1914, Esmond, Rosalind.
Testament, 1830–1881, Samuel, Eugenie.

195

	9	8	6		4	2	3	1	
6	2	4	3	1		2	5	1	4	3
9	8	6	5		2	1	3		2	1
	7	9	8	5		1	4		
9	6	8		9	1	3		1	2	4
7	8		4	6		1	4	5	3	2
	9	6	2			3	2	6	
2	5	4	1	3		3	1		1	6
9	7	8		1	4	2		1	4	2
	9	1		3	1	2	5	
7	9		3	2	1		1	3	2	5
1	6	3	2	4		6	7	4	9	8
	8	7	5	9		1	4	2	

196

Students 3 and 6.

197

7	+	9	÷	8	=	2
+		+		−		
2	x	6	÷	3	=	4
x		÷		+		
1	+	5	−	4	=	2
=		=		=		
9		3		9		

198

331, 041. These are multiples of 7 with the figures reversed. 77 (!), 84, 91 . . .

199

No. The average is 192 mph. Suppose each leg is 100 miles. The first took them one hour. The next leg took half an hour, the third a third of an hour, and the fourth a quarter of an hour. The total distance is 400 miles, and the total time taken is two and one-twelfth hours. That's 192 miles per hour.

200

201

Poster A shows Jacob (clue 2) and poster D shows Churchman, so Herbert, who's shown on the poster horizontally adjacent to the one showing "Butch" McColl (clue 1), can't be shown on poster C, nor does poster C show Silvester Jaggard (clue 2), so it must show Matthew. We now know that Silvester Jaggard isn't shown on poster A, C, or D, so he must be on poster B. By elimination, Herbert must be on poster D, and, from clue 1, Matthew, on poster C, must be "Butch" McColl. By elimination, Jacob's surname must be Wolf. So, from clue 3, "Pony" must be Silvester Jaggard

on poster B. Herbert Churchman on poster D isn't "Apache" (clue 4), so his nickname must be "Rio," and "Apache" must be Jacob Wolf on poster A.

In summary:
A, Jacob "Apache" Wolf.
B, Silvester "Pony" Jaggard.
C, Matthew "Butch" McColl.
D, Herbert "Rio" Churchman.

202

1 and 2 will knot; 3 and 4 will not.

203

204

The three squares that are the same are 3F, 7E, and 10B.

205

Horse, Sue; peacock, Joan; elephant, David; dragon, Bob; camel, Edward; zebra, Chloe; unicorn, Alan; emu, Helen.

206

36	+	12	=	48	−	26	=	22
−		−		−		−		−
20	+	5	=	25	−	17	=	8
=		=		=		=		=
16	+	7	=	23	−	9	=	14
+		+		+		+		+
15	+	11	=	26	−	3	=	23
=		=		=		=		=
31	+	18	=	49	−	12	=	37

207

Winners: Ann and Clive Dawson, director, butcher, 77. The rest were: Brenda and Pete Morris, postmistress, mechanic, 68. Rose and Len Watson, sculptor, caterer, 64. Thelma and Jack Kelly, teacher, vet, 75.

208

209

210

Triple 15
Double 6
Single 14

211

212

30 10		40 02		11 04		14 01		42 00		40 02		01 03
	40 41		31 14		14 04		45 00		52 02		22 05	
10 41		40 41		23 13		43 02		43 11		20 34		03 12
	01 53		13 41		24 21		61 11		21 33		03 42	
03 12		01 35		05 31		22 32		30 15		01 62		04 20
	05 04		13 14		23 40		10 44		30 24		33 30	
04 02		24 03		43 02		13 41		10 44		51 21		42 00
	13 05		52 02		35 10		04 41		31 41		60 30	
01 03		31 02		33 00		05 10		02 40		20 40		20 20

213

The five errors are:
1 The model's earring is missing. 2 The frill on the model's right shoulder is different. 3 The model's left sleeve has thinner bands. 4 The central design under the waistband of the skirt is not pointed. 5 The skirt has an extra band on it.

214

```
■ 1 2 3 1 ■ 1 3 2 1 ■
■ 0 ■ ■ 3 ■ 3 ■ ■ 1 ■
2 0 ■ 4 6 8 2 4 ■ 2 2
7 0 1 1 ■ 1 ■ 2 1 3 6
2 ■ 2 2 9 9 9 6 8 ■ 4
■ ■ 7 1 1 1 8 6 7 ■ ■
2 ■ 2 5 1 5 4 5 6 ■ 1
6 3 1 2 ■ 2 ■ 2 9 1 2
8 9 ■ 5 1 5 1 0 ■ 1 2
■ ■ 0 ■ ■ 0 ■ 3 ■ ■ 3 ■
■ 2 0 0 0 ■ 7 1 3 3 ■
```

The combination is 7111867.

215

Man H is the wanted man.

216

15	41	32	20	10
22	9	1	38	46
11	26	18	4	30
42	31	6	45	12
40	16	27	48	25

217

218

219

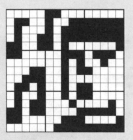

220

221

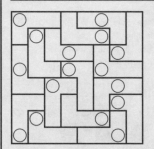

222

484

223

Figure 1 has an extra fold of material on his arm. Figure 2 has an extra detail on his right sandal. Figure 3 has more hair. Figure 4 has a wristband.

224

Red, blue, lavender, blue.

225

D. Each square has the top right quarter cut off. This leaves three smaller squares. In the next picture each of those has its top right quarter removed, and so on.

226

Chuck's date isn't Beth (clue 3) or Cathy (clue 4), so it's Alice. Thus Art is heavier than Chuck (1), who (3) is heavier than Beth's date; so Beth's date isn't Art—he's Bill. By elimination, Art's date is Cathy. Since Art is heavier than Chuck, who is heavier than Bill (above), Art is man F, Chuck is E, and Bill is D. Bill's date is Beth, and Chuck's is Alice (above); so Beth is taller than Alice (2), who is taller than Cathy—thus Beth is woman C, Alice is A, and Cathy is B.

227

228

1	+	4	÷	5	=1
+		X		X	
9	+	3	÷	2	= 6
-		-		-	
7	+	6	-	8	= 5
=		=		=	
3		6		2	

229

The 2 of diamonds, 3 of hearts, 6 of clubs, 8 of spades, and 9 of hearts.

230

```
5 0 1 0 6   7   6   7 1 2 0 9
0   5   0   1 0 2 1 1   7   8
6   7   3   2   3   3   7   8
6   7   4 0 0   2   0   6   0
2 0 1 8 5   6 1 0   1 5 1 3 1
        0     3       1   4
8 9 9 0 5     3 2 9 0 9   8
8     3 9 2 4 6   5   3 6 4
3 3 0 5 1 4     5     9 8 3
  8       8 6 1 2 3 4   1
9 1 2 0 6   1 6 8   8 3 2 4 7
1     8   5 5 0   3       8
3 5 0 1 6   2   3   3 2 1 9 8
2       8 9 2   7 0 2       0
4 0 1 1 8   9 5 6   1 0 8 6 0
```

231

BOX	BIRD	EGGS
1	BRENDA	5
2	FELICITY	2
3	DEIRDRE	6
4	EDWINA	4
5	ABIGAIL	1
6	CLARISSA	3

232

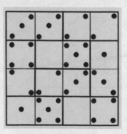

233

E, L, and 0.

234

			7	9			1	3
1	2		9	8	7		4	2
3	1	2	5		5	3	2	1
		4	8		9	1		
2	3	1		3	6	2	1	4
1	9		3	1	8		7	1
4	7	8	6	9		1	3	2
		9	4			3	2	
9	3	6	1		2	4	3	1
8	2		2	3	1		9	8
6	1			1	5			

235

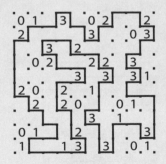

236

C		A	B	
B		C	A	
	A		C	B
	C	B		A
A	B			C

237

77	84	61	68	75
66	73	80	82	64
85	62	69	71	78
74	76	83	65	67
63	70	72	79	81

239

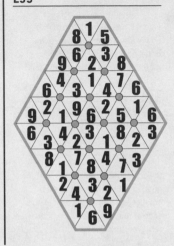

238

4	7	2	9	9	2	5	6	3	7	2
4	3	7	0	4	1	2	2	0	4	7
0	9	8	5	9	9	3	8	3	1	9
0	5	3	6	4	6	1	4	6	8	8
6	6	3	0	7	7	5	5	2	6	0
7	5	1	9	3	4	1	1	4	1	9
9	0	6	6	1	0	0	1	5	8	3
8	1	2	5	8	7	2	7	3	1	2
4	0	8	5	9	4	5	2	7	8	6
3	4	3	9	5	8	0	7	6	8	2

486

240

1	JESSE JONES	WELLS FARGO
2	FRANK FOSTER	JAIL
3	CHUCK CARSON	SALOON
4	DAVE DALTON	BANK
5	ROCKY RAWLINGS	TRADING POST

241

4	+	7	-	9	=	2
+		+		-		
6	+	3	-	8	=	1
-		÷		+		
1	X	5	-	2	=	3
=		=		=		
9		2		3		

242

```
  7 1 3 6 4 8   1 6 3 8 4 2 5
5   7   3   1   5   3       9
2 1 5 2 2 6 0   7 3 0 1 4   9
4   0   3   1     9   3 2 5 0
9 0 5 4   3 2 6 4 1 9   3   3
3   0   4 8 3   1 0 3 6 0 0
9     4   4   2 9 2 1   9   4
  5 3 8 0 1 8     3   0
  6   3   0   6 6 0 3 2 9 9
4 0 9 2 1 4   4   0     3
0     6     8 0 9   2 7 3 2 8
3 5 8   6     8   1   1   1
6   2 3 5 7 9 8   1 6 1   0
4 4 4   1   4 2 3 0   6 3 0 7
7   3 9 9 0 2   8 6
```

243

Tangles a, b, and d will not form a knot. Tangle c will form a knot.

244

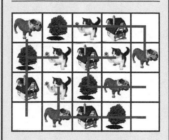

245

3	0	0	3
3	3	3	2
5	5	0	5
5	2	2	2
2	0	0	5

246

Weights A and B will rise, and weights C and D will fall.

247

248

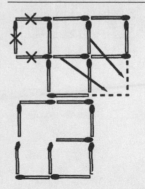

249

250

1	2	7	9	3	6	8	5	4
9	5	4	7	1	8	6	3	2
3	8	6	2	5	4	7	9	1
5	6	9	1	7	3	2	4	8
4	1	8	5	6	2	9	7	3
7	3	2	8	4	9	1	6	5
6	4	1	3	2	7	5	8	9
8	7	5	4	9	1	3	2	6
2	9	3	6	8	5	4	1	7

251

Shape D.

252

T S	8 D	8 H	K D	T C
J S	A H	K C	8 C	Q S
T D	9 C	K H	8 S	9 S
T H	K S	Q D	Q C	9 H
J C	J H	J D	Q H	9 D

253

3 3 4		6		2 7 3
6 7 1	6 1 1			9 8 7
1 2 9	6 2 0			6 5 1
	2 7 3	6 1 1	7 7 3	
	2 6 1	8 2 8	2	
	1 8 2	7 6 3	5 4 4	
2 1 6	6 1 9			2 1 9
9 0 5	1 7 2			1 7 3
2 7 2	7			7 1 6

254

13.

255

Flag, fork, candle.

256

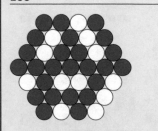

257

258

Quarterfinals	Semifinals	Final	Winner
Chelsea v Norwich	Chelsea		
	v	Arsenal	
Spurs v Arsenal	Arsenal		
			EVERTON
Everton v Watford	Everton		
	v	Everton	
Liverpool v Southampton	Liverpool		

259

4	+	6	−	1	= 9
÷		+		x	
2	x	8	−	9	= 7
+		÷		÷	
5	+	7	÷	3	= 4
= 7		= 2		= 3	

260

A	E	D	B	C
B	D	C	E	A
D	C	E	A	B
E	A	B	C	D
C	B	A	D	E

261

A, *The Old Mill*, 1964.
B, *St Aidan's Church*, 1981.
C, *Crane Bay*, 1976.
D, *Lower Woods*, 1992.
E, *Fiddler's Brook*, 1988.

262

0	4	1	5	0	0	0
5	5	2	5	6	0	1
5	2	0	4	3	3	0
6	4	2	4	3	4	4
1	4	2	0	1	3	1
1	6	2	3	6	6	5
1	1	2	6	3	2	2
4	3	5	6	5	6	3

263

Shape D.

264

Rocking horse D.

265

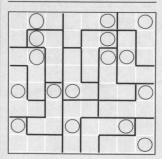

266

The weights that will go up are 1 and 4, and the weights that will go down are 2, 3, and 5.

267

Betty, surgeon, and Alice, lawyer, are sisters. Frank, surgeon, and Dave, accountant, are brothers. Carol, accountant, and Ed, lawyer, are siblings. Marriages are: Betty and Ed, Alice and Dave, and Carol and Frank.

268

B	D			C	A
A		C		B	D
C		D	A		B
	A	B	C	D	
	B		D	A	C
D	C	A	B		

269

Each square tile has neighbors—tiles that share an edge. The corners have just two neighbors, those along the edge have three, and the ones in the middle have four. For each square, check how many of its neighbors are in the same state (empty, red, or blue) as the cell itself. If the score is 0, the cell becomes empty; if it is 1 or 2, color it red, and if it is 3 or 4, color it blue.

270

	B	A		C	D
D	A			B	C
	C	D	A		B
A	D	B	C		
B		C	D	A	
C			B	D	A

271

GHOST	OF	AT	FEATURE
A	DYSART	HAM HOUSE	PAPERS
B	WINDHAM	FELBRIGG	BOOKS
C	BOLEYN	BLICKLING	HEADLESS
D	VERNEY	CLAYDON	HAND
E	LEGH	LYME PARK	FUNERAL

272

7	+	9	÷	2	=	8
−		X		+		
3	X	4	−	8	=	4
÷		÷		÷		
1	+	6	−	5	=	2
=		=		=		
4		6		2		

273

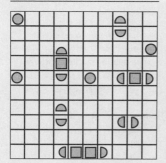

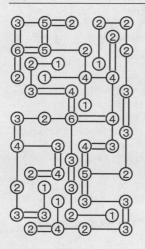

276

7	3	5	8	6	9	2	1	4
9	8	1	7	2	4	6	3	5
2	6	4	1	3	5	8	9	7
8	5	7	9	4	1	3	2	6
3	4	2	6	8	7	9	5	1
1	9	6	3	5	2	7	4	8
6	2	3	4	1	8	5	7	9
4	7	8	5	9	3	1	6	2
5	1	9	2	7	6	4	8	3

277

1	0	7	9	8	9	■	2	1	2	8	0	6
3	■	1	■	3	0	9	4	7	■	1	■	6
4	5	3	5	2	7	■	5	8	1	9	4	1
8	■	9	■	6	1	5	1	3	■	2	■	6
7	6	5	7	■	8	7	4	■	9	0	8	3
1	0	4	3	9	■	2	■	2	7	1	9	0
■	1	■	3	0	4	■	4	2	1	■	2	■
5	7	1	4	7	■	2	■	6	7	3	2	9
7	5	7	6	■	8	1	5	■	9	4	4	7
2	■	2	■	1	4	7	5	6	■	1	■	1
2	1	3	0	7	1	■	3	1	6	2	9	3
1	■	5	■	4	6	0	2	3	■	6	■	2
5	5	1	1	0	8	■	6	7	6	8	6	9

278

Architect: Mark Jones; barber: Neil
Franklin; critic: Luke Harkness;
dentist: Otto Ives; economist: Karl
Gainor.

279

Q	T	T	Q	9
C	H	S	S	H
K	9	T	J	J
C	C	C	S	C
K	8	J	9	J
D	S	H	D	D
9	Q	8	K	Q
S	H	H	S	D
K	A	8	T	8
H	H	C	D	D

280

72694.

281

282

3	2	3	9	4	6	4	8	5	5
5	1	5	3	3	5	3	7	4	4
4	0	4	2	4	9	5	6	3	3
5	4	3	6	3	8	4	5	4	7
4	3	5	0	5	2	3	4	4	1

283

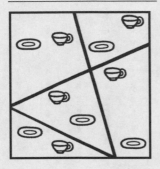

284

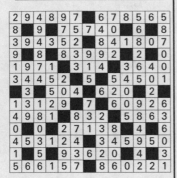

2	9	4	8	9	7			6	7	8	5	6	5
8		9		7	5	7	4	0		6			8
3	9	4	3	5	2		8	4	1	8	0	7	
9		8		8	3	9	9	2		2			0
1	9	7	1		3	1	4		3	6	4	0	
3	4	4	5	2		5		5	4	5	0	1	
	3		5	0	4		6	2	0		2		
1	3	1	2	9		7		6	0	9	2	6	
4	9	8	1		8	3	2		5	8	6	3	
0		0		2	7	1	3	8		4			6
4	5	3	1	2	4		3	4	5	9	5	0	
1		5		9	3	6	2	0		4			3
5	6	6	1	5	7		8	6	0	2	2	1	

285

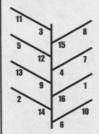

286

Belts 3 and 9 are identical.

287

3	25	1	8
36	4	49	2
9	64	16	5
6	1	7	4

288

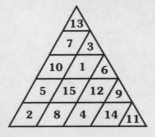

289

None of the four isolated squares is blue (clue 3), so, since the center square, number 7, is red (clue 6), and no two adjacent squares horizontally or vertically are the same color (clue 1), and there must be at least four blue squares (intro), these must be either numbers 2, 4, 10, and 12, or numbers 3, 6, 8, and 11. Two of the four squares numbered 10 to 13 are red (clue 4). If one of these is 13, the other cannot be 11 (clue 1), so it must be either 10 or 12, which would rule out the blues as 2, 4, 10, and 12. If 13 was not a red square, then the red squares would have to be 10 and 12 (clue 1), which also rules out the blues as 2, 4, 10, and 12, so, as we have seen above, they must be 3, 6, 8, and 11. Since the blue square numbered 8 has a red square to its left, from clue 2, square 5 must be white. From the same clue, square 9 cannot be white, nor can it be blue (clue 1), so it must be red. We have placed two red squares in that row, and there is another in the row above (clue 5). We also know there are two among squares 10 to 13, which makes five in all, so there cannot be any more red squares (intro), and there must be four each of the blue and white, so we have placed all the blue squares, too. Therefore square 1 must be white, so square 12 must be white as well (clue 7). Therefore the red squares referred to in clue 4 must be 10 and 13. We have identified three of the four white squares as 1, 5, and 12. Since square 6 is blue, none of these white squares can be the one referred to in clue 8. Only the colors of squares 2 and 4 remain to be identified. From clue 8, the fourth

white square must be 4 and square 2 must be red.

In summary:
1, white.
2, red; 3, blue; 4, white.
5, white; 6, blue; 7, red; 8, blue;
9, red.
10, red; 11, blue; 12, white; 13, red.

293

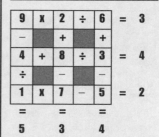

9	x	2	÷	6	=	3
−		+		+		
4	+	8	÷	3	=	4
÷		−		−		
1	x	7	−	5	=	2
=		=		=		
5		3		4		

290

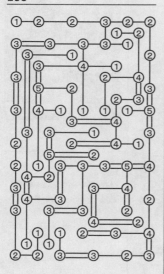

291

6 K 9 A 8 Q 4 J 2 7 10 3 5

292

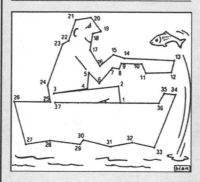

294

295

The three identical vases are the middle vase on the top line, the end vase on the third line, and the end vase on the bottom line.

296

Just place the canoe on a flat surface and spin it. Centrifugal force will carry the balls up and away at the same time.

297

24. There are six numbers on a die. In each picture, just multiply the values of all the die numbers you cannot see (they're "out to lunch"). In the third picture you have 1, 2, 3, and 5. So 4 and 6 are missing.

298

Triple 15   Double 5   Single 11

299

48	÷	12	=	4	+	40	=	44
−		+		X		÷		−
32	÷	4	=	8	÷	4	=	2
=		=		=		=		=
16	+	16	=	32	+	10	=	42
X		+		+		+		+
4	+	6	=	10	+	1	=	11
=		=		=		=		=
64	−	22	=	42	+	11	=	53

300

A6 B4 C7 D1 E3 F5 G2 H8. Score 58.

301

A	B	C	D	E	F	G	H	J	K
5	3	8	1	6	0	2	7	9	4

302

A, Enid and Fiona   B, Carol and Daisy
C, Alice and Gina   D, Beth and Helen

303

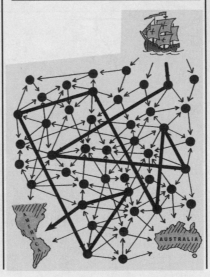

304

From the top: A, E, B, D, F, C.

305

306

1 BE DE BG BE **2** DF AF BF **3** BG CG DF BF CF **4** AG DF AG **5** BG BF AF BF **6** CG DG AE CE DG **7** AE DE BE AF DE **8** CE CG **9** BE DF **10** CG DG CF

307

6	3	2	5	0	4	3
6	5	2	5	4	5	3
5	1	4	1	3	2	2
6	6	4	5	4	6	3
0	0	0	3	0	2	2
5	3	6	6	2	5	4
1	1	0	4	0	1	1
1	3	1	6	0	4	2

308

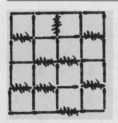

309

Print 3.

310

The lines should be drawn from 6 to 36, 8 to 29, and 19 to 45.

311

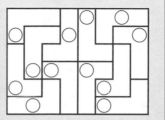

312

	A		C	B
C		B	A	
A	B	C		
	C		B	A
B		A		C

313

7	8	1	2	9	5	6	4	3
5	9	4	6	3	1	7	8	2
6	3	2	8	7	4	9	1	5
8	4	6	1	2	3	5	9	7
2	7	9	4	5	6	1	3	8
3	1	5	7	8	9	2	6	4
4	5	8	9	1	7	3	2	6
1	2	3	5	6	8	4	7	9
9	6	7	3	4	2	8	5	1

314

4	2	0	4	3	9	3	1	3	8
8	3	5	8	5	1	2	4	0	4
9	1	4	6	1	8	2	0	5	7
2	7	3	7	0	3	8	9	3	9
5	0	9	6	8	2	4	2	1	4
9	7	2	1	7	5	3	6	5	8
3	1	4	9	2	8	0	2	3	2

315

Hein was with Rudig, and Jan was with Wouter. Hence it was Roel who had no alibi.

316

B, C, and E will move up. A and D will move down.

317

0	1	3	2
1	2	3	2
2	2	0	0
1	1	1	0
3	3	0	3

495

318

D	B	A	C		
A	D		B		C
		C	D	A	B
		B	A	C	D
C	A	D		B	
B	C			D	A

319

41. In order, the numbers are 1, 4, 7,
11, 14, 17 . . . numbers that are made
from straight lines only. The shop
only stocks 1s, 4s, and 7s!

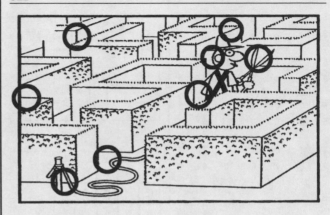

320

```
  9 4 3 2 0 1     5 1 7 3 4 8 4
9   6   7   0       3 7         2
2 3 6 1 7 1 2     4 8 2 0 6     1
0   2   3   3       2   7 3 2 6
3 9 7 9   7 3 9 9 9 8   7       0
0   8   4 2 1       1 9 3 7 6 2
7     4   1   1 7 6 2   0       2
  6 1 8 2 4 3           0   2
  3   2   2   2 7 1 9 3 8 3
4 7 6 2 3 6   1       7       1
0   1       7 2 9   3 7 0 2 2
4 0 1   3       6   4   9   9
3   7 6 0 6 3 6   2 1 4   4
3 1 1   1   6 9 1 3   9 0 3 2
1   4 8 8 7 2   3   1
```

322

Nine bunches have all three colors.

323

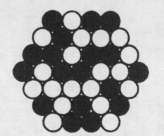

324

Q	8	T	J	J
D	D	D	S	D
T	8	K	J	A
C	C	D	H	H
J	9	K	K	T
C	H	S	H	S
Q	9	Q	8	8
C	D	S	S	H
K	9	Q	T	9
C	S	H	H	C

325

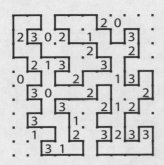

326

Eye color changed, sign on window missing, wheel nut missing, handle different color, driver's tie missing, and tire tread missing.

327

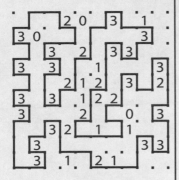

328

5 is the innermost number on strap D (clue 4), so that cannot be the strap referred to in clue 5, nor can strap E (clue 3) or strap C (clue 7), while the outermost numbers on both straps A and F must be single-digit numbers (clue 2), so the strap referred to in clue 5 must be strap B. Clue 8 tells us the 17 is not the innermost number, so, from clue 5, the strap B numbers, reading outward, must be 12, 1, and 17. So, from clue 8, the innermost number of strap E must be 18 and that on strap 8 therefore 8. We have now placed four innermost numbers, which total 43, so, from clue 1, the other two must total 21. From numbers already placed, we know these cannot be 18 and 3, 17 and 4, 16 and 5, 13 and 8, or 12 and 9, and clue 6 rules out both 15 and 6 and 11 and 10, so they must be 14 and 7. So, from clue 4, the 7 must be on strap C, and the 14 on strap A. We now know the single-digit number in the middle of strap A (clue 2) is not 1, 5, 7, or 8, nor, since the 15 is not an innermost number, can it be 6 (clue 6). It clearly cannot be 2 (clue 2). If it were 3 or 4, then, from clue 2, one of the other two numbers referred to would have to be 1, but we have already placed that number elsewhere, so, by elimination, it must be 9. We know the number

outside it is not 7 or 8, nor, since we have placed 7 and 8, can it be 1 or 2 (clue 2). We also know that it is not 5, and, since we have placed the 5, it cannot be 4 (clue 2), so it must be 3 or 6, and so must the outermost number of strap F (clue 2). But we have placed the only even number on strap F (clue 3), so its outermost number must be 3, and the 6 must be on strap A. We know the 15 is not on strap B, so, from clue 6, it must be the middle number on strap F. Clue 6 now reveals the 10 as an outermost number. The middle number next to it is 16 (clue 6), so they cannot be on strap E, which already has one even number (clue 3), or on C, which has only one two-digit number (clue 7), so they must be on strap D. Since the 2 is not on strap C (clue 7), it must be one of the two even numbers on strap E (clue 3), which leaves the 4 on strap C. Clue 7 also places the 13 on strap C, leaving the 11 on strap E. From clue 3, the 2 must be the outermost number of strap E, and the 13 therefore is the outermost on strap C (clue 7), leaving the 11 and the 4 as the central numbers on their respective straps.

In summary: (reading outward)
Strap A: 14, 9, 6. Strap D: 5, 16, 10.
Strap B: 12, 1, 17. Strap E: 18, 11, 2.
Strap C: 7, 4, 13. Strap F: 8, 15, 3.

```
   8 6 9       2 1
 8 9 5 7 6     2 1 3
 9 7     6 2 1 3 4
       9 8     2 1
 9 8 7     2 3 4 1
 2 1     7 1 5     7 9
   9 7 8 6     3 2 1
     8 9     1 2
     1 5 4 2 3     3 9
 7 8 9     4 2 3 1 8
 1 2         4 1 2
```

330

PANELLIST	GUEST	OCCUPATION	OCCUPATION
GERTA	KEN	FLEDGER'S	CRINGE
MILES	CONNIE	GRUTTLER'S	HOCKER
NOAH	ANN	CRIMPER'S	SLANT
WANDA	ENA	TADDLER'S	POSSET

331

332

E inner is given as 4, so C inner, which must be an even number (clue 4) cannot be 4 or 8. If it were 2 and D inner 1, from clue 2, B outer and H inner would both be 3, and, from clue 3, the inner 6 could only be in segment G. C outer would therefore also be 6 as would F middle (clue 4). In that case, F outer would have to be 12, which is impossible. So C inner must be 6 and D inner 3 (clue 4). So, from clue 2, B outer must be 7, H middle 8, and H inner 7, and since those two H numbers add up to 15, H outer must be 0. With the inner 6 being in C, the outer 6 must be in G (clue 3) and B inner must therefore be 5 (clue 2). To complete the B quota, B middle must be 3. We know D inner is 3, and since, from clue 4, D outer is double D middle, those numbers must be 8 and 4 respectively. F outer must be four times G middle (clue 4), and since the outer circle already has an 8, F outer must be 4, G middle 1 and F middle, from the same clue, 2. To complete their quotas, F inner must be 9 and G inner 8. C outer must be 2 (clue 4) and C middle 7. All inner numbers have now been inserted except in A, which is an odd number (clue 2), so it must be 1. To make up A's quota, the remaining odd numbers must be 5 and 9, and from clue 1, the 9 must be A outer and 5 A middle. Therefore E outer must also be 5 (clue 4) and E middle 6.

In summary:
Numbers given as outer, middle, inner.
A, 9, 5, 1.
B, 7, 3, 5.
C, 2, 7, 6.
D, 8, 4, 3.
E, 5, 6, 4.
F, 4, 2, 9.
G, 6, 1, 8.
H, 0, 8, 7.

333

Shop	Customer	DVD
Just Flicks	C. Nitt	*Gosh!*
More Movies	B. Dee-High	*Whew!*
Nite Rates	A. Blinkon	*Wow!*
Rent 'n' Rave	D. Cryer	*Hey!*

334

1 and 7.
2 and 4.
3 and 6.
5 and 8.

335

336

From left to right:
King of spades, queen of spades,
king of clubs, king of hearts.

337

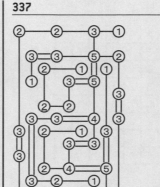

338

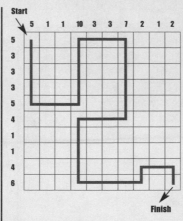

339

	Eagle	Birdie	Par	Bogey	Double Bogey	FINAL SCORE
Darma	3	5	7	2	1	65
Jackliss	1	4	8	3	2	73
Clayer	2	7	5	1	3	68

340

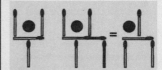

341

2	6	1	4	4	3	0	3
2	3	5	5	6	6	4	2
0	1	0	2	1	1	1	4
5	3	0	0	5	3	0	5
0	6	1	2	1	6	4	1
4	3	3	4	0	5	5	6
2	4	6	3	2	2	6	5

342

Blocks 1 and 3.

343

8	2	5	3	7	1	9	6	4
9	4	3	6	2	5	8	7	1
1	6	7	8	9	4	2	5	3
3	5	9	2	8	7	1	4	6
6	1	2	4	5	3	7	8	9
4	7	8	1	6	9	5	3	2
5	8	4	9	1	6	3	2	7
7	9	6	5	3	2	4	1	8
2	3	1	7	4	8	6	9	5

344

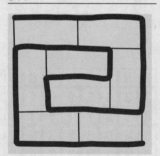

345

From the top: blue, orange, yellow, lavender, red, green.

346

Kettledrum 7.

347

2	6	0	6	0	5	3
3	3	3	5	5	6	5
6	2	0	4	1	6	6
3	2	1	4	4	3	4
5	2	4	1	1	1	6
2	3	0	2	3	2	4
5	4	1	0	0	1	6
5	0	1	0	4	5	2

348

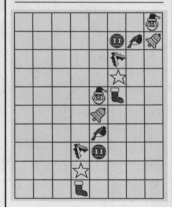

349

	B		D	C	A	
C	A	B			D	
A		D	B			C
B		C	A			D
	D	A	C	B		
D	C				A	B

350

Number 3.

351

A Hank	D Fred	G Dave
B Cary	E Bess	H Gina
C Alan	F Enid	

352

7	0	3	8	9	1	■	8	8	4	2	7	1
7	■	4	■	2	9	0	1	7	■	1	■	0
6	2	4	8	9	6	■	5	4	3	2	1	0
9	■	0	■	3	5	7	0	9	■	2	■	2
7	4	7	5	■	8	3	7	■	7	2	8	0
6	9	1	7	7	■	6	■	9	1	3	7	0
■	8	■	6	2	3	■	5	4	7	■	1	■
4	3	5	8	1	■	4	■	1	0	6	7	9
6	2	1	9	■	2	1	3	■	5	3	4	2
3	■	5	■	4	0	2	3	3	■	5	■	1
3	1	2	1	1	1	■	4	5	3	3	2	4
2	■	5	■	7	8	9	0	5	■	4	■	0
2	4	3	4	4	4	■	1	2	1	3	1	4

353

6	4	9	2	5	1	7	8	3
5	1	8	4	7	3	9	6	2
3	7	2	9	8	6	1	4	5
8	2	4	6	1	7	3	5	9
7	6	3	5	4	9	2	1	8
1	9	5	3	2	8	6	7	4
2	5	6	1	3	4	8	9	7
9	3	7	8	6	5	4	2	1
4	8	1	7	9	2	5	3	6

354

FIRST NAME	SURNAME	SUBJECT	UNIVERSITY
ANNA	JONES	MATH	YALE
BARBARA	BROWN	PHYSICS	HARVARD
CLARE	TAYLOR	CHEMISTRY	MIT
DIANA	MOORE	BIOLOGY	PRINCETON

355

356

3	6	10	1	8	4	9	2	7	5
I	C	G	E	B	J	A	D	H	F

357

358

6	5	7	1	2	3	4	9	8
1	9	4	5	6	8	3	7	2
2	3	8	7	9	4	5	1	6
5	8	1	6	3	2	7	4	9
9	4	2	8	7	5	1	6	3
3	7	6	4	1	9	8	2	5
4	2	9	3	8	7	6	5	1
8	1	5	9	4	6	2	3	7
7	6	3	2	5	1	9	8	4

359

360

SHE	SURNAME	HE	SURNAME
ANN	BRAKES	GARY	STAMPS
BELLA	NOBLE	HORACE	LYNES
CHER	DABALL	ED	COPES
DAWN	CHOVIES	FRANK	BALDY

361

3D	8C	7D
10S	6H	2S
5D	4C	9D

362

A Elmer & Harvey.
B Alvin & Frank.
C Conrad & Dexter.
D Brad & Gary.

363

6 JK 10 A 7 Q 4 9 K 2 J 8 JK 5 3

364

	B	A	C		D
	A	C		D	B
D			B	C	A
B	C	D	A		
A	D			B	C
C		B	D	A	

365

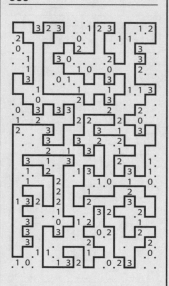

366

1 Empty.

2 Empty.

3 Informer.

4 Gunman.

5 Gunman.

367

1 D	5 I	9 G	13 C
2 O	6 B	10 K	14 E
3 F	7 P	11 H	15 N
4 L	8 A	12 J	16 M

368

Balloon C.

369

370

06243.

371

The red line must be either line 3 or line 4 (clue 3), so Riverhead must be on either line 1 or line 2 (clue 3). But line 2 does not have an eastern terminal, so, from clue 3, Riverhead must be station E on line 1, and the red line is therefore line 3. Thus, the diagonal line running between Gradwell and The Unicorn (clue 1), must be line 3. Since the blue line intersects at an angle of 90 degrees with the one with a western terminal at Molton Park (clue 2), which, we know by elimination, must be either station A or station H, it must be line 2 or line 3, but we know that line 3 is red, so the blue line must be line 2, and Molton Park must be station H on line 4. From clue 4, Potterfield cannot be either station A or station B, and we know it is not any of stations C, G, E, or H, so it must be either station D or station F, and Lampwick is therefore either station B or station D. But Wallgate must be either station B or station F (clue 1), so Lampwick, whose name is the same length, cannot be station B (clue 6) and must be station D, and therefore Potterfield must be station F and Wallgate station B. Now, from clue 1, Gradwell must be station C, and The Unicorn is therefore station G. So, by elimination, station A must be Castlebridge. So line 1 is not the green one (clue 5) and must be the yellow one, leaving line 4 as the green line.

In summary:
Line 1, yellow, Castlebridge (A) to Riverhead (E).
Line 2, blue, Wallgate (B) to Potterfield (F).
Line 3, red, Gradwell (C) to The Unicorn (G).
Line 4, green, Molton Park (H) to Lampwick (D).

372

Just write out this pattern of 49s and add the columns!

```
      49
    4949
  494949
    4949
      49
  603729
```

373

3	4	2	7	9	1	5	6	8
7	5	9	6	8	2	3	1	4
6	1	8	3	4	5	2	9	7
4	6	1	2	5	3	8	7	9
9	7	5	8	6	4	1	3	2
8	2	3	1	7	9	6	4	5
2	9	7	5	3	6	4	8	1
5	8	6	4	1	7	9	2	3
1	3	4	9	2	8	7	5	6

374

Print 5.

375

9	0	4	1	1	1		8	2	2	5	3	8
4		5		9	6	7	8	0		1		6
1	3	4	5	6	5		6	7	8	9	0	2
1		2		8	3	4	4	5		6		7
5	4	8	3		9	2	0		6	1	2	2
7	3	8	4	2		5		6	6	9	7	8
	0		5	1	1		7	3	2		3	
7	4	2	5	6		8		5	7	1	8	2
7	9	0	1		1	4	2		8	2	3	4
5		6		3	7	8	9	4		0		1
4	2	3	4	5	8		7	6	7	8	9	3
0		1		4	2	3	4	5		1		2
6	3	7	4	5	2		3	6	7	6	8	7

376

D is the correct plug.

377

Eight.

378

379

380

4	7	1	0	1	7	■	5	2	0	2	9	3
0	■	5	■	9	6	1	4	5	■	7	■	0
2	4	6	6	4	7	■	5	8	8	2	8	9
6	■	4	■	8	5	1	7	7	■	6	■	2
3	1	1	8	■	6	1	8	■	7	7	3	2
1	6	4	2	2	■	0	■	5	0	4	5	0
■	3	■	7	2	0	■	9	3	5	■	0	■
6	3	9	5	8	■	8	■	4	9	8	8	7
4	4	1	9	■	3	4	2	■	8	3	1	3
0	■	3	■	9	2	0	5	6	■	4	■	1
6	3	0	5	8	0	■	7	7	2	0	4	2
5	■	9	■	2	2	2	1	2	■	1	■	9
8	9	7	6	1	3	■	9	0	0	5	1	0

381

Top d.

382

■	■	9	8	■	1	2	■	8	6	■	■
■	8	7	9	■	3	4	1	2	5	■	
7	6	■	4	1	2	■	3	9	7	8	
9	7	8	■	3	7	9	■	■	8	9	
■	3	6	■	■	4	8	6	7	9	■	
7	5	9	8	■	5	7	8	9	■	■	
8	9	■	3	1	■	5	9	■	8	7	
■	■	7	9	5	8	■	7	8	4	9	
■	2	1	6	3	4	■	■	7	9	■	
3	1	■	■	2	3	1	■	9	6	8	
1	4	2	3	■	1	2	3	■	7	3	
■	6	4	7	8	9	■	1	3	5	■	
■	■	3	1	■	1	2	■	2	4	■	■

383

Green, orange, orange, yellow.

384

The red was in position C on Tuesday (clue 4), so since it was obviously not there on Thursday, the blue could not have been in D on that day (clue 1). Nor, by the same clue, was the red there, and since also the green could not have been there (clue 3), D must have been the black's Thursday place. So D on Wednesday could not have been black nor blue (clue 1) or green (clue 3), so it must have been red, and D on Monday must have been green (clue 2). By elimination, Tuesday's D must have been blue, and, from clue 1, C on Wednesday must have been blue. From what we have already placed, C on Monday can't be any of red, blue, or green, so it must have been black, leaving C on Thursday as green. From clue 1, blue on Monday must have been A and red in position B. Now, from clue 3, green must have been in B on Tuesday and A on Wednesday with black in A on Tuesday and B on Wednesday. By elimination, on Thursday, red must have been in A and blue in B.

In summary:
Monday: blue, red, black, green.
Tuesday: black, green, red, blue.
Wednesday: green, black, blue, red.
Thursday: red, blue, green, black.

385

5	8	9	1	3	7	6	4	2
6	1	7	9	2	4	3	8	5
3	2	4	8	5	6	7	1	9
2	7	8	4	6	1	5	9	3
9	4	6	5	7	3	8	2	1
1	5	3	2	9	8	4	7	6
4	6	5	7	1	2	9	3	8
7	9	2	3	8	5	1	6	4
8	3	1	6	4	9	2	5	7

386

2	0	1	0	3	4	■	5	5	7	8	9	4
7	■	0	■	9	3	0	0	9	■	1	■	1
9	7	1	8	7	2	■	7	2	1	7	0	7
4	■	7	■	6	9	4	8	3	■	3	■	9
6	1	2	5	■	7	3	1	■	8	4	2	2
9	4	3	4	5	■	9	■	3	0	5	1	4
■	2	■	8	2	3	■	1	4	7	■	2	■
7	1	8	2	7	■	9	■	8	2	1	3	3
7	4	0	9	■	2	5	7	■	4	0	4	1
1	■	9	■	1	7	0	1	2	■	7	■	7
6	1	0	7	7	8	■	3	0	4	0	5	0
4	■	1	■	3	9	1	3	0	■	2	■	2
4	5	0	3	5	3	■	5	7	5	8	5	9

387

Miranda is in trailer 3 (clue 4), so the woman in trailer 4, who cannot be Alicia from Cardiff (clue 1) or Zoe, the companion of Sebastian (clue 3), must be Esme. Therefore, from clue 2, Miranda, in trailer 3, is from Boston, and Desmond is in trailer 2. So Sebastian and Zoe, whose trailer we know is not 3 or 4, must be in trailer 1, and, by elimination, Alicia from Cardiff must be sharing trailer 2 with Desmond. Sebastian and Zoe are not from L.A. (clue 3), so they must be from El Paso, leaving L.A as Esme's home city. Miranda's partner is not Luther (clue 4), so he must be Paul, leaving Esme with Luther.

In summary:
1, Sebastian and Zoe, El Paso.
2, Desmond and Alicia, Cardiff.
3, Paul and Miranda, Boston.
4, Luther and Esme, L.A.

388

The top right picture should be hung with side A facing north.

389

13	24	22	10	19
7	20	16	14	2
4	18	25	21	6
15	9	5	17	12
11	1	3	8	23

390

The first place was achieved in the town competition (clue 4), so trophy B, won at the county meeting for a higher placing than the high jump trophy (clue 3), must have been for second place, and the high jump must be the event for which Karen was awarded third place. The latter isn't trophy A (clue 1), so it must be C and, by elimination, must have been won at the interscholastic competition. If it had been won in May, then, from clue 1, the 1,500 meters trophy would have been won in June, leaving the discus trophy as the one awarded in July. From clue 2, this isn't the case, so the 1,500 meters trophy, which couldn't have been won in May (clue 1), must have been awarded in July, and third place in the high jump must have been achieved in June (clue 1). From clue 2, the 1,500 meters trophy must be trophy B, leaving A as the one awarded for the discus. By elimination, this must have been awarded in May and must have been for first place at the town competition.

In summary:
A, First place, discus, town, May.
B, Second place, 1,500 meters, county, July.
C, Third place, high jump, interscholastic, June.

391

Figure a has a bracelet, figure b has a necklace, figure c has a headband, and figure d has a band on her sandal.

392

The third from the left on the top shelf, the second from the right on the second shelf down, the fifth from the left on the third shelf down, and the third from the left on the bottom shelf.

393

9	5	1	6	7	1	■	3	8	1	5	2	6
8	■	7	■	9	0	0	2	1	■	0	■	9
2	4	6	7	9	5	■	4	1	0	4	3	0
9	■	8	■	8	4	3	3	2	■	8	■	5
1	7	0	7	■	9	2	3	■	6	7	8	6
2	0	2	9	1	■	1	■	6	4	9	8	0
■	3	■	2	0	8	■	8	4	7	■	0	■
4	1	1	8	3	■	5	■	5	5	2	1	3
2	0	6	7	■	4	3	5	■	5	6	7	0
3	■	0	■	3	7	0	6	4	■	3	■	2
5	2	0	1	2	8	■	6	1	4	8	0	9
5	■	5	■	1	9	3	5	3	■	5	■	6
7	4	6	7	4	0	■	8	4	2	7	1	0

394

A:6. Multiply the number on the left by the number on the right then divide by the number below the triangle. 3 x 4/2=6.

B:15. Multiply the number on the left by 4 then subtract 1.

C:17. Divide the bottom number by 3 then subtract the number on the left to get the number on the right. 60/3=20−3=17.

D:28. Each number in the bottom half is one more than the cube of the number opposite of it in the top half. 33=27+1=28.

E:5. In each row, from left to right, the second and third numbers are found by multiplying the previous number by 2 then adding 1. 2x2=4+1=5, 2x5=10+1=11.

395

396

4	9	4	9	3	5
8	9	5	2	6	7
5	1	8	1	5	2
8	6	6	9	8	4
1	7	2	3	6	3
3	4	2	7	7	1

397

The vase was sold at booth B (clue 2). Since Elsie was running booth A (clue 4), and Norman was the customer at booth C (clue 3), from clue 1, the fire irons cannot have been sold at booth A or booth C, so they must have been on booth D. Therefore, from clue 1, it must have been booth B that was Ken's, and his customer Lesley must have bought the vase. Ted's booth was not C (clue 3), so it must have been D, leaving booth C as Mary's. Norman, her customer, did not buy books (clue 3), so he must have bought a radio from her booth, leaving the books as the item sold by Elsie at booth A. Her customer was not Ray (clue 4), so she must have been Penny, leaving Ray as the man who bought the fire irons from Ted.

In summary:
A, Elsie, Penny, books. B, Ken, Lesley, vase. C, Mary, Norman, radio. D, Ted, Ray, fire irons.

398

The letter in position III is the B (clue 3), and the 5 is on arm I (clue 5), so the letter in I cannot be any of the HAG combination, each of which is paired with an even digit (clue 1). This also rules out the letter in II as one of the combination. We now know that the H is not in any of points I, II, or III, nor can it be in either point IV or point V, since the B is in point III (clue 1). The letter in VI is a vowel (clue 6), which rules out both VI and VIII for the H (clue 1), so it must be in position VII, and from clue 1 the A is in VI and the G at V. So the number on arm II, which is directly opposite the A, cannot be the 7, since if it were, the number on arm V would have to be the 1 and the one on arm IV the 8 (clue

4), but clue 2 tells us the 7 and the 8 are on the same straight line. So the straight line whose extremities both bear an even Roman numeral referred to in clue 2 cannot be II–VI and must be IV–VIII. So from clue 2 the 7 must be on arm IV and the 8 on arm VIII. Now from clue 4 the numbers on arms V and II, which total 7, must be either 4 and 3 or 6 and 1, since we have placed the 5 on arm I. All three numbers on arms V, VI, and VII are even (clue 1), so the odd number must be on arm II. This cannot be the 1 (clue 7), so it must be the 3. Therefore the number on arm V must be the 4 (clue 4). Since arms VI and VII both bear an even digit (clue 1), by elimination the 1 must be on arm III, so from clue 7 the C is on arm I. We are now left with D, E, and F for arms II, IV, and VIII. Therefore from clue 8 the D must be on arm IV and the F on arm II, leaving the E on arm VIII. Finally, from clue 7 the 6 cannot be on arm VII, so it must be on arm VI, leaving the 2 on arm VII.

In summary:
Arm I: C, 5. Arm II: F, 3. Arm III: B, 1.
Arm IV: D, 7. Arm V: G, 4. Arm VI: A, 6.
Arm VII: H, 2. Arm VIII: E, 8.

399

4	2	5	4	6	x	2	=	8	5	0	9	2
1	0	8	9	+	6	2	2	=	1	7	1	1
2	4	÷	1	8	+	3	9	7	=	4	3	9
1	4	x	2	5	8	7	=	3	6	2	1	8
5	+	9	+	4	+	5	−	9	÷	2	=	7
1	0	0	0	9	=	1	8	+	9	9	9	1
6	7	5	x	1	9	÷	9	=	1	4	2	5
9	6	−	7	−	7	+	8	÷	3	0	=	3
6	x	1	1	5	4	5	=	6	9	2	7	0
2	8	8	9	−	5	6	6	=	2	3	2	3
4	5	+	9	0	+	4	3	9	=	5	7	4
2	4	9	−	1	6	8	−	3	9	=	4	2
2	5	x	3	6	−	2	0	0	=	7	0	0

400

Numbers 2, 4, and 7.

401

6	5	8	6	7	4
9	1	7	3	2	1
8	5	3	4	9	5
5	2	9	6	4	2
6	8	7	4	8	3
7	3	1	2	9	1

402

Pass was north (clue 5). South, whose long suit had only five cards (clue 3), cannot have been Ruff (clue 1), and, since east's suit was hearts (clue 4), clue 1 also rules out west for Ruff, whose partner had the clubs. So, by elimination, he must have been east, and his suit was hearts. Now, from clue 1, west's suit must have been clubs. We know the south player with the five-card suit was not Pass or Ruff, nor can he have been Trumpet (clue 2), so, by elimination, he must have been Bidding. So, from clue 6, his partner, Pass, in the north seat, must have had an eight-card suit. Now, by elimination, Trumpet must have been west, and his suit was therefore clubs. Pass's eight-card suit cannot have been diamonds (clue 2), so it must have been spades, leaving diamonds as Bidding's five-card suit. Now, from clue 1, Ruff must have had seven hearts, and Trumpet six clubs.

In summary:
North, Pass, spades, 8.
East, Ruff, hearts, 7.
South, Bidding, diamonds, 5.
West, Trumpet, clubs, 6.

403

5	8	5	6	5
2	5	0	9	5
4	6	6	5	6
4	6	5	3	9
1	5	3	7	6

404

405

In each triangle, the center number is the sum of the three corner numbers less the number nearest the middle of the opposite triangle. So 11 + 10 + 4 − 7 = 18.

406

Shadow 5.

407

408

Alistair is 9 (clue 4). The oldest child, who produced picture 1 (clue 2), cannot be Mary (clue 1), or Silas, whose monocled character is somewhere to the right of another (clue 3), so she must be Jennifer. We now know Silas is not 9 or 11, nor is he 8 (clue 3), so he must be 10, leaving Mary as 8. So, from clue 1, picture 2 must have been drawn by Alistair, aged 9. This face is clean-shaven (clue 1), but does not have the monocle, so it must be wearing spectacles. From clue 3, Mary must have drawn picture 3 and Silas picture 4. From clue 4, picture 1 does not have a moustache, so it must have a beard, leaving the moustache adorning picture 3.
In summary:
1, Jennifer, 11, beard.
2, Alistair, 9, spectacles.
3, Mary, 8, moustache.
4, Silas, 10, monocle.

409

No.	Name	Shots	Prize
1	Mary	7	sombrero
2	Gemma	3	gym vouchers
3	Donald	6	deck chair
4	Jane	5	parasol
5	Mike	1	swimsuit
6	Carol	2	beach towel
7	John	8	beach ball
8	Edward	4	sunglasses

410

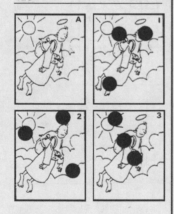

411

Picture 2.

412

413

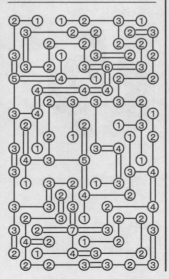

414

Order: 4–3, 7–8, 2–1, 5–6, 9–10.

415

29	33	47	61	15
57	21	25	39	43
35	49	53	17	31
13	27	41	45	59
51	55	19	23	37

416

Gretchen, who is 6, cannot be number 4 (clue 1), and number 3 is 7 (clue 4). Number 1 is a boy (clue 3), so, by elimination, Gretchen must be number 2. So, from clue 1, the child aged 7 in position 3 is the cowherd's child. Maria, whose father is an apothecary (clue 5), cannot be number 1 (clue 3), so she must be number 4, and, from clue 5, she is 5, leaving the boy in position 1 as 8. So he is not Hans (clue 2) and must be Johann, leaving Hans as the seven-year-old son of the cowherd. From clue 3, Gretchen's father cannot be the butcher, so he must be the woodcutter, leaving Johann as the butcher's son.

In summary: 1, Johann, 8, butcher. 2, Gretchen, 6, woodcutter. 3, Hans, 7, cowherd. 4, Maria, 5, apothecary.

417

Using just initial letters, such as DG for double glazing and DG' for NOT double glazing, the clues can be charted as follows:
1 DG—CH 2 RR—FG 3 ON—GD and so on. Now form the longest chain of linked facts: clues 1 and 11, for instance, give DG—CH—C' which says that houses with double glazing have central heating and do not have chimneys. Number 51, being an odd-numbered house, gives this chain: ON—GD—RR—FG—PG—DG—CH—C'—LW, using clues 3, 5, 2, 12, 9, 1, 11, and 7.
So number 51 has a green door, red roof, front garden, plastic gnomes, double glazing, central heating, no chimney, and leaded windows.

418

```
      4659
  X   7373
     13977
     32613
     13977
     32613
  34350807
```

419

METHOD	FIRST NAME	SURNAME	COMPANY
ACUPUNCTURE	ELSA	POPPIN	HI-FI NANTS
CHIN. BALLS	ELLIS	DEE	J. C. NUTTS
SITAR MUSIC	NATHAN	TEWITT	JUST LOANS
YOGA	VAL	HEEGHAM	U. B. LOOPY

420

The objects are hidden in squares d2, g2, e5, and b4.

421

A, B, D, F, H, M, N, and Q.

422

Fragments 2 and 3 are taken from the main picture.

423

Picture 1 is missing the heel of the boot. Picture 4 is missing a knot in the wood. Picture 9 is missing a potato. Picture 12 is missing a brick to the left of the ladder. Picture 2 has a patch on the knee. Picture 6 has a label on the bag. Picture 8 has a pocket on the trousers.

424

A	B	C	D	E	F	G	H	J	K
2	4	3	0	6	7	1	9	8	5

425

X	J	N	D	O
K	G	W	P	L
S	C		V	H
R	B	Z	F	T
E	Y	M	U	I	A

Taking away the Q leaves the shape of a Q.

426

1	2	6	9	3	5
4	7	8	3	2	1
6	4	2	7	4	3
8	1	9	0	4	2
2	5	3	2	1	8
7	6	1	9	2	9

1	4	4		3	1
2	9		3		5
8			2	5	6
	8	2		1	
4		5	8		3
1	3	6		1	9

427

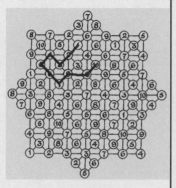

429

431

BEAR	SLEEPER	CEREAL	BROKE
CARMEN	WYN	CHAFFLAKES	CHAIR
FRED	GOLDIE	RICYPOPS	SIDEBOARD
MAMA	CHER	MUESLI M.	BOOKCASE
PAPA	DAWN	WEETYBRICKS	TABLE
TEDDY	CILLA	BRAN BITS	DESK

432

The matching ducks are: 1 and 8, 2 and 3, and 4 and 6; so the different ducks are 5 and 7.

428

430